Jungle Warfare

EXPERIENCES AND ENCOUNTERS

J. P. CROSS

Jungle Warfare

EXPERIENCES AND ENCOUNTERS

J. P. CROSS

GUILD PUBLISHING LONDON

Left: British troops wade through a Malayan river in pursuit of Communist rebels hiding in the jungle. (Popperfoto)

*To the special angel
who looks after wild animals and soldiers in the jungle
and the wild animals and soldiers themselves*

This edition published 1989 by Guild Publishing
by arrangement with Arms and Armour Press.
CN9347

Jacket illustration courtesy of *Soldier* magazine.

The illustrations in this book have been collected
from many sources, and vary in quality owing to the variety
of circumstances under which they were taken and preserved.
As a result, certain of the illustrations are not of the
standard to be expected from the best of today's equipment,
materials and techniques. They are nevertheless included
for their inherent information value, to provide an
authentic visual coverage of the subject.

Edited and designed by DAG Publications Ltd.
Designed by David Gibbons; edited by Michael Boxall;
layout by Anthony A. Evans; typeset by Typesetters
(Birmingham) Ltd.; camerawork by M&E Reproductions,
North Fambridge, Essex; printed and bound
in Great Britain by Mackays of Chatham, PLC,
Letchworth, Herts.

Contents

Introduction

The nearest most people get to warfare is watching 'instant' history on television in the comfort of their own homes; the nearest others get to it is from books. Even fewer people have a knowledge of jungle warfare. One result of American involvement on mainland Asia, in Vietnam, was to embroil all in the USA and many, many others around the world in a debate about the ethics of such a phenomenon, portrayed in a tropical, if not jungle, environment. In America much moral and psychological debris resulted from the war, yet the involvement of 'Western' powers in Asia against such an enemy was neither new nor necessarily more degrading than previous instances.

The aim of this book is to present a dispassionate and clinical record of jungle warfare. Its theme is to show how and why warfare ever had to be undertaken in jungles; leaving aside the morality or otherwise of such ventures, I am primarily concerned with the military aspects once soldiers have been committed to jungle operations. How was it that those presumed to be eventual victors – the 'superior' white races – finished up as the vanquished? What did those, presumed to be the underdogs, have that their adversaries from affluent and developed societies did not? As a military historian I write '. . . to identify the complexities and establish the perspective . . .' of jungle warfare.

'War is too important to be left to the generals', say the armchair critics, yet many mistakes have been made before and during war by politicians, with damaging if not damning effects on the outcome of hostilities. Purely to describe the conduct of war without looking at the political, social, cultural, climatical, geographical and historical roots of a conflict results in false premises being drawn, false lessons being learnt and false precepts being followed in the future. It is for these reasons that I have included in some detail these aspects where germane, especially that post-Second World War phenomenon, Communist Revolutionary Warfare.

I did practically all my soldiering in Asia and have spent ten years – thankfully not all at once! – in the jungle. I met many whom I regarded as better 'jungle hands' than I, whose experiences were more profound, whose stamina had been more sorely tested, whose deeds were braver by far than mine. By the time the British pulled out from 'East of Suez', most of these warriors (my heroes) had returned to their own country and I, a smaller fish in a fast-drying pool, was, by default, regarded as the 'expert'. It then struck me that, for those countless others who had even less experience than had I, the whole art and conduct of jungle warfare was in danger of becoming forgotten, mystique-ridden, thought of as

Above: British troops run to a Royal Naval helicopter during a troop lift. This was a common occurrence. At times Natives were also given flights when they were suitable for tasking and this created a measure of confidence so essential for victory. (Royal Navy)

Right: 'The old and the new': both armour and elephants played a significant part in Burma. The tank is a Sherman. (Royal Corps of Transport Museum)

being something only men of above-average qualities could cope with, regarded as something heroic even before the first leech bite!

I therefore felt that jungle warfare should be put in its own particular perspective of 'modified soldiering' by tracing its historical origins, its developments over the years, its operational aspects, its training requirements, the constraints of the jungle's 'armed neutrality' that mean it can never be taken for granted – in other words 'what it's all about' – so that layman and military buff alike can see it all as a whole, untainted by any hyperbole of presentation, untrammelled by ethical issues, untouched by civilian, non-combatant hand.

Prior to 1939 jungle/bush warfare was regarded more as warfare in jungle or bush that did not need any novel tactical thinking: this I have shown as background. Post-1939, to make best use of experience and research, I have analysed how conventional warfare met the challenge of the jungle in the Burma and New Guinea campaigns. There are already countless books on the actual campaigns themselves so my treatment of events there is from the viewpoint of how the various components of the military machine were utilized and what it was like for the man on the ground, rather than purely that of a campaign history.

Regarding the period from 1945, I have concentrated on the Malayan Emergency and Confrontation in Borneo in more detail than I have French and American involvement in Indo-China/Vietnam (about which countless books, pictures, films and even plays already exist); this is partly due to the latter-mentioned campaigns being more those of 'tropical' warfare rather than 'jungle' warfare.

I finish with a review of some training requirements and a bold glimpse into the future, making a plea not to forget jungle warfare, nor to commit the mistakes of the past through neglect. What I write should be read as a warning, not a predicament – a caution, not an indictment.

Fair-weather soldiers make gloomy regimental histories!

Pokhara, NEPAL, July 1988

Right: Commissariat arrangements would depend on local resources to a marked degree. (Indian Army regulations stated that, in peacetime, dry rations would be issued every week or, if the unit were remote, every decade.) Canned food was still primitive when hostilities broke out in 1914 and would have been non-existent in this campaign. Dry rations would have to be brought up by contractor and stores for the officers, such as hard liquor and linen, would have to be brought all the way from the regimental base. Apart from human porterage, records show that elephants were used. Soldiers were accustomed to mules and ponys, which would have an integral regimental complement to maintain and operate them, but elephants would have to have their own civilian handlers. Stores were first loaded then transported in great splendour, but even greater discomfort. One aspect of using these animals is that they only work for half a day. The rest of the time is spent on their getting enough fodder to sustain themselves. Even in thick country this is a time-consuming process. (Gurkha Museum)

I
SETTING THE SCENE

Left: Men of 1st Gurkha Rifles (Gurkha Light Infantry) – then troops of the Honourable East India Company, not the Indian Army – storm a stockade held by Malays in the Perak campaign, 20 December 1875. The conquest of the Malayan peninsula saw some actions in the jungle. Neither side seemed equipped to fight in wooded country for long. When skirmishing did occur, such was the nature of the terrain that hand-to-hand fighting was likely to ensue. Before the British arrived the Malay of the 19th century was more militant and was more of a pirate than a land warrior. (Gurkha Museum)

Below: During the Abor campaign on the North-East Frontier of British India (1911–14), 1/2nd Gurkha Rifles (now part of the Indian Army), operated against dissident local chieftains rather than any co-ordinated opposition, which could be fierce: the inhabitants of that area were (and still are) tough and determined fighters, even though they were neither conventionally armed nor clad. (Gurkha Museum)

1
The Background to Jungle Warfare

There were four of us on patrol late that afternoon in the Malayan jungle, myself and three Gurkha soldiers. We travelled light, with no packs and, as we only intended to be out an hour or so, no water-bottles. The jungle was thick. After an hour, just as we were about to return to our overnight camp, I heard the noise of an axe on wood. We moved stealthily forward, all senses alert, adrenalin pumping. The semi-darkness grew lighter as we came to where some trees had been felled by the Chinese Communist terrorists to make a vegetable garden to eke out their rations. We crept to the edge of the clearing, which had been fenced to prevent wild pig and deer from entering, eased ourselves over and saw two men at the far end. We crawled between the raised ridges of soil to a felled tree in the middle. I recollected that this was the first time I had crawled as I had been taught as a recruit eleven years before, in 1943.

At the felled tree I gave out my orders softly and we took aim. I fired and hit my target, thirty yards away, in the back. My weapon, a carbine, immediately jammed. The two enemy dodged the other bullets as they ran away so I got to my feet and shouted the Gurkhas' battle cry, *Ayo Gorkhali, Charge!* We chased after them, but they had not far to go to leave the clearing and get into the jungle. We followed up but lost their tracks in a maze of others. Time was against a detailed search.

They had left a rifle behind them so I turned to the one soldier who did not smoke, told him to wait behind with me and ordered the other two to return to camp.

My idea was to lay an ambush near the rifle, in case the guerrillas returned to get it. The two of us waited till dawn – no food and no water. We leaned against a large anthill. It rained most of the night. Once a tiger's growl throbbed nearby, like a death-rattle, and a mouse deer whickered in fright by our feet.

Apart from it being a very long night and, so I found out later, the rifle that of our colonel who had recently been killed in a road ambush fifty miles away, the incident was just another botched contact. It was seldom that such easy targets were come across. Why did my weapon have to jam then of all times? But at least we had had a contact after months of patrolling. We followed them up the next day . . .

JUNGLE WARFARE

Jungle warfare is something that many people have heard about but not so very many have been involved in. It conjures up visions of sweaty, dirty, heavily-laden soldiers hacking their way through dark, dank, impenetrable undergrowth, trying to avoid snakes, scorpions and a host of other creepy-crawlies with monkeys gibbering from the safety of their tree-tops and wild beasts calling to one another in the hope of a succulent meal. If it is not little men with poisoned darts lurking in the foliage to have a pot-shot at a red-faced, pack-encumbered, sweating European, it is a superbly camouflaged and cunning Asian enemy of great savagery waiting to impale the by-now-even-sweatier soldier on some dread, spiked booby-trap or rise up from nowhere and ambush him. A little 'yes' and a lot of 'no'!

Jungle warfare is, however, different from other types of warfare and is slightly special – as, indeed, are tropical, desert, arctic, mountain and urban warfare. To me the essence of jungle warfare is *when, at any intensity, certainly tactics and training, probably weapons and logistical support, have to be modified because of trees.* It is the nearest to night fighting that troops will get during daylight. In jungle warfare there are always areas where there is no 'jungle' as thick as popular imagination would have it. (Indeed, the first Gurkhas to go to London described what strange happenings of an evening they had seen in the 'jungle' of Hyde Park!) It is for this reason that mention is made of 'non-jungle' aspects of tropical warfare where considered relevant and which also makes Indo-China/Vietnam harder to compartmentalize as a battleground than Malaya and Borneo.

What is certainly true is that the jungle presents as much, many say more, of a psychological barrier as it does a physical one. The famous Spencer Chapman, in his book *The Jungle Is Neutral*, describes how some British soldiers who were left behind in the jungle died 'not of any specific disease, but because they lacked the right mental attitude'. This may have been partly a result of the Japanese bogey, but fear of the jungle is a very real one.

Even without an enemy and in calm conditions the jungle can claim victims. A potential leader in the Duke of Edinburgh's award scheme which involves physical dedication to a certain degree – a British civilian schoolmaster stationed in Singapore attached to the Royal Air Force – went into the jungle with a group of the British Army's Jungle Warfare School instructors to 'walk the course' he was to take his boys. Before an hour was out and while still in distant earshot of traffic on the road he collapsed and, within a very few minutes, was dead. Nothing wrong could be found by the doctors who examined the corpse. The only rational explanation was that he had literally died of fright.

IN ASIA AND THE PACIFIC

Countries that have been the scene of jungle warfare are chiefly in south-east Asia: Burma, north-east India, Malay(si)a, Indonesia, Borneo, Laos, Vietnam and Thailand and the islands of the west Pacific – in particular the Philippines and New Guinea. Jungle country varies from thick, tropical forest to some patches of open spaces, with a monsoon and subsistence farming in the more open cultivated and coastal areas. Military characteristics common to all jungle areas are limited visibility for both air and ground forces, scarcity of tracks and difficulty of cross-country movement by any vehicle.

In general terms there are three types of jungle: primary, secondary and coastal. Primary jungle is natural vegetation which has never been touched and has remained in its original state. Visibility is limited to 20 to 30 yards, varying according to the slope of the ground and amount of foliage present. On the tops of hills the foliage is thin and in valleys it is extremely dense. Where there is a stream that has become blocked, a swamp is often formed and this is sometimes impassable. More often than not it can be circumvented and then good navigation is required to keep on the original line. Tracks exist but were seldom shown on wartime maps. The jungle is never impassable, despite all the old soldiers' stories to the contrary. A dah (Burmese knife), a kukri (Nepalese knife) or machete was deemed necessary to cut new tracks or to remove undergrowth. This practice declined after the Burma campaign when often stealth and cunning dictated slower and less obvious movement.

Secondary jungle occurs where the primary jungle has been cleared and allowed to grow up again. The vegetation usually takes the form of very dense ferns and brambles through which it is almost impossible to force a passage. One method is to walk over it. In such places, with no high trees, it can become dangerously hot.

Along the coastal areas, the jungle often becomes more open and consists of mangrove swamps and grass that grows to a height of 4 to 8 feet, so precluding observation and holding the heat. Coconut groves are to be found near inhabited areas.

Rivers in low country are generally broad and sluggish, but in the hills they are deep and swift. Six inches of rain falling in a single night may cause them to rise twelve feet, flood the country, sweep away small bridges and tracks, and inundate camps and landing grounds.

Paddy-fields are very difficult in the rainy season, though when it is dry they present no obstacle to man, only to vehicles, because of the 'bunds' or ridges between the individual fields.

Rubber plantations vary according to their age and to their upkeep. When young they have been likened to a field of potatoes and when mature the symmetrical lines allow up to two hundred yards' ground visibility and give fair cover from the air.

Full-grown tea bushes give good cover for men but do not provide cover for artillery, vehicles, mules or elephants.

In 1943 one Indian Army training manual classified the jungle into three types – no army looks on anything, even the jungle, with civilian eyes! These were:

Dense So thick that a man on foot could not get through without cutting his way.

Thick In which a man could force his way through with the aid of a stick but without having to cut.

Thin In which a man could move at a fair pace, without cutting or damaging his clothes, by picking his way.

Types of jungle were given as bamboo, tree, palm, forest and scrub – mangrove swamp could have been added to the list.

In the same year another training pamphlet, *The Jungle Book*, gave south-east Asian and Pacific tropical rain forest countries dull descriptions. Interestingly, hardly anywhere are the jungles ever described as such, merely being called 'forests'. I wonder if the fear of the jungle permeated even the training people in far off Delhi and, by not mentioning 'jungle', the terrain would not sound as frightening as had been the case? In fact, 'normal Burma' was officially described as 'having a good road, bordered by generally difficult country'.

THE JUNGLE

The didactic note and dull tone of the training pamphlets are enhanced by men who knew the areas better and wrote about them. In a book on the fighting in New Guinea, *Not as a Duty Only: An Infantryman's War*, the author, Henry Gullet, describes primary jungle as 'sunless, dripping, curiously silent, without birds or wild animals, yet somehow alive, watching, malignant, dangerous. Men spoke quietly in the jungles and laughed seldom . . . faces gaunt and yellow. Smoky fires, lukewarm food, wet blankets, damp cigarettes and a nagging, insistent consciousness of one's physical weakness.'

In Malaya, the late Spencer Chapman was impressed with the 'absolute straightness, the perfect symmetry of the tree trunks, like the pillars of a dark and limitless cathedral. The ground itself was covered with a thick carpet of dead leaves and seedling trees; there was practically no earth visible and certainly no grass or flowers. Up to a height of ten feet or so a dense undergrowth of young trees and palms of all kinds hid the roots of the giants, but out of this wavy green sea of undergrowth a myriad tree trunks – surrounded by "buttresses" – rise straight upwards with no apparent decrease in thickness for a hundred or a hundred and fifty feet before they burgeoned into a solid canopy of green which almost entirely shut out the sky.'

While the jungle, dense, thick or thin, captures the imagination, other areas of differing terrain pose their own distinct problems of tactics and operating drills for the soldier. These are scrub, swamp, elephant grass, rice fields, cultivations such as rubber, oil palm and coffee plantations, extensive rolling countryside and opencast tin mines. The dry area in central Burma and, in Vietnam, the Mekong delta, the coastal plain and the central plateau are not jungle.

The very nature of primary jungle, its close-horizoned, all-pervading, never-ending green of trees, vines, creepers and undergrowth prevents the eyes from seeing as far as the ears can hear so voices have to be kept low and equipment so handled that it does not reverberate. It is a litany of sounds and a dictionary of sights. It is a living lexicon of lore for those who understand it. It is a state of permanent semi-twilight, gloomy even when sunshine does dapple the jungle floor with shadows, and dark in creeks and narrow valleys at noon. It is a state of permanent dampness, rain or sweat, of stifling, windless heat, of dirty clothes, of smelly bodies, of heavy loads, of cocked and loaded weapons, of tensed reflexes, of inaccurate maps, of constant vigilance, of tired limbs, of sore shoulders where equipment straps have bitten in, of a chafed crutch, of the craving for a cigarette and a cold beer for some and a cup of tea for others. At night it is darkness, with fireflies pricking the gloom with flickering lights and rotting leaves shining eerily. It is a state of mind that has to be stronger than mere physical robustness. It is a challenge. It can never be taken for granted. It is hated by hundreds. And yet for those who have the jungle as their first love, no other type of countryside can ever measure up to it for its infinite variety and the subtle beauty of its primordial nature. In Burma, even those who initially found it claustrophobic wanted to return to it after their first leave when they found the 'bright lights' too exposed and unnatural for comfort.

These 'semi-night' conditions become engrained and it is difficult to react quickly and correctly when suddenly coming out of thick, dark jungle into an open stretch of paddy cultivation or a large clearing where, even on an overcast day, the dazzle of the open sky hurts the eyes and puts the soldier at a disadvantage to anyone already there waiting for him.

Living, moving and fighting in the jungle competently and for protracted periods require the soldier to keep himself fit enough to react automatically, instinctively and instantaneously to the unexpected under all circumstances. The official Australian history of the New Guinea campaign gives examples of harsh conditions where it was not uncommon for soldiers (of 3rd Australian Division) to exist on long patrols like wild animals. 'Such conditions of rain, mud, rottenness, stench, gloom and, above all, the feeling of being shut in by everlasting jungle and ever-ascending mountains, are sufficient to fray the strongest nerves. But add to them the tension of the constant expectancy of death from behind the impenetrable screen of green and nerves must be of the strongest, and morale of the highest, to live down these conditions, accept them as a matter of course, and maintain a cheerful yet fighting spirit.'

In the highlands one group of soldiers reported taking one hour and fifty minutes to go 250 yards through thick bamboo. The two forward platoons of one company took an hour and a half to bash through 100 yards of jungle. Taking three hours to collect water when in the high hills was not rare. On one clay slope, elements of 39th Battalion took seventeen hours to cover 600 yards, cutting their way up the chute as though it were a snowfield. The slopes of Mount Lawson on Yule Island were so steep that it was possible for two men to hold a shouted conversation from one ridge to another a whole day's walk apart. Local knowledge is always at a premium; two native Papuans took 45 minutes for a journey that took the troops one and a half days, admittedly by an indirect and tortuous route.

In many parts of the jungle only men, not machines or even animals, can operate efficiently. Often the area to be covered compared with the number of troops available was so vast and empty that for long periods the fight against the enemy, Japanese or Communist guerrilla, was almost incidental. The real fight was against the enervating climate, the demanding terrain, the corroding atmosphere of unrelieved tension, of fitfulness of sleep and lack of hot meals, of disease and of accident, of having to carry everything everywhere as one side groped for the other like a grotesque game of blind man's buff. All the while the soldier had to be ready for the split second of a fleeting contact, for a few minutes of hectic action when patrol bumped patrol or, after great effort, an attack was launched or an ambush sprung.

Under these conditions, searching for the enemy, finding him unawares and dealing with him positively often entails aggression when every instinct of self-preservation warns otherwise. Then only training, self-discipline and high morale triumph as men, tired, far from base, perhaps outnumbered, possibly wounded, probably afraid, hungry and thirsty, cover those last few yards. It may be glorious to die for your country but it is far more glorious to make the other man die for his.

NATURAL HAZARDS

There are many natural hazards in the jungle to be wary of even before the enemy decides to plant booby-traps, lay ambushes or attack. Flash-floods after heavy rain can make even the driest creek treacherous. Almost every unit that served in Malaya had fatalities from falling trees or branches. In primary jungle I reckon that a large tree falls in earshot range once every 36 hours. Lying in the dark, waiting for sleep, the creaking of rotten wood takes on an ominous urgency, getting louder and louder until, in a terrifying crescendo, a dead tree crashes to the ground with a deafening, roaring whoosh which hurts the eardrums and reverberates for miles around. There is nowhere to run to, even if there were time, as the angle of fall cannot be seen. Men lie there, tense and fearful, until all is quiet except for the light pattering of leaves and twigs that continue to fall for a bit longer. No noise. Am I the only one alive? 'Are you alright? Is anyone hurt?' I ask in a strained tone – the habit of talking loudly is easily lost and leads to losing the voice speaking normally on return to base. That time nobody was hurt. Next morning we saw that all the places where we had slept were straddled by thick branches which had fallen to embrace the sleepers, not crush them. It is seldom that one is so lucky.

Insects, such as red ants, horse-flies, hairy caterpillars, ticks, scorpions, centipedes and hornets are not a constant threat, nor indeed are snakes and wild animals. British troops *hate* leeches. There have been cases where a leech has gone down the penis, so blocking the passage. This is most painful and dangerous and the fear of such a happening caused some British soldiers to wear sheaths. The worst leeches are poisonous, while giant bull leeches in swamps can suck a pint of blood at one go.

There is a case of a Malay woman who was killed by four of these creatures getting on to her body at the same time and sucking out most of her blood. I had once to resort to burning out an infection on my ankle from a poisonous leech when drugs ran out and no resupply was possible. It was either that or not walking. It took three years to clear.

Wild bees are killers as they suffocate and sting their victims to death. Wasps carry an allergy that makes the body swell, itch and feel as though it were bursting. Hornets chase anything that moves. Attacked by them, the victim has to stand stock-still in the position he was in when the wretched things started after him. It takes a lot of self-discipline not to move and a platoon of men not wanting to be stung looks like a tableau of waxworks.

Survival, to know what to eat and what not to, how to trap animals, how to fish and how to make flame without matches or a lighter, can be learnt. What is certainly true is that a soldier cannot forage for survival and still be in a position to take the initiative operationally when survival implies being the hunted, not the hunter. The greater the amount of movement, the easier it is to pick up tracks.

JUNGLE DWELLERS

Nobody in his senses would live in the jungle for choice. Those who live there do so for necessity and there are not many such people. They are the flotsam and jetsam of migratory movements, never strong enough to establish settlements where life is relatively easy. They have been left behind in remote places where nobody else wanted to live and where they could hide – in the jungle and even then they cut down the trees so that where they actually live is in the open.

Above: *Not until the 19th century did those living to the north-east of India and in Upper Burma come under the influence of a central government in Delhi. Probably of Mongolian origin, with the one-fold, epicanthic eyelids, the paternalistic British 'managed' then in a way that was understood and accepted. After 1947, the government in Delhi was Indian and minorities were not considered in the same manner. This was a different recipe for trouble, and one that resulted in a 20-year 'war' with the Mizos from the mid-1960s to the mid-1980s. In 1913 and 1914, operations continued and also embraced the Kohima area. Then unknown, it was to become famous thirty years later. The earlier 'enemy' were neither well armed nor well organized, but were brave and stubborn. A warrior poses. Tambu, 1913.* (Gurkha Museum)

Below: *Abor warriors.* (Gurkha Museum)   **Above:** *Local warrior.* (Gurkha Museum)

In this category I am thinking of such people as Naga tribesmen in northern Assam, aborigines in north Malaysia, Iban head-hunters in Borneo, natives in Papua New Guinea and Indians in the Amazon basin.

Over the centuries they have developed a resistance to the rigours, dangers and difficulties that beset such regions and which stem from aspects of terrain and climate not found elsewhere. They have developed cultures from expediency and improvisation, many relying on bamboo more than on any other one substance for building houses, making animal and fish traps, frames for drying meat, carrying water, rafts, primitive clothing, fashioning nose-flutes and cylindrical drums for dances. Their horizons, both physical and mental, are limited. There are no beasts of burden, no ploughing. For many the only milk they ever taste is their mother's and the only wheel they will have seen is a heli-copter's. To reach the age of forty is a rarity. I learnt the language of one of these people (the Temiar aborigines in north Malaysia) who only know how to count to three yet can refer back for six generations, have no generic word for 'animal' and can only relate to an object by its position from the speaker and the nearest flowing water – or where it would be if there were any!

Apart from game-wardens, loggers and others who spend protracted periods in the jungle, few other types of people have had to live there. During the war though, came the inevitable soldiers: first the Japanese Army which used the jungle as no military power had previously presumed possible, thereby elevating jungle warfare to a new status; then the Allies, who eventually managed to make the same use of the jungle and, with superior strategy, tactics and logistics, pushed the Japanese back out of it.

Since then, in what has passed as peacetime for many but not for some, this pattern has been repeated. However, instead of an invading army, the new dwellers have been those whose activities precluded them from living normal lives in villages or towns. They were the hard-core Communist guerrillas and their followers who had to use the jungle before the rest of the population in those villages and towns were ready for them. The others were soldiers of the legitimate government – sometimes with 'Free World' support as in Vietnam – whose task was to stop such people from being there, so having to live there themselves.

JUNGLE CRAFT

Before troops are committed to jungle warfare, their commanders should already know the principles of war and understand current tactical doctrines. They should appreciate what sort of enemy they are up against, his philosophy, his methods, his weaknesses, his strengths, so that opportunities can be taken and needless casualties avoided. Before a soldier can be a proficient jungle fighter, he has to know the basic rules of soldiering in combat, namely tactics, various battle drills and how to be a marksman. Once he has a fair grounding in these, he has to learn about the properties of the jungle: the limited vision, the gleaning of information from sound, the restrictions to mobility, the difficulties of supply and how all these affect his fighting ability and that of the enemy. Jungle craft is of vital importance.

In Burma, the term jungle craft implied 'the ability of a soldier to live and fight in the jungle; to be able to move from point to point and arrive at his objective fit to fight; to use ground and vegetation to the best advantage; to be able to 'melt' into the jungle either by freezing or intelligent use of camouflage, both 'sight' and 'sound'; to recognize and be able to eat native foods; and to live as comfortably as possible by, for instance, being able to erect temporary shelters so have a dry sleep. He should be able to recognize instantly the cry or call of disturbed birds. His ear should be attuned to normal jungle noises to detect and differentiate between natural and man-made sounds. He must learn to rely on his observation of broken twigs and branches, of trampled undergrowth and of disturbed mould, to detect the recent presence or proximity of humans. He has to use his sense of smell (it is a curious fact, but the Japanese soldier possessed a peculiar, unpleasant odour which was most persistent). He must readily recognize the danger of tracks converging at watering places, cultivations and habitations and to approach such areas with caution. He must learn to move through the jungle in darkness and be able to retrace his steps, to move silently, to avoid stepping on rotting logs and twigs and otherwise giving away his presence to the enemy.' That goes for all jungle, not only in Burma.

No jungle experience is quickly or easily won nor is self-confidence, but without both no battle will be won either. Without that most expensive commodity of all – the well-trained infantryman – no territory can be securely held, regardless of the sophistication of the machines used during all the jungle fighting to date. It has been found, time and time again, that the better soldiers are trained, the higher is their morale.

EARLY SANCTUARY

Man has always used the forests as a sanctuary against oppressors, a means of creeping up on enemies and for providing for his larder, so skulking in the bushes and hunting expeditions for food must be older than recorded history. All the wiles and tricks of fieldcraft that a lack of long-range weapons dictated to those whose quarry was man or to a hungry hunting group would have been second nature and of life-preserving importance to be ignored at its peril in the open; under the canopy of thick trees that provided a shelter and asylum for both hunter and hunted, the lore for survival became even more dependent on innate reflexes, automatic and immediate, and superior woodcraft – then and now. The introduction of harvesting crops placed less reliance on everybody having to be apt trackers and ambushers and gradually, over the centuries, such skills became vestigial, if not redundant, until civilization blunted many of man's finer instincts for survival.

One of the earliest allusions to cover from view being provided by thick undergrowth is in the Book of Genesis, with the description of Adam and Eve in the Garden of Eden, complete with living off the land and a snake. Only after the Fall did man have to consider security precautions, camouflage, adequate deception measures, immediate-action drills and fall-back positions when in such tree-girt conditions!

A primitive warrior has always had advantages over better trained and more sophisticated troops in wooded areas. In Europe, Germanic tribes, lurking in dark forests, gave the Roman legions (which, by then, contained many non-Roman troops) much trouble, retaining the initiative and, with fewer men, tying down significant numbers of troops. The tribes were unable to make use of this advantage so the invaders won. In Asia, centuries later, the Vietnamese did exactly the same against the French (whose forces in Indo-China also contained a minority of Frenchmen), and the Americans. This time the invaders lost. In neither case were the wooded areas the scenes of final victory, however important they had been during the campaign. It has always been postulated that the superior initiative and intelligence, both individual and group, of the more civilized army resulted in a decisive result for them when conditions of fire power and terrain were equal. Whose national pride was hurt the most – the French, or the Americans in having presumed that they could beat the Vietnamese; or the Vietnamese for being taken as inferior when they beat both the others?

The philosophies of the armies of the West and of the East differ as much as do the mentalities of the people who think them out. Although indigenous armies, having their bases in the woods, could always cause a problem of ambuscade and harassment to an occupying army, the threat they posed there was never critical until they were able to beat their opponent's 'main force' army out in the open. Eliminate your opponent's army by your superior strategy, tactics and discipline and what had been theirs was now yours. It seems fair to say that military commanders never viewed forests, woods and jungles as deserving special treatment in their own right – until they did it was a case of warfare in the jungle rather than jungle warfare.

THE INFLUENCE OF THE FOREST

When Wolfe fought Montcalm in the dense Canadian forests in the 1750s, the British Army redcoats were outpointed by Indian redskins who were allies of the French and were naturally adept in the arts of ambuscade and concealment. 'The best fighters were white half-breed settlers who combined the courage and steadfast determination of the white man with the agility and cunning of the redskin . . . The close scarlet ranks of the English were plainly to be seen through the trees and the smoke; they were moving forward, cheering lustily and shouting "God save the King".' It did not save them from taking heavy casualties. 'Both men and officers were new to this blind and frightful warfare of the savage in his native woods.'

The outcome of one of history's decisive battles, the turning-point in the war between the British and Americans, can be put down to General Gates's men taking advantage of forest conditions, so beating General Burgoyne (who was no military slouch) at the Battle of Saratoga in 1777.

From 1793 to 1795 there was a series of peasant-royalist insurrections in La Vendée, a heavily wooded area in the west of France against the revolutionary government. The First Republic called for the removal 'from the insurgent territory [of] all inhabitants who had not taken up arms, because some, under the guise of neutrality, favour the rebels, while the others (the smaller groups), although loyal to the Republic, also provide assistance which they cannot refuse in the face of compulsion'. (Orders from Republican Army of the West, 1793.) Lessons learnt then served as a warning to the British in the Burmese war of 1885–92 of what to avoid when operating against ardent natives in their natural wooded terrain. The French were faced with a similar situation in Indo-China in the late 1940s and the early 1950s and started to relocate the widely-scattered peasant population in new fortified settlements. It was only spasmodically applied because it proved difficult and costly. The British in Malaya had the same problem and solved it by resettling squatters in 'New Villages'.

Forest conditions were taken advantage of in the Cuban and Puerto Rican campaign in 1898. Under Lieutenant-Colonel Roosevelt, American 'Rough Riders' used fire and movement, and excellent fire discipline, in thickly wooded country. The Spaniards, who lost, stated that they had 4,000 men; the Rough Riders had 543 and lost eight killed and 34 wounded. Such parallels were evident when one side surprised the other by skilful use of similar tactics in post-war Asian guerrilla wars.

In 1943, jungle fighters in the Pacific theatre were told about the raiding tactics that brought victory to the renowned Mexican raider, Emiliano Zapata (?1877–1919) and the orders he gave to his fighters: 'We may get scattered, and then every man must use his own judgement, but my general orders are: "Never engage the enemy except from cover, ambush him, flank him, draw him on, tease him, lure him into pursuit, exhaust him, cut back on him when he is exhausted, fade away. Do nothing that you're supposed to do; do everything that no one would dream that you'd do. Keep cover, shoot straight, and never let up."'

Hints for a Bush Campaign, produced in 1901 as a result of the fourth and last Ashanti Campaign (1895–6), lays great stress on the comfort of Europeans. 'It is of the greatest importance in such a bad climate that officers and men should be spared as much worry as possible, that their meals should be regular and that columns should arrive at the end of the day's march in such time as to allow every European to have a bath. Except when actually marching through the enemy's country . . . it is a good plan to utilize the hammocks of the field hospital to carry Europeans during the heat of the day. Half the Europeans might be carried from 11 a.m. to 1 p.m. and the remaining half from 1 p.m. to 3 p.m.' This had its dangers as is shown by this incident:

'An officer, while being carried in a hammock, saw the muzzle of a gun peeping out of the bush laid straight at his stomach and not a yard off. He could just see the dim outline of a savage pulling the trigger and was so petrified with astonishment that he simply lay still and watched the man, as he thought, empty the contents of the gun into him. He saw the flash of the priming as the flint struck the pan, and made sure [sic], he was a dead man, but by an extraordinary piece of luck, the gun missed fire, but before he could draw his revolver the savage was away off into the bush. All this happened in a flash and it so unnerved him that for the next three days, sleeping or waking, he held a loaded revolver in his hand.'

That resulted in 'there being one golden rule to follow in fighting badly-armed savages in the bush and that is, "Don't give your enemy any leisure to reload his gun, but keep him on the move and press home your attack with the bayonet."' That sentiment is still ever-green.

Even as late as 1930, British officers and non-commissioned officers of the Royal West African Frontier Force were advised to stay on tracks through the jungle and keep out of the jungle itself as it was too severe for Europeans.

Men of those times would have heartily agreed with the sentiment of what Grant Taylor, the American-Irish policeman who eventually ran gangster Al

Capone to ground during Prohibition, said about there being only two kinds of gunmen – the quick and the dead. None of the historical fighting in woods, bush or scrub, however, qualifies as jungle warfare as it is known today.

EUROPE AND ASIA: DIFFERENT VIEWS, SIMILAR SENTIMENTS

The roots of the crushing defeats of so many non-Asian armies by Asians from the mid-20th century onwards, as well as Asians of one philosophy beating Asians of another – the Chinese civil war for instance – are embedded in history and are worth examining.

Long before the prowess of Roman legions became legendary in Europe and Asia minor, a remarkable man in eastern Asia had worked out how best to overcome an enemy: the Chinese military philosopher of about 350 B.C., Sun Zi, had laid down principles of war. One of the best known of these is this; 'Break the will of the enemy to fight and you accomplish the true objective of war. Cover with ridicule the enemy's traditions. Exploit and aggravate the inherent frictions within the enemy's country. Agitate the young with the old. Prevail if possible without armed conflict. The supreme excellence is not to win a hundred victories in a hundred battles. The supreme excellence is to defeat the armies of your enemies without ever having to fight them.'

Just over two thousand years later, the great Communist leader, Mao Zedong (Tse-tung), aspired to win China from the Nationalists. He had many problems on his hands, both political and military, with severe handicaps of logistics, support and, in the earlier stages, manpower. Being a firm believer in Sun Zi's philosophy, it is no great surprise to find him adhering to the old maestro's principles and becoming victorious. He quotes them in his famous *Thoughts* and Chinese Communists related them to their armed struggle in the jungle. During the Second World War, engrossed though he was with his own problems, he learnt from Western weaknesses. He saw Westerners' craving for creature comforts as self-inflicted 'sugar-coated bullets' hastening their eventual collapse.

Military eccentricity and unconventional methods have often paid dividends, whether the commander be Roman general in the 2nd century B.C. or Vietnamese guerrilla leader in the 13th century. In the former case, Fabius Maximus beat Hannibal, leader of the Carthaginians, by avoiding a pitched battle, being content to wear the enemy's troops down by harassing them on every possible occasion. In the latter Tran Hung Dao defeated Kublai Khan, the Mongol emperor, by similar mobile guerrilla tactics that included avoiding a 'head-on' battle. In 1287 the Mongols were defeated, 300,000 of them being routed, in the Red River area near Hanoi.

For many of those in Europe, war began to be seen as chivalrous and heroic, certainly in the upper echelons of society. By the 12th century, the crusaders had pushed the eastern border of Europe – now synonymous with Christendom – into Asia, its limit merely reflecting the fortunes of the religious campaign of the day. Thus it was that Europe became a concept with a fixed eastern limit and Asia, by default, a non-concept, a vast beyond, a geographical vagueness, with very little meaning other than describing the larger, non-European part of that vast landmass. Even the word 'Asia' is found only as a loan word in most Asian languages and is understood only by a handful of Asians. Although their meanings were lost before the time of Herodotus, the 'Father of History' who lived in the 5th century B.C., the probable derivations of 'Europe' and 'Asia' are from pre-historic Semitic-Babylonian – *asû* meaning 'to rise' and *erebus* 'to set', so have no other significance than the daily phenomenon of the sun's passage. Darwin thought that Europeans were descended from gorillas and Asians from chimpanzees, a not unattractive thought in some respects.

All major political ideas have come from Europe, while all religions, especially those of the Book, have come from Asia. (In modern times, many Asians and Africans in British-held lands came to see Christianity as a cover for colonialism, especially with the Church of England having obligatory prayers for the British monarchy.) The present Dalai Lama wrote about a glass curtain between Europe and Asia which, by causing haze, discoloration and distortion, prevents a clear perception of one another.

The ensuing arrogance in the belief in the supremacy of ideas, culture and many other matters, including those of a military nature, that emanated from Europe over those of Asian origin, seems to have been a constant since the 12th century (although Chinese arrogance in respect of everything and everyone non-Chinese is so much older and more persistent). It brought its own eventual downfall in the mid-20th century, mainly in the jungles of Asia.

In the 18th and 19th centuries this belief in European superiority was constantly reinforced as the colonizing European powers established their trading settlements in Asia without any insurmountable difficulty from local troops. The climate was often a greater hazard to the uninvited and unacclimatized visitors – in the early days of British involvement in India, for example, mosquitoes were thought to be good for a person's health as they sucked impurities out of the blood! The intruders came by sea and, apart from any local opposition, any threat to a particular territorial area would likewise come from the sea, the enemy being another European power – except for Russian encroachment on India over the Khyber Pass from central Asia.

Although the eastern armies were numerically superior to the Europeans they were no match for them: the Europeans acted as a team but the Asians acted as individuals. Organization and discipline were very poor, leadership was by example and there was no proper chain of command for passing on orders. When the King of Bali was killed in action against the Dutch all his soldiers committed suicide rather than continue fighting because dying was the last thing the king did and there was no one to give any orders to the contrary. The habit of rigorously and meticulously following the commander's actions under every circumstance showed an inflexibility which is still a characteristic in many, if not all, Asian armies today.

The early Europeans came in a frame of mind to succeed. Before Portuguese explorers set out for the unknown, they attended their own requiem mass. Hundreds of years later, soldiers of North Vietnam also attended their own funeral with full rites before moving to the south to fight the Americans. Some had their skins tattooed to read: 'Born in the north to die in the south.'

Trade being the aim of the Europeans, their territorial expansion was directed at the minimum required for this to be maintained in a framework of law and order. People generally were not interested in the hinterland unless profit

Above: Communications would be limited and comparatively easy along the grain of the country on established footpaths and along the rivers. However, the rivers needed crossing and, certainly during the monsoon, fording them was either out of the question or too perilous to be worthwhile. (Gurkha Museum)

Centre: From earliest recorded history camps susceptible to attack were surrounded by a wall, the more important and permanent, the stronger and more heavily defended. When the undergrowth made an approach by hostiles more likely, a watch-tower would be erected and sentries posted. This picture shows the Indian Army stockade, complete with flag, at Wakching, 1913. (Gurkha Museum)

could accrue. The upper reaches of, for instance, Burma were better left untouched if the only result were a China that would react to hinder trade. Over the years jungles, the tropical rain forests of south-east Asia, were seen as an impenetrable barrier, a place to be avoided, not as a battleground.

Skirmishing in Asia beyond India, sometimes in jungle terrain, took place during colonial expansion. Five times from 1824 to 1886 British troops were involved in Burma along with local upholders of law and order – Eastern Frontier Rifles, Myitkyina Military Police and Naga Hills Battalion (among whom were a number of Gurkhas from east Nepal) to name but three. In Malaya, during one of the least known campaigns – the Sungei Ujong war of 1875–6 – a Victoria Cross (VC) was won by a Captain Channer, of the Bengal Staff Corps attached to the First Gurkhas. The 3rd Regiment of Foot (The Buffs), with detachments of the 10th and 80th Regiments, along with a half battery of gunners from Hong Kong, the First Gurkhas and a company of the Bengal Sapper and Miners were involved. Conditions were 'very trying' and, in this instance, a 3-day approach march through thick jungle was undertaken. Some small stockades were captured and the attackers suffered some casualties.

On 20 December 1875 Captain Channer won his award for, in the scathing words of one British historian, 'leaping over a stockade on a Friday [the weekly day of prayer] and driving away a few Malays from their cooking pots'. Another historian described it as 'a courageous action'. Channer 'had gone forward with a few men . . . [and] seeing his opportunity, rushed a stockade which commanded the rest of the position'. A road bearing his name is in Seremban, not so very far from the scene of the action.

SAVIOURS OR SAVAGES?

In Indo-China, from 1858 to 1884, the French pushed in from the coast in their quest for expansion, trade and glory. They established a series of forts or strong

Above right: Improvised ranges could be easily made in areas where there was little danger or worry of hitting locals. Peacetime budgets never allowed as much practice in firing live ammunition as was necessary, and expeditions against hostiles was when much-needed practice could be achieved. The men shown at musketry practice, in Tam Lu, 1913, are sitting down to shoot: firing from the prone position with long grass around means that virtually no target can ever be seen. (Gurkha Museum)

posts – some in jungle – from which they tried, never very successfully, to dominate the surrounding countryside. The French presumed that their influence would spread like an oil-slick from where they had established themselves, bringing the benefits of colonial rule to places not as yet under their control. Indeed the Americans also used the 'oil-slick' concept when they started their pacification policy in that ravaged country, having found out how very sticky was the 'tar baby' of 'Brer Gook' – Uncle Sam versus Uncle Ho.

The arrogance of the French towards their colonies has been well documented; the cruel exploitation, the brutal maltreatment and contempt of the Tonkinese, Annamites and others in Indo-China shown during that phase sowed the seeds of bitterness and frustration, as well as a burning desire to be rid of them. General Vo Nguyen Giap, in September 1945, said that the French had built more gaols than schools, more prison camps than hospitals, more barracks for their colonial army than houses for the people; in that month, Ho Chi Minh said that the French had forced the use of opium and alcohol on the Vietnamese to weaken the race. Such bitterness does not accrue overnight. From personal experience, I know these feelings not to be the product of some partisan historian's imagination: for instance, to shop without rancour in Saigon, in 1945, I had to speak French well enough to be understood, but badly enough not to be taken for a Frenchman. It was bitter irony for so many Vietnamese that, when the northern Communists did prevail, Communism was as much a failure as it has been everywhere else, with its mismanagement, corruption, privileges, repression, intransigence and cruelty only differing from previous colonial rule by being applied by Asians, not by Europeans.

British colonial characteristics have been described as a blend of 'racialism, arrogance, aloofness and greed'. In the idiom of the times, such traits were often observed between the social classes in Britain itself, so it is not surprising that they were duplicated abroad. At least the British who worked in the colonies bothered to learn the local language, unlike the French who, certainly in the forces, never spoke anything except French. 'If the native soldiers can't speak French, they go hungry,' was one remark made to me by a French officer who heard me speaking Urdu to an Indian soldier and Nepali to a Gurkha. The British, in the main, liked their Asian colonial subjects and treated them paternally for the most part. Some British officers and colonial civilians came to love their men so much that they wholly identified with them and, on having to leave them, suffered premature death of a broken heart, helped on by overdoses of gin. Going on pension from the old Indian Army was known as 'leave, pending death'. Rubber planters in Malaya regarded the Malays as 'making good pets'; in Borneo the British had almost total empathy with the Natives of the hinterland.

THE EFFECT OF THE FIRST WORLD WAR

The Great War of 1914–18 saw, certainly in Europe, a type of protracted, static, linear warfare that permeated the future thinking of many military minds. This, to a calamitous degree, ossified development of tactics and training as much as did the financial constraints that were introduced into Britain after the 'war to end all war' had been won, even though in the following peace a disinterested observer might have been excused for not realizing that war was to be no more.

During that time there had been no military activity in south-east Asia of any overriding importance and, anyway, who in Asia posed any threat to the 'White Man and his Burden' (which was written about the Americans in the Philippines, not the British Raj in India) where native troops were only any good with Europeans, preferably British, of the officer class? It was regrettable, in the minds of the military, that some British people still sullied their hands in trade by being 'box wallahs', but the sun never set on the British Empire – some Indians said that was because not even God trusted the British in the dark – and it was obvious that, apart from Queen Victoria promising the Indians eventual independence when she allowed the Congress Party to be a vehicle for such a movement, elsewhere things were set fair for the foreseeable future.

That frame of mind was patently obvious at the outbreak of the Second World War: through no fault of their own, troops in India were facing across the North-West Frontier in anticipation of Russian involvement; troops in Singapore were facing the sea; and what few troops there were in Burma initially trained for desert, not jungle, warfare. In 1941, the War Office in London said that it was a waste of effort to send troops to Burma and a visiting Ministry of Information official sympathized with young British soldiers that they would see no action there. Nowhere was there any urgency displayed in the provision of fully authorized quantities of small arms, support weapons, ammunition, stores or spare parts for infantry battalions. Nowhere was there any realistic training. Nowhere, so it seemed, was there a spark of urgency, dedication or preparedness in the direction whence disaster eventually came – from the Japanese in south-east Asia – over the seas and through the jungle, not from the Russians over the barren North-West Frontier. This lament of imperfections could be repeated for all other branches of the armed forces in Asia. As for that basic and vital commodity, Military Intelligence, it did not seem to exist with a large or a small 'i'.

JAPANESE: JUNGLE GIANTS

The Japanese brought jungle warfare out of its subsidiary role and to prominence. They successfully exploited it to make up for their unequal military strength and weaker industrial base compared with the Western democracies. To redress this imbalance the entire Japanese thrust into south-east Asia and the Pacific was planned to take advantage of climate and geography, and their armed forces for such an enterprise were specially designed to compensate for the West's conventional forces' numerical superiority. Even with the superb bravery shown on so many occasions by the Japanese, it is doubtful if they could have been successful in such places as Burma and New Guinea without 'jungle warfare'; nor would they have been defeated on land had the Allies not become adept jungle fighters in conjunction with superior military hardware and logistics.

Japanese expansion in south-east Asia had been a threat since 1932, but their defeat at the hands of Russian and Mongol troops on the border of Outer Mongolia and Manchuria in 1938 was not the least of the factors which decided them to turn south. Their dedication to training in the islands of Taiwan and Hainan developed jungle tactics (in concert with the native population for 'live enemy'), and rewarded them handsomely, even if the troops deployed in Malaya had recently been in Manchuria (prairie-like terrain with a temperature range of below 40° Celsius to above 40°) which was the opposite of tropical jungle. Their solid preparations over the preceding years to find out all they could about others' dispositions and ability generally to withstand such a sweep south from Japan – doctors, dentists, barmen, barbers, masseurs, photographers and tattoo experts as agents in all the main towns of (and often in military camps themselves) their target countries – not only paid great dividends but was as meticulous in planning and preparation as were the Allies' indifference to and unawareness of the real and ugly situation that had reached its own point of no return and had acquired its own momentum.

The Japanese aims seem to have been oil in the Dutch East Indies (modern Indonesia) and security of sea lanes, so Malaya, Borneo and the Philippines had to be taken. Burma would not have been a concern if it had not been the overland route into China from India. Between December 1941 and April 1942 the Japanese had occupied Malaya, Singapore Island, Burma, Bataan, Sumatra, Java, nineteen other provinces of the Dutch East Indies, the Philippines, New Britain and the northern Solomons. For permanent consolidation of all their gains, the Japanese needed to eliminate Australia, but they did not bypass New Guinea and the surrounding islands, they pushed through them. Had they gone straight for the Australian mainland, it is possible that they would have won the war. Despite such speedily acquired and unprecedented gains, there was still no conclusive result and, like a man on a moving bicycle, they had to keep going to maintain momentum and balance.

These spectacularly quick successes, against an enemy who thought that the Japanese were second-rate soldiers – short-sighted, bad shots, afraid of the dark, so short-legged that they could not easily walk over rough ground and whose almond-shaped eyes could not see through bomb sights – had virtually destroyed any faith that the colonial population had had in their masters' ability to defend them or their families, had put paid to the belief in the white man's superiority and invincibility, and had severely dented the morale of all British, Australian, Dutch, French, Indian, Gurkha and Burmese soldiers serving in the Burmese and Pacific theatres. The Japanese were supermen, experts in the jungle in a way never previously imagined, invincible, brave to a degree unsuspected and malignantly cruel in a manner few had ever contemplated modern men could be. They also despised the softness and lack of military endeavour in their enemies. They used the jungle as a conduit of movement; the Allies tried to fight the jungle and the enemy, and, to start with, were unsuccessful against both.

The great problem for the Allies in planning counter-offensives was not so much the intrinsic quality of the Japanese troops, equipment and generalship but the jungle, a shield for the Japanese, that had to be penetrated before getting to grips with them. It was just as much a mental as it was a physical barrier to the vanquished. This frame of mind had, in fact, never fully permeated those units with high morale. During the retreat through Burma in 1942 for the Gurkha battalions of, for example, 48 Brigade, offensive action against the Japanese was the norm. These 1,700 men managed to kill 25 per cent of the enemy, some 500 men, at a cost to themselves of only three killed and seven wounded. Their rearguard action, at Kyaukse, was belatedly described as the 'most brilliantly fought of the entire Burma war'. This, however, was never publicized, so the outside world was only to learn that successful action against the Japanese could be taken as a result of the first foray by General Wingate and his Chindits. The gain was much more than purely military and that was great enough, with jungle warfare now elevated to its proper place in the strategy and tactics of military thinking as a serious and separate form of combat in its own right. It was also psychological in that the barrier erected by both the Japanese and the jungle had been penetrated effectively.

In an aside, there is no doubt that Wingate impressed people. Whether they liked him or not, they could not ignore him. In 1988 he was still remembered when, as a subaltern, he went riding to hounds in Dorset. He was frantically untidy but very brave on a horse, with a penchant for swimming his steed across rivers that left the other riders nonplussed. But it was his eyes that caught people's notice; with piercing gaze, he gave the impression of being fired by an inner compulsion seldom seen in others.

The Japanese outran their ability to organize any further advances, either towards India to the west or to invading Australia, New Caledonia and New Zealand to the south and south-east. As for India, the Japanese seem to have been under the impression that the Indians were only waiting for an excuse to rise up and throw the British into the sea. The thought that the Indians would not have welcomed other occupants of their land, even though they were Asians, does not seem to have struck them. Despite their propaganda about the Co-Prosperity Sphere of Greater East Asia, their aims were primarily of self-interest.

The Japanese successes in the Pacific campaign brought with them problems that may not have been fully appreciated in the planning stages of that enterprise, as has been pointed out in *Green Armour* by Osmar White, an Australian war correspondent. Just as the Germans baulked at invading Britain in 1940, because of technical difficulties, so the Japanese could not make a positive move immediately after their successes because they were unwilling to commit extempore invasion forces to so technically difficult a project as leap-frogging the Arafura Sea and New Guinea without insurance of cover by land-based aircraft which they lacked. This delay allowed the Australians to rally.

Although initially bemused and nearly beaten by the Japanese, later the Australians definitely got the upper hand in the jungles of New Guinea. So successful and so well geared to prevailing requirements and conditions was their conduct of jungle warfare and training for it that General Slim wanted officers of the British and Indian Armies to be attached to them in significant numbers to reap the benefit.

Initial victories were won by the Japanese navy and army, the latter mostly in the jungle. Although the Japanese lost the opportunity to conquer half the world when the Allies won the naval battle of the Coral Sea, in the final analysis victory for the Allies only came when heartland Japan was so bruised that the political will to continue the fight was no more. The turn in the Allied fortunes in the jungles of Asia and the Pacific were sufficient only for peripheral victories; the decisive hammer blow had to be made where it hurt most – by definition as near the heart of the country as possible.

Japan would not have surrendered on 15 August 1945 without the dropping of the atomic bomb twice on its soil earlier in the month. It is very probable that the war would have dragged on for another two years or so with, who knows, as many if not more casualties to the Allies and the enemy as were caused by these latest weapons of mass destruction. But dropped the atomic bombs were; the totality of the war embraced force even to that unheard-of extent and at a price many later considered was too high.

Once more, after victory in 1945, was it believed that the 'war to end all war' had been fought and peace would prevail for ever: the idea of such horrendous weapons being used again was something that no sane person could contemplate. It was equally true that none of us on the ground in Asia at the end of the war would have believed it had we been told that jungle warfare would be the staple military diet of a significant part of a number of armies, including the British, for many years to come – in my case ten years 'under the canopy'.

The United Nations Organization (which unkinder wits describe as 'a high-level platform for low-level propaganda') started off as the earnest of mankind's intention to settle quarrels and disputes amicably and without resorting to bloodshed. Alas for such pious ideals! Since 1945 the world has been witness to more wars than at any other period in history, especially the type called 'brushfire', a picturesque but inexact term for a small, anti-government war in the Third World. It was as though those countries that did engage in hostilities saw the suicidal folly of generating fighting to the pitch of sophistication that characterized the Second World War, although the fighting in Korea in the early 1950s and on the Indian subcontinent in the 1950s and 1960s was ferocious and intense. Those who felt it their mission to get rid of one type of regime (often colonialism) and replace it by another (just as often Communism) could ignore the nuclear dimension of retaliation as they planned their campaigns that, to a large extent, took place in the jungles of Asia. Even then mere acquisition of territory was not seen as being sufficient for victory.

Metropolitan governments found themselves in the unenviable position of being unable to react to this new situation in as crisp and positive a manner as they would have liked. The quest for freedom from colonial rule, for self-determination and for independence in Indo-China clashed with the wishes of

France – when the French had no intention of voluntarily handing over its territory to anyone – and the adherents of Ho Chi Minh, who were equally sure that they would evolve their own destiny in which France would play no part. The British Government found itself unable to hand over power in Malaya to the Malayans as long as there was a second contender to rule in their place, the other being the Communists.

As far as Britain is concerned, full-scale hostilities such as in the Second World War have not occurred since 1945. British government policy has a wide military template, however, and operations involving jungle terrain include: prophylactic deployment to deter aggression – Belize since 1978; prevention of internal (Communist) aggression against the legitimate government of the country – Malaya from 1948 to 1960 and Kenya in the early 1950s; counter-action against an internal rebellion – Brunei in 1962–3; prevention and deterrence of external aggression from a foreign power in aid of a friendly power – Malaysia from 1963 to 1966.

Other countries have had to face military and political problems involving unconventional military action in all sorts of terrain. For example, apart from Indo-China, the French were heavily involved in Algeria, where they used the lessons of their defeat in Indo-China to try effectively to counter the situation there. The Filipinos had the Hukbalahaps (originally standing for the People's Anti-Japanese Army, 'Huk' for short) insurrection on their hands from 1945 to 1952 before ever the New People's Army (24,430 strong in August 1987 and supported by 1.7 of the 55 million Filipinos) and Muslim separatists started anti-government activity. In the mid-1980s the Americans were active in their own reading of a, to them, disadvantageous situation in central America and had recourse to unconventional warfare backed by conventional weaponry. Even the Russians in Afghanistan found that their conventional military machine was inadequate for the task in hand – indeed, had it not been for the helicopter, whether used as troop carrier, gunship or scout, all such campaigns would have given the underdog a better chance of holding out longer and maybe not losing at all.

DEFINITIONS

These aspects of unconventional war have spawned their own crop of differing names to describe situations that, on the face of it, seem depressingly similar. Unconventional military action has been described as low-intensity, irregular or guerrilla warfare, with insurgency, insurrection, rebellion or revolution also applying as labels. Jungle warfare is not in that list, because all those facets of an armed struggle can take place in any type of terrain, including jungle.

It is in this context that the use of special forces must be mentioned. Every army has them and every army has protagonists and opponents for and against them. The Chindits in Burma were not special forces, far from it (although they won four VCs, three of them posthumously), but the role they had to play was special, even though some senior commanders felt that, militarily, the use of scarce resources would have been better spent in the main offensive, not on a 'side show'. The British have a love/hate relationship with 'private armies' yet make a better job of operations requiring them than do most other nationalities.

Undoubtedly there are certain tasks that do need special troops with specialist training – the British Army's 22 Special Air Service Regiment (SAS), the United States' 'Green Berets' and such units as the French Composite Airborne Command Groups in Indo-China, for example. If armies had at their disposal all the money they required it might be possible to train all combat troops to carry out every sort of task. However, peacetime armies are not profit-making organizations; if they were, they would soon be out of business.

It is worth giving brief definitions of those terms which cover military activities of an **unconventional** or **unorthodox** nature, as some of them overlap. A **guerrilla** is a member of an **irregular**, usually, but not necessarily, politically motivated, armed force that combats stronger regular forces, police or army; an **irregular** is a soldier not in a regular army. Both guerrilla and irregular make use of unconventional methods and tactics and, for the purpose of this book, only the term guerrilla will be used. **Insurgency** and **insurrection** are one and the same, with an **insurgent** in international law being seen as a person (or group) that rises in revolt against an established government or authority but whose conduct does not amount to belligerency. Plenty of room for grey areas there!

Rebellion and **revolt** are also synonymous for all intents and purposes, both implying resistance to a government or authority by force of arms. For the enthusiast and not pursued here at all, French military thinking goes even further

Right: Most communicating was done by runner. However, during the normal campaign season there was always enough sunlight for messages to be flashed by heliograph at some time during the day from the flat areas near rivers where a main camp was erected to a picket on any open piece of ground in the surrounding hills. This method was still in use as late as 1947 when the author was serving on the North-West Frontier, then India, now Pakistan. (Gurkha Museum)

and talks about **subversive** and **partisan** warfare, with the assertion that **partisan warfare + psychological warfare = revolutionary warfare**.

The last term, **revolutionary**, is the most important of all and is the one that is used in this book. This is because, apart from its meaning of **the overthrow or repudiation of a regime or political system by the governed**, it also has a special meaning in Marxist theory – **the violent and historically necessary transition from one system of production in a society to the next, as from feudalism to capitalism**. It is **Communist Revolutionary Warfare (CRW)** – first used in its present sense by Mao Zedong (Tse-tung) in 1936 – and its counter that have been the cause of so much fighting in the jungle and have resulted in tactics in jungle warfare being improved upon over the past four decades.

For the Communists, revolutionary warfare is not so much a war for territory but for people; it has a 'social dimension' otherwise unseen except in religious wars of conversion. It embraces political, economic and cultural strands, the first two of which are as important as or maybe more important than any military policy. This is shown in their armed forces having political commissars at all levels who outrank their military equivalents, even in action if they consider it necessary. Some Asian revolutionaries never forget its political side, as illustrated by Mr Le Duc Tho, of North Vietnam, who became famous in 1973 when he negotiated America's withdrawal from Vietnam with Mr Henry Kissinger. He regarded negotiations as a form of protracted revolutionary warfare. Mr Kissinger once told him 'I admire your ability to change impossible demands to merely intolerable demands and call this progress.' The Western world seldom seems to grasp the fact that the Communists still remember what Lenin said in 1917 – that politics equals war minus bloodshed and war equals politics with bloodshed.

The terminology used for operations to counter Communist revolutionary warfare (and guerrilla warfare) is normally **Counter-Revolutionary Warfare**, but may also be **Counter-Insurgency**, abbreviated to the first two letters of each word, **COIN**.

There is some confusion over the terms **bush, forest** and **jungle**. Bush is a word used far more in Africa, Australia, New Zealand and Canada than in Britain. The dictionary will say that 'bush' means an uncultivated or sparsely settled area, usually covered with trees or shrubs, or indeed a forested area and woodland generally; 'forest' is a large wooded area having a thick growth of trees and plants; while 'jungle' is an equatorial forest area with luxuriant vegetation, often almost impenetrable. Such niceties have not been observed by many, and use of any of them reflects the fashion that pertained until the Burma campaign rather than impenetrability of thickly wooded terrain.

Tropical warfare should not be confused with **jungle warfare** as the former refers to one of the world's climatic regions, not necessarily to peculiarities of terrain. Conventional war is just as possible in the tropics – the Torrid Zone – as anywhere else although people might tend to connote tropics with jungle and monsoon conditions rather than with, say, desert, the countryside around Calcutta or the Peruvian coastline.

Jungle warfare is, as we have seen, slightly special. Besides the significant effect it has on fighting and administration so, of course, do the climatic conditions and characteristics of the combatants.

2
Climate and Combatants

TROPICAL CLIMATE

Jungle warfare does not normally take place in a climate that is bracing, crisp and refreshing but where it is enervating, stuffy and unhealthy. The nearer to the Equator, the less variation there is. Dawn and dusk are always at about 6 o'clock. In the tropics there are no seasons with summer and winter; monsoons mark the only difference in weather, making it wetter and a bit cooler when actually raining. Day temperatures hover around 32° Celsius and at nights a sheet for cover is all that is needed. A natural, unbroken sleep is not easily come by. Sweat is a constant; damp a tedious companion. Thirst is never far away. Too much liquid spoils the appetite. The best part of the day is the very early morning. After that the dead hand of the tropics offers only inertia that needs a positive physical and mental effort to combat effectively.

Hot, damp climate shortens the life of material objects and lessens the efficiency of machines – in which Americans have always put boundless faith. Untreated meat has to be eaten the same day. Rice turns sour about eight hours after it has been cooked. Stitching of clothes rots, rust appears overnight and, in the monsoon, mildew grows on leather between dusk and dawn. Prickly heat rashes make the body uncomfortable and the temper short. Bugs proliferate. Frogs and scorpions find the inside of footware the best place for them (but not for the person who, without first holding both shoes or boots upright and tapping them firmly on the floor, tries to put them on in the morning!). Nothing is dry, all is damp. Ceiling fans, intended to cool, swirl hot air; if turned on high enough in offices to dry the sweat, a harassed desk worker is constantly going through the motions of a one-armed paperhanger. Paper sticks to the hand and ink easily blotches. Only in those havens of cooler weather, the hill stations, are conditions mitigated.

By the 1950s air conditioning was a perk of senior officers and most soldiers never experienced it at all. It was gradually introduced into British troops' barracks and canteens, but proved to be a 'two-edged weapon'. I found that soldiers who did not live in air conditioning were better able to withstand the rigours of hard jungle training than were those who did. These latter had to make a physical adjustment each time they left their coolness and, on their return to it, had to make adjustments in reverse. The only soldiers to die on hard physical training that I knew about had air conditioning in their accommodation. Living in the jungle is a far cry from living in canned air. Fair-weather soldiers make gloomy regimental histories.

For Europeans in the tropics a different approach to eating and drinking is necessary. Heavy, starchy meals in the middle of the day make the eater comatose and lethargic – yet the wisdom and experience of the pre-war Indian Army, where breakfast between 9 and 10 o'clock after a couple of hours' work, no lunch as such and a meal in the evening produced as fit a bunch of soldiers as any, was never accepted by the British Army in the tropics. A curl of the lip, a look down the nose and muttered remarks of 'hill top' and 'gone native' greeted any such suggestion. Yet few British troops were really fit. Of all the Asian races I have met, the Malays appear as the most idle by European standards and they have a heavy midday meal. Reluctance to try local fruits and vegetables, not serious as such, puts a strain on supply resources and may make it harder than otherwise for a soldier to survive. A large meat ration agrees with non-tropical troops as well as Asians when they can get it. As an Indian Army training pamphlet put it:

'Was ever Tartar fierce or cruel
Upon the strength of water gruel?
But who shall stay his raging force
When first he rides then eats his horse?'

Much has been done in the way of making rations light-weight and ready to eat after heating. In earlier days, rations were monotonous and short of calories, consisting of raisins, biscuits (probably with weevils), processed cheese, corned-beef, powdered milk, sugar and tea. When chocolate was introduced into Gurkha rations the men refused to eat it, believing it to be made from blood. Others experiencing Indian chocolate for the first time were not even as kind as that! Many British soldiers were not clever at mess-tin cooking and found it a chore. Even when they were adept, dry fuel and clean water were not always easy to find. The smell of cooking could jeopardize security.

A glimpse at 'how it was done' has been provided by an old soldier from the Chindit operations, Private J. Lindo of the King's Liverpool Regiment, who wrote: 'The Yanks have a very sweet tooth and it showed in the "K" rations with which they supplied us . . . There were three packets . . . daily, breakfast, dinner and supper. We were supplied with five days' rations at a time, which in most cases had to last us twice and sometimes three times as long. They became so boring that all kinds of concoctions were thought up.

The processed cheese (ugh!) was mixed with the crushed biscuits, the bouillon powder added and mixed with water. On the order at dusk, "light fires", we were all like beavers. The "cheese bouillon" was placed over one fire whilst your "oppo" brewed up. By the time the order came to "douse fires" we had a hot meal . . .'

The soldiers even made a cake with biscuits, lemonade powder, fruit bars and chocolate that could be eaten on the march! Private Lindo is indeed right when he says; 'Yes, the Tommy can adapt to any climate or conditions. His ingenuity is amazing.'

Without sufficient fluid intake the body dehydrates. Before the Second World War the teaching was to drink as little as possible, a pint or two a day with salt tablets added 'prevents heat exhaustion which would otherwise kill you', said the doctors. Some units in Burma carried two water-bottles and the troops were only allowed to drink from them when there was potable water handy for an immediate refill.

This attitude about water intake eventually changed, thanks to a new generation of guardians of our health from civil practices, and we were exhorted to drink as much as we could and abjure the salt tablets. This 'prevents hardened arteries which would otherwise kill you', they said. Alcohol, whatever its proponents argue to the contrary, apart from seldom quenching a thirst, makes tropical conditions harder to tolerate in the long term. Not often (even once was once too many) those who were unable to live a normal life except by hard drinking broke down from alcoholic remorse and had to be evacuated in a strait-jacket. At the other extreme were those who drank large amounts of fresh lime-juice. After six to eight months this, as often as not, gave the imbiber gallstones.

Everything is affected in the tropics: food, matches, cigarettes, radio batteries, equipment, aircraft and pyrotechnics, to name but a few items. The mind changes into a gear of acceptability when entering the jungle that would be unthinkable in camp, while having a sweaty body and wearing dirty clothes that become second nature. Smokers find it hard to realize just how much they stink compared with a non-smoker. Smell remains in the air for longer than normal. I have smelt cigarette smoke one hour after a platoon had moved off after a rest – the men had sat down near a swamp and the smell of the smoke had not moved. Tobacco used by the guerrillas had a different smell so I knew it was my soldiers who had been smoking.

WILD LIFE

Wild life in the forests of all monsoon rain forest countries was seen as similar to that in Burma, where 'the forests contain an infinite variety of trees and plants; palms and rubber trees are numerous, cinnamon, cloves and nutmeg occur in the wild state, as do melons, cucumbers and pumpkins'.

Sometimes there were unseen dangers: in 1941 there was still a peacetime garrison at Port Blair in the Andaman Islands of a company of the North Staffordshire Regiment, which was reinforced, in January 1942, by 4/10th Gurkha Rifles. Major C. M. A. R. Roberts recalls that 'we spent our time digging defensive positions to defend Port Blair. The worst enemy was malaria. Our defensive positions and the area generally were later bombed and strafed by the Japanese and I remember watching in horror as "C" Company's position in a coconut plantation on a promontary overlooking the harbour disappeared with a tremendous rending sound in a huge cloud of red dust and smoke. I called the company commander on the field telephone. He said the bombs did not do too much damage but the falling coconuts were terrifying.' (Some of the 'inhabitants of the Andaman Islands' forests' were described as 'friendly but unreliable', some as 'hostile and will shoot on sight', yet others as 'semi-friendly but cannot be relied on'.)

Troops were told that, 'regarding wild life any of the following may be seen [in Burma] and some may be used to supplement rations; they should however not be relied upon; wild elephants, gaur, mythun (a cross between gaur and domestic cow), wild oxen, rhinoceros, deer, wild goats, wild pigs, Himalayan black bears, Malayan sun bears, tigers, panthers, monkeys, badgers, otters, ant-bears, cats, jackals and wild dogs. The Burmese eat iguanas, tortoises and snakes. The rivers and lakes contain vast quantities of fish . . . There are many kinds of reptiles.'

Maybe so, but some are not always easy to recognize. At 7 o'clock one morning, deep in the jungle of north Malaya, I was sitting on the bank of a river some 50 yards wide. It flowed in a wide curve. I suddenly heard a noise that sounded like the mewing of gulls; borne by the current from the far bank, I saw a long, thin, black snake which had curious bumps equidistant along its entire length. Each bump was making a noise and I called for my men to come and see it. None of us could fathom what kind of snake it was, but it did seem as if the reptile had swallowed a number of piglets whole and the wretched things, still alive, were trying to escape. The current carried this creature past us, towards the near bank, where it hit a rock. It split in two, the tail end swimming on gamely but the front part disintegrating, each bump all of a sudden growing four legs and moving independently. We were spellbound and it was only when each moribund 'piglet' stood up and scampered away on two legs did we realize that we had seen a family of monkeys crossing the river – too wide to jump from tree to tree – holding on to one another's tail, being carried over by the current.

Animals are not normally a hazard. The Malayan buffalo is aggressive towards Europeans (something to do with their body odour) and the wild bison towards everybody. Animals are normally more afraid of men than men are of them, yet they have to be treated with respect. Malayan tigers will only become savage when their cubs are threatened. An Australian SAS trooper on patrol in Indonesian Borneo was killed by an elephant because he frightened it by firing his weapon at it. The teaching is, 'if you have an elephant charge you, try and run away downhill'.

These animals can turn sour unexpectedly: two soldiers were trampled on by an enraged elephant. As one man escaped the other was seized yet again and impaled on one of the tusks, suffering severe injuries. The soldier was critically ill for a fortnight, but six months later had made a complete recovery.

Elephants, however, are normally placid. I had taken some men out for a night ambush on a rubber estate during the period of the full moon. We were in three groups, with myself at the farthest end of the line. Nothing had happened by the time set to lift the ambush, so I started back to meet up with the other groups. Even in the waning moonlight I could see that one man was extremely shaken.

I asked him what the matter was but he was unable to speak. His friend told me that he had been lying motionless, watching the road to his front, listening to the noises that never cease – twigs dropping, branches snapping, insects, small animals. Suddenly he felt warm air in his ear and thought it was his section leader who had come quietly over to see if he were awake. He put his hand up and there, *Ram! Ram!*, was an elephant's trunk. He glanced up and saw the animal standing over him, investigating him tentatively.

The soldier whispered to his section commander, agonizingly, 'Send it away, send it away!' The NCO, acutely conscious of what an angry elephant could do, responded by collecting as many twigs as easily came into his reach without moving his body and threw them, almost conciliatorily, at the elephant. Agonizingly slow seconds passed. The elephant lifted one of his front legs and stepped over the recumbent Gurkha, now emulating rigor mortis, so petrified was he. Then over came the other front leg and finally, after an eternity of a few more

Above: Dutch troops crossing a stream in Java, their pack-horses laden with pieces of equipment. (Popperfoto)

Right: Dutch troops assembling a mountain artillery gun in jungle terrain on the island of Java, Dutch East Indies. (Popperfoto)

seconds, both back legs. The elephant then moved off to where it was joined by its mate and offspring. That was at 9 o'clock; by midnight, when I met him, the man was being helped along, still almost in a state of trance, unable either to believe his luck or, in his heart of hearts, that it had not all been a frightful nightmare.

A sentry of 1/6th Gurkha Rifles, in pitch-dark jungle, inadvertently leant against an elephant's leg, presuming it to be a tree. Being lightly touched on the ankle, then the knee, did not worry him unduly but when he found his rifle trying to move upwards, he became alarmed and pulled it down abruptly. The next thing he knew was that he was flying through the air and even the renowned Gurkha discipline was unable to suppress a squawk of pain when he landed in a thorn bush. The NCO, who had a rope tied round his wrist for silent communications, nearly lost his hand. It was only the next morning when the sentry was shown a pile of dung that he changed his story from being attacked by an evil spirit to an as-frightening-but-more-prosaic elephant.

A patrol came across a baby elephant that had fallen into a hole. They dug it out and, being hot, took out their water-bottles for a drink. The baby elephant made frantic efforts to get at the water, so parched was it. The soldiers emptied all their water into a 'basin' formed from a poncho cape so that the dehydrated creature could drink its fill. When they moved off, the elephant followed them, making so much noise that the soldiers had to abort their mission.

Birds flying towards men can indicate that they have been startled by other men. They, and monkeys, can be misleading, especially when ears are tuned to listen for a particular sound or set of sounds. I have deployed a company in thick jungle to surround and attack what we presumed was the enemy building a camp. We crept towards our target, tensed at the prospect of a fruitful contact, only to be violently disappointed to discover the unusual combination of a woodpecker feeding off some tree ants, and monkeys, with sticks in their paws, beating the branches of trees. More than once has a stream that gurgled over stones caused the lead scout to report voices!

Animals have been used by security forces. The Japanese had some horses in Burma. Mules were extensively used by the Indian Army and were of the greatest value, adding considerably to flexibility of movement. They had, sadly, to be 'de-voiced' to prevent their giving away the presence of troops by braying. Tracker and patrol dogs can be of great value but are apt to wilt in the heat. Carrier pigeons were one answer for remote outposts in French Indo-China and Borneo. Elephants have been tried in Burma and Malaya. The most unsuitable animal that was ever sent to Burma was the camel. The demand for a few of these cumbrous creatures turned out to be a garbled message on another topic!

HEALTH AND HYGIENE

As ever, the jungle effects tropical hygiene as it does everything else – excess of sunlight and heat, the prevalence of disease-bearing insects and 'the grossly insanitary habits and customs of the natives'. In the jungle direct exposure is minimized, but the danger of heatstroke is often accentuated by the hot, moist atmosphere and the lack of air movement. Sudden chilling of the body as a result of resting in wet clothing or from cold night breezes is liable to be specially dangerous.

At one time in Burma malaria was so prevalent that the mosquito was doing the work of the Japanese. It was only when commanding officers were sacked because of a high rate of malaria in their units that the problem was kept in check. British troops found mosquito-nets too much trouble to carry so had to use an evil-smelling cream that did not last all night. When a battalion was in tents the duty officer would check that the men had smarmed the stuff on by opening the tent flap and sniffing, little realizing that it was, in many cases, the tent pole that had been annointed, not the men!

In areas remote from habitation malaria and infective bowel diseases were rare, but the incidence of septic scratches and minor injuries was certain to be high. In the jungle, more than anywhere else, hygiene is a matter for the individual. This point has always to be impressed on everybody from the beginning. At first sight the disposal of excreta was not thought to be a problem. Each man carried a pick or a shovel and after a pit had been dug in the evening, a wooden frame would be erected over it. The pit was filled in next morning. Fouling of the ground, especially in camps on the Lines of Communication (L of C) from India to Burma was a danger to health. Temporary latrines must be dug and filled in before troops move off.

On active service health has to be maintained for troops to be effective, but it is not easy to maintain a high standard of personal hygiene with so few facilities. In a medical survey of troops in the Malayan jungle, conducted from August 1954 until July 1955, skin diseases, especially among British troops, were the most prevalent sickness. Forty-six cases per 1,000 were reported from old-timers, while every person who went into the jungle for the first time was noted to have been affected. The chief troubles were ringworm on the feet, secondary infections from abrasions or bites, boils, impetigo and prickly heat. This was not too surprising in relative humidity of 90° Fahrenheit. Pressure from wet clothing and equipment exacerbated conditions.

Scrub typhus, of which 120 cases were reported during this time, was no threat once mite repellant was rubbed into clothing. Heat stroke and heat exhaustion were rare. Malayan jungle temperature does not seem to exceed the critical 83° Fahrenheit, but the intense heat in *lalang* (thick, exposed, long grass) did claim victims.

Leptospirosis, caused by bathing in rivers in spate after flood waters had washed animals' (particularly rats') urine from their holes in the banks, claimed two deaths in 120 cases during the period under survey.

Malaria was hardly ever reported where suppressives were taken: Mepacrine (which gave people a yellow tinge and, Japanese propaganda said, made one sexually barren) and, after the war, Paludrine, which only tasted foul. In the Burma campaign camouflaged face veils blurred vision but the troops found that if they inked over the part they looked through they could see clearly. Gloves, though provided, were hardly ever worn. Officers scarcely ever got malaria and the theory was that it was whisky that prevented it. One bottle was allowed each month and many got rid of it so quickly that no other preventive was needed!

A scratch that would heal in a day or two in a temperate climate becomes a festering sore in that same time unless stringent measures are taken. A cold takes weeks to shake off. Basic drugs and first aid equipment have to be carried; preventive medicines have to be taken. In the lowlands of New Guinea malaria, typhus, leprosy, hookworm, yaws and many types of skin disease were prevalent. Apart from those medical hazards, the soldier ought to know what to do for fractures, sprains, animal and snake bites, drowning, burning and contact with poisonous trees.

Acclimatization was as much a subject for controversy in Burma as it was thirty years later when reinforcement of Malaysia by British troops after the pullout from 'East of Suez' was under discussion. In the 1940s it was thought that seasoned troops needed about six to eight weeks of gradual conditioning before undergoing prolonged physical exertion in the tropics. Recruits required longer. (In Malaysia the optimum period was six weeks.)

If it is hard to adjust to the physical side of tropical life – and it is never easy – it is far harder to inculcate the correct mental approach that is essential, at times vital, for soldiers on active service in a jungle environment. For any untrained, unacclimatized, untried soldier, especially a 'townie', great physical and mental efforts have to be made before a measure of military competence can be instilled and confidence enhanced sufficiently to have an even chance of being successful. Instead of four-footed game hunted by one side only, both sides of the two-footed variety are hunters and hunted, let alone the problems of living and moving that have to be overcome before the fighting aspect can be seriously tackled. High morale is ever-important.

MORALE

Against an enemy as ruthless as the Japanese, probably one of the greatest factors pertaining to morale was the knowledge that casualty evacuation was efficient so wounded men would neither be captured by them nor left to die forsaken – a sad feaure of the withdrawal in 1942.

The best British battalion in the Malayan campaign of 1941–2 was the Argyll and Sutherland Highlanders. It is a recorded fact that this was the only British unit seriously to train in the jungle. What is not so well known is that after the outbreak of hostilities, the commanding officer sacked all the rifle company commanders and replaced them with younger men in their early twenties. These were the forerunners of a breed of officer that had yet to make an impression in the rest of the army that was still suffering from a restricted budget, unrealistic training, class-consciousness and time promotion. They worked wonders. At the end of the war 203 men returned to Scotland from captivity and, at a regimental reunion forty years later, 200 of them were present. A wonderful record!

Apart from belonging to a good unit and good health, the correct frame of mind when in the jungle is imperative for high morale which is often hard to sustain: the jungle surrounds one the whole time, there is no fresh air, no view, no end to it. The soldier carries his house on his back and it is always heavier at the end of the day than it was in the morning! At night a change of clothes can bring relief, but I have known it to rain every day and night for a month, to rain without stopping for seventy-two hours at a time and, on one occasion, with only a break for a quarter of an hour in five days and nights – no dry clothes then. It

Right: This photograph was taken during the Allied attack on the Japanese-held village of Satelberg, New Guinea. The troops moved at dawn behind the spearhead provided by the Matilda tanks; here a wounded soldier is carried back from the action to the rear area for treatment. (Popperfoto)

Right: However thick the Burma jungle was (and in many places it was not as thick as popular imagination and old soldiers' tales would have one believe), it was always much sparser after fighting had swept through it. Shellfire was responsible for many of the leaves being blown off the trees. Years later in Vietnam, the Americans would try to get rid of it altogether using chemical warfare and bulldozers. This is Garrison Hill battlefield (Kohima?); it is dated 1 September 1944 which suggests that this photograph was taken a very long time after the battle. (South East Asian Command)

Right: Looking back from 'Scraggy' to 'Malta Hill', from which the famous feature was attacked. In the foreground is equipment which the Japanese had left behind in their hurried retreat. (Gurkha Museum)

is at times like these that a man remembers what the sergeant-major said: 'You shouldn't have joined if you've no sense of humour!'

In *Defeat into Victory* Field Marshal Sir William Slim devotes fifteen pages to this subject. In essence the Great Man wrote that morale consisted of the spiritual, the intellectual and the material, in that order: spiritual is not the same as religious, but belief in a cause and a contempt for death are prerequisites. The British are shy of talking about spiritual things, this trait being most marked in the English, then the Welsh and the Irish, and least of all the Scots. Indian races are more ready to respond to abstract grounds as all religions, local patriotisms, and military tradition are part of the everyday fabric of their lives. Gurkhas are the most stolid of all audiences. At basic level, morale embraces food, pay, leave, beer and mail. I once talked about morale to the Field Marshal and he gave me the firm impression that an officer with low morale was not a good officer.

The Welsh seemed able to retain high morale. Certainly 2nd Welch in India when war broke out did. They trained long and hard. Their strictest order was never to talk, always to whisper. They were never attacked at night by the Japanese who howled and yelled, crashing about near their perimeter, trying to draw their fire. Company Sergeant-Major John Edwards remembers how everything was always done in pairs so that men were never alone. When they used the bayonet, as individuals, they favoured the silence of concentration rather than the noise of abandon.

The Welshmen kept their sense of humour. One of their most prized possessions was a zinc bath they had found somewhere and was carried on one of their forty mules (they also had fourteen elephants). One day the bully beef stew was cooked in an old Burmese cemetry and a cook saw a skull, bleached and ghostly, on the ground. He hid it in the stew and caused quite a commotion when he served it to some unsuspecting soldier! Edwards remembers how improvisation played its part when he found out that the best cup of tea 'I had ever tasted' had been strained out of the cook's sock, which he put back on after the brew was over.

Men shaved every day, keeping a drop of their morning tea to soften the bristles. After the war, soldiers of 1st King's Own Yorkshire Light Infantry were ordered not shave in the jungles of Malaya but nobody liked it and the order was changed back in a few weeks.

My own definition of high morale reflects the post-war campaigns and it is, 'the willingness and ability to give of one's best when the audience is of the smallest'. In other words 'to go those last few yards'. I also see that for dedicated Communists, being atheists, it is political not spiritual motivation that impels them.

EQUIPMENT

Soldiers can only be expected to give good results if they are clothed, equipped and rationed sensibly. In the early days of the war in Burma troops wore shorts with turn-ups that could be tucked into their stockings at night. These garments were unpopular (they held the water after crossing rivers) and the turn-ups were cut off. In 1941, during the retreat in Malaya, apart from wearing khaki-coloured uniforms and heavy hobnailed boots, British troops also carried great-coats, steel helmets and respirators in addition to packs, haversacks, groundsheets and blankets.

By the time I joined my battalion of Gurkhas in Burma everything that could be made green was. I remember being particular impressed to find even towels, underwear and toilet-paper were all green.

In New Guinea the Australians were similarly overburdened to start with, but they later discarded steel helmets, respirators and all extra clothing, less a pullover and a spare pair of socks, with blankets and towels cut in half. They retained their gas capes as being better against the rain than groundsheets. Not for the first time did the soldier find a better use for certain items of kit than the original design. They discarded their bayonets which got in the way when patrolling and were useless for digging. This put them at a distinct disadvantage in hand-to-hand fighting when the Japanese made a bayonet charge against them.

Australian troops in Malaya wore bayonets. In 1942 Lieutenant-Colonel C. G. W. Anderson gained a VC, having made a bayonet charge against the Japanese during the Muar battle. In the mid-1960s he returned to Malaysia, as it had become, to tell us about his experiences. We were at the very place where he had temporarily routed the Japanese and, softly yet very eloquently, he mentioned that he had led another bayonet charge in German South-West Africa in the First World War. He was debating the merits of a quiet and a noisy bayonet charge and asked us, his audience, which we thought the better. In the embarrassed silence that ensued as we all waited for someone else to answer first and tell him that he was a man in a boys' league, I noticed a car slowing down as it passed along the road that had been built after the war, near which we were standing. It was flying the flag of the recently accredited Japanese Ambassador, the first since the war had ended!

Another battlefield narrator was a company commander from a British battalion of that time, 2nd Loyals, which had gone to reinforce the Australians. It was clear from his harrowing account of what went wrong (there was nothing they did that went right) that ordinary movement was hard enough but, impeded by unnecessary and heavy clobber, fighting was far harder than it ought to have been. Reliance on transport and a peacetime mentality drastically slowed down the British soldiers. They were bemused by the speed of the lightly equipped yet horrifyingly efficient Japanese, who took only a quarter of an hour to cook and eat their meals and whose only standard piece of equipment seemed to be mackintosh capes with hoods. In 1942 the soldiers of 2nd King's Own Yorkshire Light Infantry went into battle in Burma in the same dress as they paraded in India – khaki shirts and shorts, thick woollen hosetops (stockings without the feet, known in Gurkha units as 'footless'), hobnailed boots and pith helmets.

When operations in Malaya started in 1948 hobnailed boots and gaiters were worn because canvas jungle boots of calf length had yet to be produced. Special light-weight equipment was not available until the mid-1950s and, significantly, it was Australian in origin.

AIR

In modern warfare aerial superiority can often be a decisive factor in victory or defeat. From the air the jungle looks like a carpet of cabbages and it takes much time and experience to navigate an aircraft with accuracy. In the tropics all aircraft have payload and ceiling limitations. If, in a temperate climate, the ceiling of an aircraft is say, 10,000 feet, it could be much less in the tropics where the air is too thin for a similar performance. Mountains rise to 8,000 feet, are often cloud-girt and constitute a hazard, especially when having to drop supplies to troops operating in them. Pilots found it very difficult to know where the air currents were so that they could get their runs over the dropping places as needed.

Even when such tiny spaces in the jungle were found there were difficulties that the pilot would not have expected. In 1952 my company was taking aerial resupply in Malaya. In those days only smoke marked the dropping zone; panels and marker balloons came later. I was not near the set when the following conversation was monitored by battalion headquarters: 'Valetta for Ground. Put up smoke!' called the pilot. 'Ground for Valetta. Wilco. Out,' answered my Gurkha operator. Nothing happened for a while and that conversation was repeated twice. Finally the angry voice of the pilot came crackling through, 'Valetta for Ground. Smoke! Smoke! Smoke! Smoke! Over!!' It was getting late. 'Ground for Valetta,' radioed the Gurkha. 'Wilco. Wait out.' I got back to the set just as the aircraft flew away, still with our rations on board, to find a puzzled Gurkha signaller lighting the cigarette the pilot had insisted he smoke, then calling, '. . . Smoking. Over.' (That was almost on a par with the corporal in 2nd Royal Welch Fusiliers who, when on patrol, was overheard to say, 'Jones, don't you go down that track or else we'll have to take you home lost!')

Away from the mountains in New Guinea air support was difficult when 'planes skated, skidded, staggered, slithered, rocketed their way through air that was as rough and solid-seeming as an angry sea'. Turbulence at heights adversely affects all aircraft and the first generation of helicopters especially suffered. Whereas in Europe a light aircraft can rise 700 feet a minute, in the tropics 300 feet is the limit. Another limitation for airmen over the jungle is when guns are registered using smoke as this slows down the process.

During the Second World War there was no helicopter support. Since then this versatile flying machine has changed the face of military operations as much as any other piece of equipment – as much as the '7-league boots' of fable – with, in the 1960s, America developing vertical attack by helicopter-borne troops.

Air support has also provided such controversial aspects as bombing and spraying defoliants. In Laos the American-sponsored Thai secret army (Thai Unity Forces) needed B-52 strikes on bends in the road ahead of the troops as they advanced, as well as in their rear to maintain forward momentum. Movement through bombed jungle is very difficult; bombed swamp limits speed to less than a hundred metres an hour.

THE ASIAN ENEMY

Then there is always the enemy, an Asian enemy, with stricter codes of conduct, different standards of ethics, higher levels of tolerance to discomfort, hunger, pain and fear. For him there is no front line, no fixed line of communication, no obvious direction of approach. He has no set numbers but has infinite patience, he moves quicker and better at night, his camouflage is better, he is more determined with his zealous beliefs, he eats and sleeps less and carries more than does his 'civilized' counterpart. He is ruthless and can be cruel, he uses fear as a weapon – usually not the decisive one – and he is careless of life (his own and ours). There are millions of him.

As for fighting, so much depends on the scale and type of warfare. In the Second World War the Allies fought against the Japanese on land, in other people's countries. Their hold on the entire Pacific region was weakened when they lost the Battle of the Coral Sea, but they still had to be prised from their territorial conquests by fierce land battles. On mainland Asia, territory for territory's sake had to be captured from or denied to the enemy. Strategy was global. Complications were caused from the very top in Burma by the Americans insisting that there be a land campaign to link up with China, and the British, especially Mr Churchill ('I hate jungles, which go to the winner anyway'), who wanted to substitute an amphibious operation against the tip of Sumatra as a stepping-stone to the recapture of Singapore. There were also complications in the Pacific with the Australians favouring decentralized planning and the Americans (who were in overall command) preferring it to be highly centralized.

Further down the scale of military thinking ideas also differed. In December 1941 the High Command in Malaya was not the least interested in anything as unconventional as guerrilla warfare. It 'seemed an extravagant and impracticable notion'. The idea of stay-behind parties consisting of Europeans and Asians was vetoed, if for no other reason that that it would be bad for the morale of Asians if the Europeans showed by such drastic action that they feared a victory by the enemy. On the other hand such ideas found some favour elsewhere, for instance Wingate's 'Chindits' in Burma and the Americans' smaller 'Kit Carson's Scouts' or 'Bushmasters' in Vietnam. Fundamentally these formations were not unconventional, but only an extended version of the old cavalry foray into enemy territory. Basic tactics – fire and movement having to be co-ordinated, artillery support requirements, all-round defence or whatever – only needed modification for the jungle and were never to be forgotten if success was to be achieved.

Controversy over Wingate still rages and, for the most level-headed appraisal of his achievements and failures, I can do no better than to recommend *Orde Wingate and the Historians*, by Peter Mead. Wingate was responsible for: the philosophy of Long Range Penetration into the guts of the enemy; the exploitation of air supply in jungle terrain; the use of air support to replace artillery.

Furthermore, he put an end to the myth of the Japanese soldier being a 'superman'. Mead quotes what the Japanese Fifteenth Army Commander, General Renya Mutagichi, wrote: 'On 26th March I heard on Delhi radio that General Wingate had been killed in an aeroplane crash. I realized what a loss this was to the British Army and said a prayer for the soul of this man in whom I had found my match.'

In Burma whole formations would be committed at the same time, yet often it seemed to the men on the ground that it was only their company that had to be ready to attack, counter-attack, defend or withdraw so thick was the jungle. In New Guinea, the razor-backed mountains were so narrow that a battalion could be in a defensive position one-man wide.

Above: One of the defended positions on the slope of 'Linch Hill' which was taken together with 'Scraggy'. Lance-Naik Dambar Bahadur Sunwar of 4/8th Gurkha Rifles is inspecting a Japanese bunker. Many are the stories of derring-do from that time that the old pensioners in the hills of Nepal still relate: war was hard but you were fed, looked after when you were hurt, your companions were fit and active like you and there were decorations to be won and promotion to be earned by 'Jap-hunting'. (Gurkha Museum)

Below: Making sure that no Japanese were left to fight again was quite a gauntlet to have to run. It was against the Japanese Code of Honour to be captured alive; a prisoner of war was as good as dead. They fought on until the last, having to be flushed out of positions long after the main action had ended. (Gurkha Museum)

THE JAPANESE

In view of the superman image that the Japanese quickly created for themselves, it is surprising that such a man as General Wavell, in 1942, regarded them as a second-rate enemy and seemed to anticipate little or no danger from them in Burma. This under-estimation of the Japanese and an over-estimation of British and Indian troops' ability to defeat them was a serious error of judgement – certainly at the stage of the war when they so often seemed invincible. Yet British forces did often fight very heroically. I think the one event of the Burma campaign that engraved itself in people's minds more than any other was the blowing of the bridge over the river at Sittang. More than 35 years later, in the hills of Nepal, those who had been there and left on the far bank would inevitably bring it into their conversation, with a shake of their head and a far-away look in their eyes, within half an hour of any reminiscing.

The Japanese, like other nationalities, have two definite strands running through their character. One shows them to be an aggressive, materialistic people who are not easily daunted; the other reveals them as capable of subordinating all to the spiritual values that generate acts of self-destructive bravery on a scale seldom seen in modern times.

In Japan race and nationality are the same thing. They unthinkingly offend Asian multi-racial societies. In Burma their frugality, energy and capacity for hard work earned them speedy rewards. They were quick, had excellent camouflage and an eye for ground. They fought with savage and, at times, hysterical fury. They were very brave. If fifty Japanese were holding a position, forty-five of them would have to be killed before the rest would kill themselves and the position could be taken. Contrary to what was often thought, they were not naturally at home in the jungle, nor were they born fighters, the majority of their soldiers being urban dwellers. They were slaves to habit, much noisier than were the Allied soldiers. Most were rotten shots and they preferred to rely more on artillery and mortars than on small arms. At night their positions were most difficult to spot. On the march they were careless and easy to surprise.

From the beginning they gained the initiative, by thorough preparation. When fighting the Chinese they sometimes aped them so causing them casualties, as they did when fighting the British by disguising themselves as Burma Rifles soldiers.

The Japanese held their enemies in 'overwhelming contempt'. Their predilection for looting, raping and wanton bombing, and their obsessive cruelty to prisoners were feared beyond measure. However, their belief in *yamoto-dameshii*, the Japanese spirit that sees death in battle as man's finest destiny, did not compensate for material shortcomings and was counter-productive. Their own discipline was brutal. They were alien in the countries they invaded, although many Asians were happy to see white men humbled by Asians. The Burmese premier, U Saw, said, 'We Asiatics have had a bad time since Vasco da Gama rounded the Cape.' Among the Burmese as distinct from the hill tribes – Chins, Kachins and Karens, who were friendly and good fighters – the British could count on no general support. The Burmese of lower Burma were on the whole apathetic, wishing only to keep out of the way of the fighting. There was an actively pro-Japanese group of Burmese but that was estimated to be not more than 10 per cent of the population.

The strength of the Japanese Army lay not in any special aptitude for jungle warfare but in the morale of their soldiers. The men were 'hard, frugal and bestial'. Such obedience and ferocity would make a European army invincible. After the battles of Imphal and Bishanpur, General Slim talked about the supreme courage and hardihood of the Japanese soldiers. He knew of no army that could have equalled them. The Japanese soldiers committed suicide, blowing themselves up in front of or under tanks to disable them. 'This desperate form of courage was something that we knew little of and saw with amazement, admiration and pity.'

Although it was seldom if ever apparent to the Allies in Burma, there was a fundamental fault in Japanese generalship. This was a lack of moral, not physical, courage. There were pernicious personality clashes between commanders. Leaders at the top would not admit mistakes for fear of losing face. They ignored sound logistical planning and outran their supplies to their eventual detriment. Many officers suffered from tactical rigidity once they had lost the initiative.

Staff work was rudimentary. No one under the rank of captain had his death reported and they were heedless of casualties. Administrative troops were non-existent. Tim Carew in *The Longest Retreat* writes: 'There were no clerks, fitters, cooks, signallers, military policemen, medical orderlies, field bakeries, field post offices, pay offices, dental mechanics or hygiene sections.'

Viewed from Malaya, the Japanese were seen as very security-minded and very afraid of the dark. Spencer Chapman wrote that the Japanese troops that he had seen were good second-class material, well-trained and poorly equipped. He further notes that it was unprecedented for Japanese troops to be on jungle operations as far away from the road head as two days' journey.

In New Guinea Japanese officers were as prone to make mistakes and incur official wrath as in any other army. For instance, Major Takamura (III/102 battalion), was relieved of his command: 'There is still insufficient understanding and zeal in execution. It is a regrettable fact that with the lack of clearness of understanding, there have been many instances of failure to get any practical results. To be specific: there is a lack of quick, reliable transmission of orders; slowness and lack of comprehension in carrying out plans; leaders are lacking in eagerness to serve; they are not strict in their supervision of their subordinates; and there are those whose sense of responsibility cannot be relied upon. Reports are greatly delayed, some are not straightforward and frank and there have been much carelessness and many mistakes in various investigations; hence opportunities to advance our objective are lost.'

General Nakano upbraided his senior and middle grade divisional officers on their lack of willpower, their poor leadership, their prevalent whines, their feeble morale, their lost prestige, their lack of attention to detail. They had 'forfeited their trust and confidence because of the contradiction of their words and deeds'.

Japanese soldiers were everywhere respected as doughty fighters. The Australians saw that they ignored the limitations which jungles normally imposed on others. They ate less food, needed less in the way of shelter, transport and creature comforts. They were able to counter the enervating effects of the tropics. They improvised well and, when the going was good, they did not succumb all that quickly to disease. They were ready and willing to die for their emperor. As the Japanese themselves once put it: 'After drinking the *sake* graciously presented to the divisional commander by the Emperor, the unit vowed anew its determination to do or die . . . and demonstrated the unique and peerless spiritual superiority of the Imperial Army . . . All those who fell severely wounded committed suicide by using hand-grenades and, of the total of 186 men, all except 58 became guardian spirits of their country.'

The Japanese went on record as being 'willing to sacrifice ten million men to win our war'. Even allowing for a measure of hyperbole in that boast, how many of those who opposed them were willing to make sacrifices of a mere fraction of this amount?

Their soldiers' weaknesses lay in individual stupidity, with their 'leadership in adversity as unintelligent as it is courageous'. One case (of many) was when troops followed the same track each time they went in a particular direction and each time they crossed the same open ground to look at their dead comrades. They were needlessly easy targets and the Australians took full advantage of this in New Guinea.

In Burma an officer-led patrol of 2nd Welch climbed a low escarpment and surprised two Japanese machine-gunners, capturing them and their weapon. They had been told that no one could climb the cliff so had not resisted them, when unbelievingly, they saw men do just that.

The Japanese regarded their soldiers and machines as equally expendable, the only difference being, which could contribute the most to what had to be achieved? This was a view-point not shared by their opponents. The Japanese had to resolve, 'to die as martyrs, to burn with sincerity, be especially brave and calm, see an opportunity and act quickly and dispassionately'. Even with such exhortations, when the troops' normal meagre daily rations – two and a half pounds – were not available and they were so consummately tired that they could not go foraging, they resorted to desperate measures. Twice at least were traces of cannibalism found.

Being urban bred they were not used to looking after themselves and wastage rates were very high. 'The captured Japanese position was nauseatingly filthy, with an overpowering stench. The habits of some Japanese soldiers in occupation were worse than those of many animals; and this poor sanitary discipline no doubt accounted for the high rate of sickness,' says the official Australian history. Not only was hygiene discipline appalling but, unlike in Malaya, so was their security. Time and again complete lists of units and officers, till then unknown to the Australian authorities, would be found on dead bodies in the front line.

A prisoner of war was as good as dead and was the ultimate disgrace. *Hara-kiri*, ritual suicide by disembowelment with a sword for those who carried them, was infinitely preferable. Each Japanese soldier carried a grenade with which to blow himself up rather than face capture. For instance, during the battle for the Mariana Islands in June 1944, 40,000 Japanese were killed or committed *hara-kiri*, with only 1,000 captured.

The only live Japanese soldier I came across in Burma was unable to walk; he scared me by asserting that there were many thousands of troops in the direction a Gurkha patrol had gone. In the event it transpired that he thought I had asked for his army number!

THE CHINESE

Although the Japanese and the Chinese are both Asians with much culture in common, their armies were vastly different. The Allies felt it imperative that China be kept in the war at all costs. Some of those costs were the lives of Allied soldiers.

The characteristics of the overseas Chinese (guerrillas who fought in the Malayan Emergency of 1948 to 1960 and who were so active on the Thai–Malaysia border until the late 1980s – and who so hated getting wet it was best to attack them when it was raining) were not the same as those of the Chinese troops who fought in Burma, formed bodies of military men in an uninstitutionalized army. The philosophy of these latter was different both from that of the former and of the Japanese. The central Chinese army did not become involved until after any regional 'war lord' army had taken so many casualties that it posed no threat to it.

In the 1940s Chinese formations lacked much that a modern Western army finds essential. For instance the Fifth and Sixth Chinese Armies had no services at all – rations, rail transport, fuel for vehicles were all British-supplied. There were no tanks, no artillery and no medical services in the accepted sense, and only a rudimentary system for casualty evacuation. Both divisions had one vehicle each, the commander's staff car. The Chinese staff was not interested nor was it adequate to handle six, later nine, divisions. A sense of timing was utterly foreign to them. When Chinese divisions did have artillery, it was central to all tactical thinking.

Whereas the Japanese had spent much time and trouble on their 'intelligence' preparations, the Chinese had done nothing. Everything Burmese was foreign to them; food, currency, politics, way of life, attitudes, beliefs. All was a closed book that remained forever shut. The impulse for 'combat efficiency and the offensive spirit, like the Christianity and democracy offered by missionaries and foreign advisers, were not indigenous demands of the society and culture to which they were brought', wrote Barbara Tuchman in *Sand Against The Wind*. The whole Burma adventure was foreign to their thinking.

The Chinese do not feel any military solidarity when it comes to fighting. They prefer to go about their tasks with guile and subtlety rather than by normally expected tactics. Chinese military officers usually did not involve themselves in any responsibility for the outcome of a battle. The proverb 'good iron is not used to make nails nor good men to make soldiers' is most indicative of Chinese military thinking.

Chinese troops could be tough, courageous and ruthless. The Fifth Army records troops carrying 120 pounds and marching thirty miles without a halt, but does not say what the state of the troops was at the end. They had defeated the Japanese in a major battle. Their discipline was generally good by oriental armies' standards, except that of labour units. As nothing was provided, hoarding became 'a cultural imperative' and they stole everything. They were seen as 'genial thieves', their monthly pay being about thirteen pence a month. They could be galvanized into action by the thought of money. They were told that they would be given US $50,000 if they took Taunggyi. This they did, collected the money and disappeared.

CSM Moore, a Chindit veteran, recalls constantly hearing about the Chinese refusal to move or take part in action. On two occasions they had supplies dropped a mile in front of them to make them move. Referring to the battle of Mogaung, Private Lindo recalls that the Chinese came in at the end, 'but took no part in the actual fighting, the hand-to-hand stuff. Imagine how the Chindits felt when it was announced that American-trained Chinese troops had captured . . . Mogaung. How bitter we felt . . .'

THE GURKHAS

All men can be incredibly tough on the battlefield. One example of physical stamina from Burma is of a Gurkha. Havildar Manbahadur Limbu, 'D' Company, 1/7th Gurkha Rifles, was shot through the spleen, slashed on the back of his head by a Japanese sword, then walked sixty miles to catch up with his battalion. The medical officer said that by the laws of medical science he should be dead. Manbahadur grinned and asked to be returned to his platoon.

When 2/1st Gurkha Rifles was captured in Malaya in 1941 the soldiers were put in gaol. To escape was very difficult. One rifleman decided his best chance was to volunteer to join the Indian National Army (Indian soldiers who joined the Japanese cause, turncoats as the British saw them) and then escape. This he did, walking through the jungle, past the Japanese, then the British lines, and on into India. Penniless, ill and in rags, he made his way across 1,200 miles to the First Gurkha regimental depot in the foothills of the Himalayas in early 1945. Limping the last five miles uphill and taunted by children, he stumbled towards the headquarters office block. Ignoring people trying to stop him, he went into the adjutant's office. Saluting, he reported his number, rank, name and battalion, then fell into a dead faint.

In such a fragile state he was not allowed to be interviewed for a week. He was the first man of 2/1st Gurkha Rifles who had escaped. He could tell the authorities the fate of every officer and man in the battalion. (In the ensuing trials of the Indian National Army, officers and men involved were graded 'black', 'grey' or 'white'. This soldier was a material witness but, as he had 'volunteered', he was graded 'grey' and his evidence about Indian soliders he had met in captivity was disallowed. The breach of trust, as he saw it, by the British after such agony endured for so long, was unbearable and he hanged himself in remorse.)

Then there was the remarkable story of the 2-taper, Naik Nakam Gurung, of the same battalion. He was hurt and had to hide. His company commander, Captain C. G. Wylie, had gone forward and another Gurkha officer tried to comfort Nakam Gurung. 'Stay where you are. The British forces will return soon,' was the message which burned in his brain. His other friends later went in search of the company commander and also disappeared. 'You'd better wait, the company commander expects one of us here,' they had said.

Days turned into weeks, into months. Only the man himself and the angel that looks after wild animals and soldiers on operations knew how he managed. About six months later he had given up hope. He had probably heard disquieting rumours during one of his desultory contacts for essentials from some frightened villagers, and formed his own conclusions. One day he was sitting in a cleft in the branches of a big tree where he had made himself a temporary shelter. It was the end: black despair, and the loss of the will to live, forced him to plait a vine rope, make a noose and put it round his neck. He tied the other end round a branch and jumped off. The vine snapped and he hurt his leg as he hit the ground. He then took his rifle and tried to shoot himself, but it misfired. 'I am ordained to live,' he thought.

He was periodically visited by Chinese guerrillas and slowly the years passed. Peace was declared but he knew nothing about it. The Malayan Emergency started and he continued farming his cleared patch of jungle. The aircraft he heard were still flying against the Japanese, so it was said. And one day, about eight years after he had been told to wait, a patrol of Gurkhas came across him. Talking among themselves they said, 'What a scruffy-looking man, not worth capturing is he?'

The lone man suddenly realized with a surge of hope flooding all other emotions that they were speaking his own language and he was alone no longer. The patrol's suspicions had to be allayed. They had taken him for a guerrilla and the fact that he spoke Nepali meant that he might be a spy. 'We ought to kill you,' they said.

Nakam Gurung tried to explain how it was he was in the jungle. 'Told to wait?', said the patrol commander, scornfully. 'Who is your officer, then? If you can't tell me that we will shoot you as a spy'. Now came a curious coincidence – the adjutant of 1/10th Gurkha Rifles, whose patrol this was, in a different battalion, in a different army, fighting a different war, was the officer who had given the order to wait so many years before. And when they met, the soldier, in utter sincerity and simplicity, said to Major Wylie, 'I knew you wouldn't forget to send for me!' Both men broke down and wept – the soldier never knowing that the patrol was, in fact, on the wrong compass bearing in the first place!

The tailpiece occurred when Major Wylie, returning from the conquest of Mount Everest in 1953, paid a visit to 2/1st Gorkha Rifles in India. He met Havildar Nakam Gurung, then promoted to three tapes, who said he had been given nine years' back pay, but as the service had not counted for pension he was not going to waste all those years waiting in the jungle.

(A Japanese doctor with the Chinese guerrillas in Malaya was killed in the middle 1950s and another Japanese gave himself up in the Philippines even later.)

THE AUSTRALIANS

A prime example of Australian stamina in New Guinea deserves to be quoted in full. In July 1943 an observation post in a place called Sepu was overrun before dawn. Private B. R. Roffe, of 2/7th Independent Company, a farmer of Balah, South Australia, displayed extraordinary fortitude. In the first burst of fire from the Japanese one bullet went through his left bicep, across his chest between skin and ribs and stopped short on the right side. Another pierced him behind the left

Right: During the British advance down the Paleb-Tamu road, some of the hardest fighting took place round the hill feature known as 'Scraggy', captured by men of 4/10th Gurkha Rifles. Here the Gurkhas are clearing this grim position; the remains of Japanese dead, equipment and caved-in Japanese bunkers were to be seen everywhere. Pollution of the air and ground by men, dead and alive, was a problem alway to be faced after a battle had been fought. Sanitation in Japanese bunker positions was non-existent and it was often impossible to evacuate the wounded and dead. Apart from those dangers, a Japanese counter-attack was always to be expected after one of their positions had been captured. (Gurkha Museum)

Right: Bombay Sappers and Miners hard at work maintaining the road – a vital task at any time, especially during the monsoon. (Gurkha Museum)

Right: As the Japanese retreated on the Assam-Burma front, they blew up bridges and damaged roads wherever possible. It was the task of the Sappers to restore communications as quickly as they could. Here, the road to Tamu having been blocked by a landslide, ammunition is rolled down the slope of the hill. (Gurkha Museum)

knee and another went through his left buttock. The Japanese officer leading the attack then pounced and hacked at Roffe with his sword, severed his left deltoid muscle twice, gashed the left side of his head, stabbed him between the neck and left shoulder, cut the back of his left wrist, almost severed the left index finger, gashed the inner side of his right arm above the elbow and at the inner side of his right elbow.

> This [wrote Roffe later] happened in a very brief space of time with no opportunity for resistance on my part and the blow on my head disabled me considerably. I came out of a daze to find my attacker standing a few feet away and out of sheer desperation I attempted to tackle him. I advanced unsteadily, abusing him in a rather ungentlemanly manner, while he drew a long-barrelled pistol and aimed it at my chest. Fortunately it misfired and while he was still gaping in amazement I seized the opportunity to retire hastily to the cover of the jungle. A few badly aimed shots followed me, but I managed to keep clear and, although I had not progressed far by nightfall, felt that I at least had some hope of getting back to the [main] ambush [position at Limbien]. I bathed my wounds as best I could and propped myself up against a tree for the night. My only hope of finding my way seemed to be on a track which we had carefully avoided on the way down. The next morning I was able to find this track by taking direction from the sun and followed it at a respectable distance, reaching by nightfall a point where we had camped overnight on the outward trip. Clad only in shorts and boots I spent a most uncomfortable night in pouring rain, trying to keep some of the weather off (unsuccessfully) with leaves.
>
> The third day was the most difficult as the only water to be had was what had been caught in fallen leaves the night before. Apart from a few bites of green paw-paw I had not eaten since before the attack. The going on the third day was all uphill but I managed to reach Limbien by nightfall and much to my relief found that we were still in possession of that point. The natives soon organized a *kunda* vine and sapling stretcher and a message of my survival was radioed to Bena [or Garoka] from where the 2/2nd Company Medical Officer, Captain McInermy, immediately set out to render aid. The next morning I was moved off from Limbien to Guibi where we spent the night. It was there on re-dressing my wounds that [it was] discovered my head was fly-blown. Having seen these pests successfully removed from sheep with kerosene and having no other medication effectively to attack them, some kerosene was found and duly applied with good results . . . The top of my index finger which had become infected was then removed.

THE BRITISH

There are many examples of British stamina to be found but the one man who epitomizes fortitude (among so many, including those prisoners of war on the 'death railway') is Spencer Chapman. He survived beyond the normal human capacity for survival, living, as he did, in the Malayan jungle for about three and a half years. He overcame dangerous illnesses (once for two months, including a period of unconsciousness for seventeen days with no one looking after him); he once took twelve days to cover ten miles of jungle and, on another occasion, went barefooted without food for six days. Twice wounded, captured by both Japanese soldiers and Chinese bandits, and able to overcome many other hardships, he was indomitable.

SELF-ASSESSMENT

This is how CSM Moore saw his men 150 miles behind the Japanese lines:

> On the move the priorities of our British squaddie never ceased to amaze me. His top priorities were the next bivouac area and the next cup of char. His second priority

was preparing to face the enemy. On the move not a piece of dry twig was left behind on the track. Every other man resembled a scarecrow, branches and twigs everywhere. Within minutes of bivouacing, fires were lit and char made. The sight of this performance will never leave me. Dozens of 2-man fires, one man holding the mess-tin, the other fanning the smoke away with his bush hat. Tea was made within a couple of minutes of halting.

He concludes by saying that in his view,

there can never be a better example of the qualities of British troops (and Gurkhas who took part) than that displayed at the battle for Mogaung.

Private Lindo says that the British soldier is noted for his humour, especially in adversity. He remembers the occasion when a stream ran through the column's bivouac area.

We took advantage of it, stripping off and washing our stinking bodies . . . We took it in turns to wash. One man came back from bathing with his towel around his waist . . . We were cleaning our weapons when [the man] started to give a cabaret act. Keeping his towel in front of him like a fan . . . he started to sing and dance, flicking his towel up now and again to show his private parts. Everyone was laughing at his antics when suddenly there was a burst of gunfire. Everybody took cover except the naked man who was trying to get his trousers on while holding on to his rifle. What a dilemma! . . . He never gave any more concerts after that, although the firing was accidental.

Some of my friends in British battalions told me that, as the war wound to a close, the wartime British soldier saw no point in going on patrol with the risk of being killed, captured or wounded at that juncture. Many British battalions were organized in three rifle companies, based on a soldier's demobilization number. Only those with six months' clear service went on patrol. That was not the case for those battalions that had high morale and good discipline as CSM Moore pointed out.

In 1945 the Chindits reformed after a break in Dehra Dun. We were visited by General Auchinleck with the sad news that we were breaking up. We were due to go home but the General asked us to volunteer for parachute duties as an example to all the men of the column. With a few exceptions all the column took a pace forward.

And CSM Moore's punch line is, 'Are they mad? No, just British.'

In a remarkably frank assessment of the Australian soldier in *Green Armour*, Osmar White sees him '. . . above everything else, a realist. He has too much horse sense to make good cannon fodder. The "death or glory" idea fails to move him. He believes wholeheartedly that it is much better to be a live dog with the will to bite – and a bite or two left – than a dead lion with no will or bite at all. He can see no virtue in stubbornness for the sake of stubbornness, nor in discipline for the sake of discipline. Give him a logical objective and competent leadership and he is one of the most dangerous and resourceful fighters in the world. But employ him on a task or in a manner beyond the limits of intelligent patience, and he makes a poor defender of last ditches.'

In the end it was the 'old traditions of courage, determination, self-sacrifice, team-work, initiative, endurance – and humour – that enabled Aussies to triumph over a fanatical enemy and over rugged and pitiless terrain and the rigours of a tropical climate'.

It is interesting to see what the Japanese thought of their enemies; they considered British troops as indolent, effete and out-dated, and Indians and Gurkhas as cowardly and disloyal.

In a document written for the edification of the Japanese soldier, the author, commenting on American tactics said:

> The American forces are slow and steady. They cannot attain a decision by one small test. Individually or sometimes in small units, sportsmanlike adventure will be attempted, but generally they are very steady and advance step by step and will not attack unless they are positive that they will not lose. Once they attain confidence, however, they will display gallantry far beyond their expectations. It must be expected that when this is attained they will change to extreme caution as in the normal state generally of all foreigners.

As the Australians saw him, the American soldier tried hard and learnt fast. He was equipped more lavishly, though not more effectively, than his Australian counterpart. His *métier* was to capture enemy positions which had been flattened or blasted by a previous bombardment. (I observed exactly the same tactics in the 1970s with the Thai Unity Forces in Laos.) The Australian jungle soldier, without the Americans' array of support weapons had to rely more on his individualism, common sense and stamina. That the Americans themselves understood the difference is evident from this quotation from *The Jungleers: A History of the 41st Infantry Division:*

> The Australians and Americans fought entirely different campaigns. When the Australian infantry lacked immediate artillery support, they would storm and take the objective by sheer perseverance and bravery . . . The Yank style of fighting was to wait for the artillery to come up and let the big guns blast the enemy positions as barren of all life as possible. It saved many American lives and got better results, although it took longer.

(In fact, the casualties of US battalions in this campaign were usually heavier than those of the Australian battalions involved.)

Brigadier Calvert wrote that there was not much wrong with the African soldier.

> If he'd had his own long-term British officers, if there had been any real desire of white South Africans to have him as a good soldier and to be proud of him, as in the Indian Army, he could be as good as the best Asian troops. But not all Africans are saints.

Gurkhas said that Africans were careless and noisy, did not put sentries out during periods of rest, or take many other precautions.

Soldiers from the Indian subcontinent came from areas far apart and different. Because they lacked imagination and the ability to express deep truths, they were less influenced by the 'dirty' side of war. Being, in the main, peasants, they were more tractable in infantrymen's country than many British troops who were born and bred in a 'concrete culture'. Certainly, for the Gurkha, it is wrong to say that he knows no fear. He can get very afraid, but more often than not it is the fear of fear that keeps him going when the fear itself would have stopped other troops.

II
CONVENTIONAL
WARFARE IN
JUNGLE TERRAIN

Previous page: *Men of 4/10th Gurkha Rifles march through Prome, central Burma, May 1945. (Gurkha Museum)*
Above: *These Matilda tanks are carrying out training manoeuvres in New Guinea during the Second World War prior to going into action against Japanese strong points in the Finschhafen area. (Popperfoto)*

Below: *The farther away from trees the gunners were, the easier it was to support the infantry, but very often the jungle enclosed the gunners too. When a piece became stuck in muddy conditions there was often only the brute force of the soldiers to manhandle it out. This was an all-too-common occurrence during monsoon conditions. (Royal Artillery Institution)*

3
Major Phases: British and Japanese Methods

Never before had the white races been given such a trouncing as they were by the Japanese in south-east Asia and the west Pacific in 1941 and 1942. Much time, effort, money and treasure were spent, and many lives and limbs were shattered, before those white races could turn the scales on their Asian enemy and beat him. Nothing has been the same since for any of the direct participants. Very few people in those regions were unaffected by the turmoil of those times.

BRITISH TACTICS

Individual campaigns have been written-up in great detail by both victors and vanquished, but chiefly by the former and always to justify the survivors, so it is said. There is a military dictum: 'There are no bad men, only bad officers.' Here I merely attempt to portray, in considerable detail, what it was that the soldier, individually or collectively, and his officer, had to know to bring this victory about. As I myself only came in at the tail end of the Burma war, much of my knowledge is that which I learnt but never used under completely similar circumstances. I have liberally refreshed my memory – and added to my own knowledge – by talking to those who were there and studying the manuals produced to fill the many gaps. I pay my respects to the unknown authors of *The Jungle Book*, the military training pamphlet that the Indian Army produced in September 1943. This reflects the improvement of morale in the army after its blistering defeats in 1942, and is the first attempt to portray conventional British military thinking for jungle warfare.

INFANTRY

Infantry was and still is the paramount arm in the jungle owing to its comparative mobility. Well-trained infantry can dominate the jungle. Special training, however, is necessary to accustom troops to the strange conditions of jungle life. This training, then and now, must inculcate the ability to move quickly and silently, to find the way accurately and with confidence, to shoot to kill at disappearing targets from all positions on the ground, out of trees and from the hip, to carry out tactical operations in the jungle by means of battle drill without waiting for detailed orders. Above all, the highest pitch of physical toughness was, and still is, essential for everyone involved and the leadership of junior commanders must be confident, offensive and inspiring.

However realistic a soldier's training is, it is only when in action can a fighting man's true worth and ability be measured. It is not surprising, therefore, to find failures. Refreshingly, one training manual admitted this by stating that: 'Not one man in fifty can lead a patrol, so if you can find out who are leaders before operations commence, you have found something vital. This resolves itself down to getting rid of poor leaders despite personal likes and dislikes . . .'

An American officer in the South West Pacific is quoted as saying: 'I have had to get rid of 25 officers because they just weren't leaders. I had to make the battalion commander weed out the poor leaders. Our junior leaders are finding out that they must know more about their men.'

The feeling of loneliness and the bad visibility in the jungle tend to make men jumpy if they have not complete confidence in themselves. In Burma, the 'pair' system was prevalent: this entailed two men always being together. There were severe penalties when the basic rule was broken; punishment when found out by one's superiors or death when found out by the Japanese.

General Briggs of 5th Indian Infantry Division issued 'Five Commandments' to his soldiers:

1 Be determined to kill every Jap you meet, then some [more Japs].
2 Be determined not to let the Jap frighten you with ruses and induce you to disclose your positions and waste ammunition. Ambush him and do unto him as he would unto you.
3 Be determined to hold fast when ordered, whatever happens. The Jap will then have to give you the target you want, while our reserves are on the way to help you.
4 Be determined to carry out to the letter every task given to you, whether on patrol, in attack or defence. No half measures. Plan for all eventualities, after anticipating enemy reactions. Plans cannot be too thorough. Be observant and suspicious.
5 Be determined – even fanatical.

Mortars frequently had to replace artillery in support of the infantry owing to their greater mobility. They had to be used boldly to reduce the distance to the observation post (OP).

Anti-tank weapons were of all sorts; rifles, guns and grenades, hand-held or fired from a discharger cup affixed to a rifle. Apart from their normal employment they were used at short range against pillboxes and bunkers as well as against Japanese tanks.

Grenades were the favourite weapon of the Australian soldier and indeed were carried in all campaigns. The close nature of jungle terrain enhances their value. In defence the grenade has an advantage over all other weapons in that its silent delivery does not disclose its point of origin and thereby give away the position of the thrower.

Grenade-throwing in thick country has its hazards for the thrower who has to be careful that the missile does not bounce back off a tree at him. I know of a case (it was after the war) when an officer from a European theatre came to my battalion in Malaya. He said he wanted to throw some grenades so arrangements for this were made. He ignored the warning about the danger of hitting a tree and threw his first grenade at some branches to show that it would penetrate them. It bounced back, exploded and blinded him in one eye. He returned to the unit some months later. Determined to regain his confidence he threw another grenade under the same circumstances and was blinded in the other eye.

In Burma armoured personnel-carriers were particularly vulnerable in the jungle and were never to be employed in a tank role. When used forward they were always to be protected by infantry. They were frequently very effectively employed in bringing such items as ammunition, water and cable to the forward troops, and to assist in the porterage of heavy weapons over difficult or vulnerable routes to their positions. Their use would jeopardize silence if such were a requirement.

In a letter written to me in 1987, Major C. M. A. R. Roberts (late 10th Gurkha Rifles) said:

> We reached Imphal in November 1943 via Ranchi where I remember we had a tremendous demonstration of fire power one day. As 25-pounders ripped up the ground ahead of us and Hurricanes tore overhead with all guns blazing, two Gurkha soldiers standing just behind me commented laconically; 'Like popcorn,' said one. 'More like goats farting,' said the other.
>
> . . . I have a record in my notebook of the time and the distances we marched over mountains and through jungle, crossing rivers and fighting battles on the way. There were, according to this now yellowing document, 29 stages, and whether we stuck to them or not I cannot remember, totalling 325 miles from Imphal to the Irrawaddy. And those are just the map distances. God knows how far we walked over the ground. And I was told when I was at school that I had flat feet and unless I did something about it I would not be able to walk by the time I was 21!

ARTILLERY

Artillery in jungle areas was hampered as regards observation, communications, movement and gun positions, but in the case, for example, of anti-tank work, the problem was not so great. Basic principles pertained; for instance, concentration of artillery fire was as sound in the jungle against the Japanese as it had been proved to be in North Africa, and the needs of the infantry always to have close support, no matter what type of country was encountered, had to be constantly borne in mind. It was not sufficient for the Forward Observation Officers (FOO) to accompany an outflanking attack, relying on wireless (not radio in those days!) to get through to the guns. A proportion of artillery weapons had to go too to give that close and guaranteed support to which infantry was entitled.

Guns in this context included any weapon with which field or mountain artillery was equipped, namely 25-pounders, 3.7in howitzers or mortars.

To be effective against the Japanese in the jungle, artillery support had to be provided rapidly. Information of enemy units was always at a premium and contact could occur at any time or place, so actions developed very quickly with no preliminary warning. This meant the necessity for close liaison with the troops whom the guns were supporting. FOOs had to remain well forward and in close touch with battalion or company commanders. They had to be prepared to make and carry out immediate fire plans without reference to their battery commanders. It paid dividends for infantrymen to be able to act as FOOs in emergencies.

Except in dense jungle, suitable gun sites for mortars and 3.7in howitzers were to be found in clearings. This would allow mortar batteries to provide support in the initial stages of an attack which the howitzers would strengthen when they could be brought into action.

25-pounders were used when opposition was heavy, but their movement was largely confined to roads and tracks. In thick country positions were difficult to find. The immediate vicinity of straight and open roads was generally avoided to minimize enemy air attacks. This meant that reconnaissance parties from 25-pounder batteries and regiments had to move well ahead of the guns to find suitable observation posts and gun areas in good time. Because of the Japanese habit of attacking from anywhere, the guns also had to be ready to fire in any direction. This added to the difficulty of finding suitable positions for them. Thick country always poses the problem of observing shell bursts. Ranging by smoke, air burst and sound were normal, helped by aerial photographs and accurate maps.

The Japanese dug themselves deep and their prepared defensive positions were strong. To be effective artillery fire had to be intense. This meant that frontages had to be very narrow and areas for concentration small. The thicker the country, the slower the rate the infantry could move, so barrages had to conform. Sometimes it was possible to register likely forming-up places of Japanese counter-attacks, but in all cases registration of areas to the flanks was essential.

Dominance in thickly enclosed country often hinged on control of a central road along which artillery was based in depth for defence. It, as ever, had to be ready to fire all round. Protection of gun sites was of great importance. For anti-tank artillery the field of fire often consisted of a narrow lane cut through the jungle to a distance of only forty yards from the road along which enemy armour was expected to move. Anti-tank guns were more often used against Japanese bunkers than armour.

Night firing seems to have resulted in Japanese panic, according to an escaped prisoner. He described how, as the first rounds of gunfire arrived, the Japanese, officers and men, dropped everything and ran for such places as stream beds and rock crevices. There they stayed for some time after the shelling stopped.

ENGINEERS

Jungle conditions do not necessarily imply a new engineer role nor do they alter principles of engineer work and organization. It was found, certainly in Burma, that, apart from large concentrations of resources usually being impracticable, there were never enough sappers. Improvisation was often the only way to fulfil a mission.

Much engineer effort was spent on making and improving communications, road making and bridging. Jeep tracks had to be corduroyed and upgraded. The many waterways in jungle terrain needed crossing-places developed for taking heavy loads. Sappers had to look out for bridging sites. Culverts and drainage systems were required. Water storage cisterns, tarpaulin water tanks, water points and pumping equipment were needed.

The Japanese tried to deter or delay advances and the engineers were required to recognize and remove enemy mines and other delaying devices, such as booby-traps.

As well as constructing strong points for their own forces, engineers were often called on to deal with enemy strong points and this entailed training for the assault with the infantry.

ARMOUR

I can do no better than to quote General Slim on the use of armour in jungle:

Tanks can be used in almost any country except swamp. In close country they must always have infantry *with* them to defend and reconnoitre for them. They should always be used in the maximum numbers available and capable of being deployed. Whenever possible penny packets must be avoided. 'The more you use, the fewer you lose.'

5th Indian Division, fresh from the desert, had to learn that frontal assaults were costly. Tactics were based upon those of tanks. This meant that troops manoeuvred to seize ground which was, or could be made, so vital to the enemy that he was forced to attack. Encirclement, hooks from left or right flank, and guile were to replace the more direct assault.

The regimental history of the 10th Gurkha Rifles for March 1944 is revealing when it describes the first occasion that the Japanese used tanks in the war in Burma. Whatever the higher command may have known, the sudden appearance of enemy medium tanks and guns in the Kabaw Valley at Minthami in March 1944 was a surprise to the troops, and the atmosphere of tension and uncertainty which surrounded their advent has been graphically described by Major Mike Roberts:

The next day, 13th March, that 'something' which had been expected so long, and which was now crystal clear to us, if it was not to Brigade, happened. At 1800 hours, as the sun was nearing the hills in the west, Jap guns fired from Htinzin at a gun position just behind our hideout. The first Jap guns we had ever heard. The first Jap shells ever to pass us by in anger.

An uncomfortable silence followed. [One of my platoon commanders, Jemadar] Narbir, ever crafty, changed his position. We packed our belongings, saddled the mules, and stood-to. Posts on the Sunle Chaung kept a sharper look-out over the wide, stony bed of the river. Nothing happened for a long while. Perhaps half an hour. Then we began to feel an uneasiness in the air. A man would be strapping up his pack, and would suddenly hesitate and then stand up as if he heard something. Then everyone would stop and listen for a while, and shake their heads and go on with whatever they were doing. But it would come again. Something in the far distance, throbbing, undefined.

I called the 2nd Border [Regiment] company, on my right and asked them if they could hear any odd noises down south. They replied that a patrol had reported tracked vehicles in Htinzin. So that was the answer! Not only had the Japanese some infernal machines that could penetrate the rocky fastnesses of the Atwin Yoma jungle, but they also had tanks and guns in Htinzin, and, the latter having rung the gong for the first round to begin, the former were advancing into the ring.

I told Narbir this news, but he merely said 'Hunchha [OK], Saheb,' and asked me if I would like any eggs.

I then went down to the Sunle Chaung and reassured myself that the banks were too steep for tracked vehicles to pass, and sat for a while and meditated on the plan for our withdrawal.

I . . . wandered back to the hideout, where the men were waiting, tensely, in their trenches, while the mules stamped and swished their tails and reflected on

Left: 'The road is in view of the enemy and so the tanks move off it on to a jungle track', writes Major Roberts of 4/10th Gurkha Rifles. The place is unknown. General Slim's maxim for the use of tanks was: 'the more you use, the fewer you lose.' (South East Asia Command)

Left: Soldiers of a British battalion (identity unknown) move up through Monywa. (South East Asia Command)

Left: Being a fit Gunner meant more than just being able to do your job well. Provision of ammunition to sustain an infantry attack, for instance, needed very detailed planning, while, in a fluid situation, keeping everything together was quite a business. The more men needed to hoist a gun around, the fewer there were available for other duties – ask the Battery Sergeant Major! (Royal Artillery Institution)

whatever mules do reflect upon in such crises as these. The sound of the tanks was constant now. Waxing and waning, now muffled, now sharp and clear, but never ceasing. The sun was setting as they came out into the open on the south side of the chaung, opposite Sunle . . . So we waited whilst the darkness engulfed us. There was no enemy movement across the chaung, and soon the full moon rose, allowing sentries to relax a little. And in the stillness of the night the roar and clatter and squeak of the tanks seemed unhealthily close. They appeared to be, from the sound of them, level with us now, on our right, as if they had occupied the Border company position and were driving up the road. There was no firing, only the roar of the tank engines echoing down the corridors of teak. Sometimes a great gust of noise would terrify the mules, making them strain at their bridles and stare wide-eyed into the darkness. The men would stare uneasily and look at me, wondering what I would do. Still no enemy moved across the chaung . . . The tanks were past and behind us now. The moon cast a slanting light through the high jungle, and the paths were clear to see . . . We set off in a long line, heading north, parallel to the road.

We were soon level with the tanks again and they seemed terribly close. (I afterwards discovered that they could not have been more than fifty yards away at times.) The jungle was thicker than I had expected and we had to cut for the mules at times. The tanks were a blessing here as they drowned the noise of our cutting. After some hours of extremely slow progress we blundered out on to [the road] . . . The tanks were only a short way behind, and with each surge of noise the mules would blunder, terrified, off the track, fighting against their wretched drivers, who struggled to drag them back as quietly as they could and without breaking the line of march. They had a hard time that night but they never let us down once. It was now 0200 hours and I moved on up the road cautiously, making for the road junction a mile or so south of Maw. We reached the junction at 0400 hours, and threw ourselves down among the fallen teak logs there for an hour's sleep after the nerve-racking march of the night. The relief of being away from those tanks after prowling flank to flank with them up the length of that Sunle road was greater than can be described.

In his letter of 11 September 1987, Major Roberts wrote:

One of the things I remember about this particular action was that on 12th March or thereabouts, I could hear the Chindits' planes going in overhead. That'll keep the Japs quiet, I thought.' It didn't. This aspect of the jungle war gets all the publicity nowadays. Personally I think it was a waste of time and effort, and took away some of our best NCOs. At the time it was quite clearly contributing very little to the main XIV Army effort.

About five days after this we had a terrific scrap at 5 in the morning defending a 25-pounder position. Apart from the fact that we clobbered the unfortunate Japs and took an officer prisoner, what sticks in my mind was the appalling noise – hugely magnified by the echoing jungle.

AIRCRAFT

Aircraft found the jungles difficult terrain to work over. Pilots could not easily reconnoitre for the army or identify targets. They attacked their own troops on more than one occasion and troops shot down their own aircraft. Target indication was in its infancy and was often achieved by smoke which was unreliable. Apart from missions of lethal intent, aircraft were of the greatest value to the troops on the ground in reconnaissance and supply work. The concept of joint work was not developed to the extent that became common practice after the war.

Aerial photography was of two kinds. Apart from when a pilot would take photographs to supplement first impressions of anything he thought merited further study, they provided regular cover of certain areas for intelligence purposes and helped commanders plan attacks. This was particularly important when maps were inaccurate. This use of aircraft was a relatively new departure and was found to be of greater use than had been expected, especially for artillery and engineers.

It was the supply aspect of air effort that played such a dominant role in the Burma war by allowing troops to remain where they were and fight it out although they were surrounded by the Japanese. It was often very difficult to get supplies on to the target and pilots made it a point of honour to perfect such missions.

Expensive and dangerous though it was, aerial resupply prevented the Japanese from invading any farther into India than they did, and Chindit operations were planned and executed round the air aspect. Such was the nature of the campaign and the low priority of the theatre, air support concentrated, for the most part, on routine supply dropping.

Parachutists were dropped at Elephant Point near Rangoon in the closing stages of the war. This was on open terrain as the technique of jumping into trees had not been thought out. There were two other drops that have never had much publicity: one in upper Burma in late 1942 and the other in the Arakan in 1943, before the rains. For this latter about twenty Gurkhas, dressed as natives, were dropped to get information about the enemy. They had to make their way up to Imphal. Their wireless broke down and they were given up for dead soon after their drop. I have only met one survivor and he vividly remembers the desolation of abandonment as it seemed at the time. When eventually they all made their return, they looked so jungly and unmilitary that they were very nearly shot by their own side. My friend's hope was that some use was made of what information they did manage to procure.

THE FOUR PHASES OF CONVENTIONAL WAR

Traditionally the British Army has seen that there are four phases of conventional war. These are the advance to contact, the attack, the defence and the withdrawal. The principles of these four phases were never in dispute in the campaigns in Asia and the Pacific, but the terrain and the different type of enemy led to modifications. These need to be described for better understanding of the fighting.

1. The advance to contact
The advance through the jungle usually consisted of movement on narrow jungle tracks or native trails. Often both were liable to deteriorate rapidly even under foot traffic. Roads were available in some areas and even the all-weather type suffered from heavy use. Often lack of roads led to every item of equipment having to be portered.

When possible the advance was made by separate columns in approach-march formation along all suitable lines of approach. This afforded opportunities for rapidly outflanking the enemy while preventing any similar attempt by him.

Often speed was essential as the advance became a race for successive tactical objectives. (Whenever I think of speed in a military context I remember what the late Lord Wavell wrote about it. 'Speed is an expensive commodity. Alike in battleships, racehorses and women, a comparatively small increase in speed may double the price of the article.') Columns used to advance on a narrow front. In a rapid advance in thick country it was often not possible to secure the flanks since flank patrols were not able to keep up with troops moving on tracks. Then the drill was to put out strong detachments to the front and pickets on transverse tracks. Flank protection was essential when passing through open cleared areas. When halted every body of troops had to secure itself from attack from any direction by all-round defence.

A constant problem in thick country is the unreliability of maps. Air photographs often fail to reveal hostile troops. The passage of information was slow as the main method of relaying it from forward patrols was to wait for them to return to base. Information from local inhabitants could be obtained, sometimes for cash, but was often suspect.

Being leading scout was the most nerve-racking experience. Most British battalions changed their leading scouts every ten minutes, their leading sections every twenty, their leading platoons every hour and their leading companies every half-day.

On the ground it was never so straightforward. A diary was kept by a British officer (the late Major A. C. Bickersteth) of 10th Gurkha Rifles and published privately, after the war, under the title, *One Damned Thing After Another*. His battalion, 4/10th Gurkha Rifles, was detached from 32 Brigade and sent on an individual task, to establish a position behind the Japanese on their main L of Communication near Shwebo, east of the Chindwin, and 'make a nuisance of themselves with ambushes'.

December 18th, 1944. We started on our show today. The first march was south, on up the Pondaung Chaung and over a saddle into the headwaters of the Makkadaw Chaung, going as far south as Pawlaw (the first village after leaving Webon on the Pondaung Chaung).

The men, as usual after a day or two's rest, were slow off the mark this morning. I was leading company and had to march at 0830 hours but only just got away in time. First halt was in the area of Brigade HQ where the brigadier was wishing the CO good luck . . . We stopped at 1200 hours to wait for the R[ecce] Group. The going was very trying now as we were walking in the loose sand of the dry chaung. I made my company move pretty quickly. We crossed the saddle about 1240 hours and descended through more 'teaky' jungle to Pawlaw. Actually I had a half-hour halt at 1140 hours just before reaching the camp area which . . . had [been] laid out.

We now seem to be well into the dry belt as the chaung is wide and waterless. However we did find water – a little in a small chaung running down by the village (deserted obviously for a year or so). So here we dug some holes and produced some water, five gallons of milky white fluid, all of which was given to the mules. The battalion came in slowly, the baggage column not till very late.

We found a patrol of the Northamptons here . . . CO ordered that no slit trenches were to be dug tonight as the men must get what rest they can. A cold night.

December 19th. We were marching east and partly south today mostly over trackless, jungly and hilly country. I was rear guard and so covered the battalion out, sitting on the far side of the village. I also had to arrange for a message drop, but the aircraft never came. Eventually left Pawlaw at 1015 hours at the tail of the baggage column. Subedar Mahser and a platoon of D Company have gone straight down south to Pyingaing to try and beat up what Japs they can tonight. (It was the following night that Mahser and his platoon had such a successful ambush and killed about fifty Japs.)

The route we took led over a ridge and down into a dry sandy chaung, then up another one (we were on no recognized track) through thick jungle mostly bamboo, creeper or thickets. We had a long halt about 1230 hours. Far hungrier and thirstier today than in all the marching so far, while a tendon in my knee is weak and was hurting slightly. On over a saddle, along a knife-edge ridge and down into the Thanbo Chaung . . .

. . . again we did not dig slit trenches. Camp was in a very dark bit of jungle near one of these open spaces of cleared jungle . . .

The men trying all night to fill up the big canvas tanks with water.

December 20th. Not a good start. First there was trouble over getting enough water and rations (the water, too, pretty foul). However, was at last ready by 0930 hours . . .

. . . had arrived at 1330 hours, and now allowed the company two hours in which to cook tea, have some food, and collect and leave behind heavy kit, like blankets and extra clothing. I go with two days' jungle ration only . . . I have a difficult route to follow along these awful ridges. I saw the CO just before I left and then set off about 1545 hours with my company and thirteen mules carrying reserve ammo., PIAT [Projectile, Infantry, Anti-Tank], mortar and ammo, and pioneer explosives.

The going was very slow as I had to cast and recast my route. We must have started off from much farther back than we thought. The CO had given me his idea of the map reference of the water point where the battalion was stopping, but it must have been miles out. Anyway by 1700 hours, after marching along these knife-edge ridges, I thought I had reached [the] point [I should have] and so went west into a nala which I found to my surprise was running north. However as it was now dark I decided to bed down. No water here, and no blankets so beastly cold. Slept in a 6-inch deep slit trench in sandy ground by a dry chaung very uncomfortably.

The target was not reached for another two days.

2. The attack

Attacks generally are of four types and the wars in Burma and the Pacific were no exception. There are the encounter battle, frontal or flanking attacks, attacks against minor resistance and attacks against prepared positions. Each has its own variations.

The encounter battle results from offensive tactics locating enemy positions without being detected first. Surprise is therefore one major benefit. Speed is essential to prevent the enemy from reacting to nullify what has been achieved till then. During the preparatory stage, troops not in contact with the enemy must be so disposed that they can resist and immediately counter-attack any endeavour by the enemy to outflank or envelope them.

The nature of jungle terrain necessitated attacks being made on a narrow front so that control could be maintained. Patrols covered the gaps between units. A firm base and a strong reserve were always a requirement.

Once the troops had been committed their momentum had to be maintained. To halt and try to take cover was always fatal. High casualties and failure to take the objective always resulted.

Frontal or flanking attacks were more deliberate than the encounter battle. The frontal attack was employed when time or the nature of the terrain did not permit outflanking or when the enemy was overextended. It was often made astride the axis of advance as this simplified control and direction, and enabled supporting weapons to be employed quickly.

Any flanking attack is more difficult than a frontal attack but is often more decisive. It was constantly used by the Japanese, and flanking movements by them were a worrying feature of their advance down the Malayan peninsula, giving the defenders there the impression that they were outnumbered when that was not the case – except locally.

British tactics for a flanking attack, certainly during the Burma campaign, required that the force be divided into four components. First there was the fixing element, which secured the track or some other tactical feature and fixed the enemy. The second and third components were the outflanking elements which made the main attack on one or both of the enemy's flanks or on his rear. The fourth component was the reserve that ideally was big enough to cover either or both of the other two forces as well as countering any hostile reactions.

To maintain control and to check direction, short bounds were necessary. Checkers of direction and distance were specially detailed. Bounds were fixed by time, by distance or by movement from one feature to another that could be seen and pointed out on the ground.

In those days great reliance was placed on laying signal cable for communications. Wireless communications were unreliable and always required a back-up. Men were detailed to unwind and lay cable as the troops advanced.

Once contact was made deployment was automatically carried out according to rehearsed and known battle drills. Often the attack was a series of engagements by small parties at close range. By then there was not much that the commander could do to influence the course of the battle except by effective use of the reserve. Anticipation and a keen sense of timing saved many a situation. The reserve worked better as a complete unit, not in penny packets.

Attacks against minor resistance were normally made by the advanced guard to dispose of the enemy. Once again prearranged battle drills so often held the key to success. Leading sub-units obtained cover by leaving the track at once and making their own way towards the enemy. At this stage great reliance has to be placed on junior leaders.

Sometimes it was desirable to bypass minor resistance. Then the original advanced guard fixed and isolated the enemy while the main body continued to advance with a new advanced guard by making a detour against the enemy. Such operations were common in New Guinea which was more rugged than many parts of Burma. In one typical action at Kokada, the advanced guard took four hours to deal with the Japanese. Twenty-four Australians were killed in developing the attack, but only six men were killed in the five minutes it took to overrun the Japanese position. Between 150 and 200 Japanese were killed.

Attacks against prepared positions made it necessary to develop a plan which included the fullest possible use of all supporting arms and weapons. Over the months operations in Assam and the Arakan showed that formal frontal infantry attacks supported by a barrage and made against organized Japanese positions were rarely effective and often costly.

Thorough reconnaissance to determine the location of enemy strong points, including the exact position of automatic weapons, is always of the utmost importance, whether in the jungle or not. On many occasions it may be necessary to fight for this information, possibly by staging a preliminary attack. Patrols and observers by day and patrols right into the enemy's lines by night can find out if they are well led and use cunning and strategem to draw the enemy's fire.

Special features which patrols and observers were told to examine Japanese positions for included all high ground from which observation and a good field of fire could be obtained. Trees, particularly at road or track bends, culverts, the edge of clearings, the openings underneath native huts and the roofs of buildings all had to come under scrutiny. Areas on the flanks of restricted approaches, such as dry stream beds or a single route through swamps or heavy jungle always needed close attention.

As for the artillery, the maximum possible concentration was always needed. A thick barrage on a narrow front was often the best type of support.

A limited objective was often assigned to ensure proper consolidation and adequate mopping-up.

The value of air support often depended on the extent to which troops and pilots had worked together in jungle areas, especially in the area in which operations were taking place. In those days the indication of targets to pilots (by smoke, flares and other signals) and the reporting of targets by pilots presented special difficulties and were only overcome by 'previous combined training amounting to close personal friendship'.

When tanks were available and ground was suitable for their use they were of both moral and material value to the close support of infantry, even more so if their employment came as a surprise. The heavy gun of the large types of tank was particularly effective against Japanese bunkers. The opportunities the jungle afforded for the action of tank hunting parties demanded, however, that infantry and tanks worked in even closer co-operation than in more open country and it was rarely advisable to dispatch an echelon of tanks alone to the objective.

Attacks against prepared positions were serious affairs and the preparatory phase needed several days for completion. It was during this time that a detailed knowledge of the target was built up. Once that was done the troops had to get into positions from which to launch the attack. This involved such measures as protection of forming-up positions and start-lines as well as gaining approaches to the Japanese positions. As always accurate maintenance of direction was essential. Supporting weapons had to be moved into position and concealed. Flanks had to be protected. Wire had to be gapped and minefields identified. Deceptive measures were part of the plan so that the time and place of the attack remained secure for as long as possible.

Infantry pioneers or engineers had to clear gaps through wire defences. Such special assault parties blinded enemy pillboxes and bunkers by sandbags or explosives placed in loop-holes. The first wave of infantry passed through to the objective killing as it went but not halting to mop-up. It consolidated immediately, pushed out patrols and prepared to meet the inevitable counter-attack.

Other pioneer or engineer parties and moppers-up followed closely on the infantry. Bunkers were destroyed. Moppers-up completed the task 'with bullet, bayonet and bomb'. In fact, under such conditions, it was necessary to kill most of the Japanese before the defensive position could be taken. The Japanese would have to be killed until only a handful of survivors remained. These would then kill themselves rather than be taken prisoner.

The Japanese were in the habit of bringing down defensive fire on their own positions. It was therefore unwise to remain on that position for any longer than necessary. Consolidation was required to prevent the recapture of the position by

Right: Locals look on at an overturned Gunner vehicle. Recovery was always a problem, especially when there were no solid foundations for pulling anything out. Many vehicles carried their own tow-chain. One of the advantages of the jungle was that there were many trees that could be used to winch out vehicles. (Royal Artillery Institution)

Below: Lance-Sergeant Lenthall, MM with Signalmen Hatch and Thomas laying a line between Brigade HQ and newly liberated Hopin, Kohima-Imphal. (Royal Signals Museum)

the inevitable Japanese counter-attack. A pre-arranged fire plan would need to be made in advance as time was always at a premium on such occasions. Tools and supporting weapons had to be brought up to ensure all-round defence in depth prior to the next move forward.

Without exploitation much effect of the attack would be lost. The plan for this phase would be dependent on several factors, some of which were: the extent to which the enemy had been broken or demoralized by the attack; the depth of the enemy position; the necessity for seizing quickly any tactical feature beyond the immediate objective; the artillery support required to cover consolidation; the time available, bearing in mind that an attacking force had to have sufficient time in which to form a defended area for the night. The aim, however, was always to establish a firm base first and, when that had been done, to deliver the subsequent thrust as rapidly as possible.

Whenever rehearsals had been carried out, great dividends were always paid.

On 21 January 1945, 4/10th Gurkha Rifles put in a moonlight bayonet attack, from a very strong, bunkered position on a slight rise that covered Teizaung (near Myinmu to the west of the Irrawaddy). Major Tony Bickersteth continues in his diary:

> It was now 0930 hours and I was still two miles from Wunbye [where the Japanese were] when the airstrike came in – too soon for me to be near enough to see the immediate effects . . . I moved east along the railway till I . . . reached a cart road, [which] was narrow with thick hedges on either side. 4 Platoon had hardly advanced 200 yards before two Jap LMGs opened up on it from the neighbourhood of [a] pagoda.
>
> There followed a rather abortive battle (it was getting on for 1500 hours at the time) till 1630 hours . . . The responsibility of running a battle is the worst thing I know, because if you make a mistake you lose men's lives and lose, too, superiority over the enemy, so I was hot and sweaty and very tired by the time the CO came on the air again, telling me to consolidate for the night on the ground gained, and keep the enemy occupied with patrols and jitter parties . . .

Major J. Nettlefield, commanding 20th Battery of 24th Mountain Regiment had this to say about Kohima:

> There was not one tree standing that was not blasted and splintered; the more primitive houses were knocked flat, and others were holed and battered beyond recognition. The place stank. The earth everywhere was ploughed up with shellfire, and human remains lay rotting as the battle raged over them. Flies swarmed everywhere, and multiplied with incredible speed. Men retched as they dug in, and a priority task was to clear up as far as possible. But even then the stink hung in the air and permeated one's clothes and hair. It made one realize once again how sub-human the Japs were. A bunker was found in which about twenty men had fought and lived for several days – a bunker littered with their dead companions and their own excreta . . .

3. The defence

Defence, like the other major phases of war, cannot be thought of in a vacuum nor can it be an entity on its own. The Japanese were still 'supermen' when the training manual from which I quote was written. Great pains were being taken to inculcate an offensive spirit. Talk of defence was frowned on, especially the 'passive defence' mentality of sitting down and waiting for trouble. This was never to be permitted. Although training in defence had to be undertaken, its concept was one of 'temporary assumption' except when it was in the form of protection at rest on completion of a day's advance and at the end of each day's fighting.

As is so often the case in military thinking, when offensive action is being taught all the cards are in the hands of the attackers. When defence is the subject under discussion, it is the defenders who turn out trumps. Never was this dual thinking better brought out than when 3/7th Gurkha Rifles was ordered to convert to a parachute battalion. A film, showing just how easy it was to parachute, was sent to the battalion and shown to all the men. The sky was full of paratroopers drifting lazily and easily down to the ground. The commentator remarked, '. . . so you can see how easy it is to shoot parachutists out of the sky before they can do you any damage!' Luckily English was not one of the Gurkhas' languages then!

The very essence of defence in dense country was that it had to be both mobile and aggressive. Defended localities were required, their chief purpose being to provide firm bases from which mobile elements could operate for laying ambushes, for offensive patrolling and for immediate counter-attack. Strong reserves, prepared for offensive action, had to be located where they could move immediately to any threatened locality.

The most common type of defence was the occupation of a position for the night, sometimes known as harbouring. Two hours were needed to complete preparations before dusk. The harbour was organized as a perimeter defence, with the force being divided into three parts. Half was detailed for perimeter defence of which a third would be deployed in depth to counter infiltration. One quarter would be in reserve for immediate counter-attack to expel any penetration. The remaining quarter was for counter-offensive action, such as patrols, snipers or listening posts outside the perimeter.

Slit trenches had to be dug for each rifle and Bren gun group to give protection against enemy bombing, artillery and mortar fire. They also permitted the maximum use of hand-grenades which are so effective as night weapons. Fires were not allowed at night and cooking had to be done while it was still light. Soldiers knew how hard it was to find dry kindling so if they found any when on the march they picked it up and stuck it in the back of their packs.

To preserve ammunition Australian soldiers used to throw clumps of earth in the direction of suspicious noises. If more noise was heard it was taken to be an animal. If there was silence, it was considered hostile.

Fields of fire were developed by cutting lanes for all weapons to be fired. These also helped increase fields of view and, when time permitted, some form of obstruction (such as *panjis* – pieces of bamboo with one end in the ground and the other tipped and hardened, which did a lot of damage to anyone who trod on them) to be planted. Where possible the fire lanes were to be cut knee-high in the form of tunnels. The approaching Japanese soldier would be unaware that he was entering into a defensive post. Security would be maintained unless the enemy was crawling.

Trip-wires made from vines or creepers, booby-traps and warning devices (often large dry leaves that crunched when trodden on) were used to prevent silent infiltration. The weapons to dispose of enemy infiltrating such a post at night were the bayonet and the grenade. Firing was generally forbidden. The usual aim of enemy fire at night was to discover the position of sentries and posts, to disturb the defenders and to inflict losses. If his fire was not returned he would be unsuccessful in the first two and probably in the third.

'Stand-to', as ever, took place at dusk and first light. However, in July 1944, a serious warning was given by higher command as, 'Some units, particularly headquarters, are very bad in this respect. An officer or senior NCO must be made responsible for going round at the appointed time to ensure that troops are standing-to.'

Active defence was seen as another type of defence. The enemy usually sought to outflank a position. These tactics often entailed the disadvantages of a long advance, with long routes of supply, difficulties of communications, and movement in country which was not known to the attackers. The defenders, on the other hand, were fighting on ground of their own choosing and with centralized reserves.

The main problem of defence in the jungle is the prevention of infiltration. To overcome this, patrols and snipers had to operate forward of localities. The role of these patrols was both to find out the enemy's strength and direction of approach and to harass and hit him should he approach. Patrols were also given the task of denying the enemy reconnaissance of the position. In this they could be helped by snipers.

In the case of mobile detached forces, trails were to be avoided and a suitable position could often be found in an extra thick patch of jungle. Protection would then be provided by a system of all-round localities with pickets on the likely approaches and vantage points, and local patrols. Unless the force was very small it was not advisable to camp in one locality, since that gave the enemy an opportunity to surround it and to concentrate his fire on the necessarily crowded space inside. The lay-out of localities in the form of a starfish had the advantage that the reserve was placed centrally and communication ran outwards from the centre. This arrangement also made infiltration difficult and dangerous.

Positional defence was used when a more permanent type of defence had to be undertaken. Under such circumstances the position selected had to be on ground of vital tactical importance which could not be bypassed with impunity.

Since artillery support was generally limited, such positions had to provide for the maximum use of all infantry weapons, particularly the flanking fire of automatics. The defence was then built round the automatic weapons, using the minimum number of men necessary to operate and protect them. The posts had to be mutually supporting and sited in tactical localities both laterally and in depth. Localities had to be self-contained and with sufficient water, rations and ammunition to enable them to last for several days without assistance. Advantage was to be taken of natural obstacles and of the opportunities the jungle afforded for the erection of artificial obstacles. Communications had to be arranged both laterally and in depth to provide for the rapid movement of reserves. The additional time available for the preparation of the position allowed considerable clearing of fields of fire and this came high in priority of work to be done.

The conduct of the defence had to be aggressive. That was achieved by allotting as large a proportion of the force as possible for counter-attack. When the time arrived for launching the counter-attack, speed was imperative. In order to be able to be as slick as possible previous reconnaissance and rehearsal were essential. In dense jungle it was sometimes necessary to cut tracks beforehand and in any case routes had to be marked.

4. The withdrawal

The manual is explicit on this fourth phase of war. In bold letters it proclaims that **THERE WILL BE NO WITHDRAWAL.**

In fact withdrawals should be comparatively easy because the denseness of the jungle often precludes immediate and visual contact. During Chindit withdrawals, each column acted as flank protection for the others. Wide dispersion offered troops higher prospects of living off the land and so there was that more possibility of reaching safety.

Major Tony Bickersteth wrote this about one withdrawal in which he was involved during 1944 from the Wittock area of the Kawbaw valley:

> What happened very shortly is this: On 12th evening the Japs began attacking Wittok. At that time the Border Regiment had moved into reserve with us and 114 Jungle Field Regiment, were in the Wittok position. We established a post also with Carriers and Pioneers . . . about half a mile back along the road behind the 114's position.
>
> Japs continued shelling the area for four days and used their tanks. During that time our battalion, with the Border Regiment, twice had orders to move . . . the second occasion being for a long-distance counter-attack against Htinzin. Both orders were cancelled. Several battles went on, one in which A and C Companies went out and attacked an enemy AFV [armoured fighting vehicle] harbour and killed plenty of Japs . . .
>
> On 17th evening [the] code word . . . came through . . . to withdraw right back . . . The Jeeps with the Mortars were escorted back . . . by the tanks and got clear away up the road save that one jeep trailer blew up on a mine and a mortar was lost. The Carrier party also left that night, had a battle, then closed . . . the following day, [18th]. The Border Regiment had the brunt of the attack, but the situation would have been O.K. and the enemy ambush liquidated, if it had not been that a grenade landed slap among the mules. These panicked and everyone scattered . . . That night the battalion in its various bits was attacked five times, and the enemy's tanks on the road came into play, though they didn't actually open fire.

From 23 March to the end of the month the battalion stayed where it was.

> March 31st. This was the hell of a day. The orders are now that all battalions will leave tomorrow morning . . . and that means B Echelon (i.e. nearly all the transport and Q) moves today at 1200 hours as well as the mules. Had great difficulty in getting the mules away. They were supposed to leave at 0800 hours, but the usual morning shelling delayed things. However, I got in nearly every company's ground-sheets, mosquito nets, and blankets and, owing to the hard work of the Quarter-master Jemadar . . . we eventually got the bundles tied up – even A Company's who are out. But the mules from C Company didn't turn up. In the end I had to send the Transport Havildar off without them and they followed. As it was, it was 1000 hours before any of them got away.
>
> Then on top of that came the loading of the trucks. This luckily I had been able to arrange at slightly more notice, and the ammo (essential), cooking equipment, men's blankets, some of the mess, etc, were loaded by 1130 hours as I intended, though there were several things I was unable to get away which I should have liked. But the trucks couldn't take them. However I think we have got enough off . . .

Then came destruction – of all compo-pack rations, mule rations, some left-over clothing and tents, and post-ammo. Burning and blowing up were not allowed, so we had to 'render everything unserviceable' with water and by using kukris to cut it.

Had the four trucks I have kept back loaded and then saw to A Company's kits. Unfortunately when they went off the other day they went merely to clear the ridge, and one platoons's packs were still here. Shelling was going on but the remaining section of A Company went up . . . taking most of the stuff. There was plenty of shelling this afternoon, one shell landing near [the company commander's] bunker, just before he went off. Rather shaking.

C Company is getting most of the shelling, but only a casualty or two. Our mortar detachment up there did very well. We were able to send up plenty of bombs to these and told them to fire off as many as they could. They fired the lot, about 130, and kept the Jap gun pretty quiet. In fact I don't think that gun fired again.

. . . Nearly everything except mortar ammunition was destroyed, and all the men's kits and bedding were away so no one had anything to sleep in tonight. To bed tired enough about 2100 hours after a scratch meal on compo-pack rations – very good really.

Then at [midnight] one of these ruddy firework things went off. We are to leave them in our positions before we go, with a time pencil attached, so that after we have gone the sounds of firing will still be heard from the position . . . There was then an explosion . . . which was reported as an anti-personnel mine so everyone was stood-to. In front of my position there were then two explosions following each other pretty closely. May have been anti-personnel mines but I think some of our men got windy and chucked grenades. Anyway I heard no movement and we soon stood down again, and I got some sleep.

April 1st. Left (or rather 'evacuated' – tactically, 'withdrew from') Moreh today and returned to Shenam. A bad business as always in a withdrawal – destroying stuff: ammo and rations, which we weren't allowed to blow up . . .'

JAPANESE TACTICS

That the Japanese were brave was never in doubt. Their tactics, however unimaginative they were at times, struck fear into the hearts of troops fighting against them in Malaya and Burma. It is now known that the strength of the Japanese in Malaya was less than the number of the combined Allies yet, even forty years after the war and despite evidence to the contrary, many of those who fought against them during those anxious and heart-rending days still do not believe this to be so. The Japanese managed local superiority of numbers and outflanked positions, thereby giving an impression of having many more troops than was the case.

Behind the scenes not everything went as smoothly for the Japanese as had been imagined, though that was not apparent at the time. In the flush of victories as sweeping as any in modern history that did not matter particularly. One of the best books written about the Burma campaign, which reads with the urgency of a good thriller, is *Burma, The Longest War, 1941–45*, by a man who was one of the few Japanese interpreters on the British side, Louis Allen. This provides fascinating details of what it was like from the Japanese point of view. However, for a general appraisal of how the Japanese operated and how this was relayed to junior commanders opposing them at that time, it is wise to turn and see what publications of the period made of it all.

Attacks showed similarities. The Japanese, when operating on the Ukhrul road, '. . . invariably preceded an attack by firing two green Very lights across

Right: *The way back into Prome. Men of 3/1st Gurkha Rifles wading over a river. Such was the climate that clothes would dry quite quickly on a person, that is until they were once more as wet with sweat as they had been with river water or rain. Footwear suffered badly though, and could incapacitate a man fairly rapidly.* (SEA Film Unit)

Right: *Lochan bridge on the Tamu road which was blown up by the retreating Japanese and rebuilt by the Sappers. One of the dangers in this type of situation was the mines and booby-traps left behind by the Japanese. By now all soldiers in Burma had learnt that the 'front line' could, in fact, be anywhere.* (Gurkha Museum)

Right: *When the bridge near Pobong was destroyed, pioneers from the Pardikot State Forces put up a suspension rope-way in no time and troops were able to maintain the momentum. Indian troops are crossing this rope bridge, but it was a slow process and one that could be delayed by bad weather or enemy snipers.* (Gurkha Museum)

the defended positions. Attacks were often poorly organized and sheer weight of numbers rather than tactical skill would be relied on for success.

The Japanese were noisy in attack. During the assault shouting and screaming were common. At first our troops did not know how to react, there being enough noise anyway. Our teaching was to make noises when bayoneting anyone [or that seemed the idea during bayonet training!] and actually in the charge, not indiscriminately.

The idea then caught on that a 'counter-noise-barrage' would raise the morale of the defenders and make the Japanese believe that a counter-attack was being launched. The anathema of losing face often led the Japanese to increase their endeavours to try and take a position, leading to even more fanatical and suicidal attacks being attempted.

Before any attack was mounted, they usually tried to locate positions of light machine-guns by trying to draw their fire. Soldiers would deliberately expose themselves by day or shout as they moved about noisily at night.

Even very thick wire round a position would only be a deterrent. The Japanese would tear themselves through it, regardless of casualties and wounds. One method of clearing wire was to dig in tanks, at night, sited to fire on the wire with the aim of sweeping it away as the assault came in. On other occasions guns were sited at very close range for the same task.

Assaulting troops were often led by officers, armed with a sword, in the leading wave. Swords had a mystical quality that transcended their being a mere weapon. (More than forty years later, families of those officers who lost their swords during the war have associations in Japan to help any who want to return them to their original families. The sword I had surrendered to me after the war had been in one family for 250 years and has five nicks in the blade as a result of sword-to-sword combat. I offered to return it if given material for this book.)

On operations on the Silchar Track it was observed that the enemy put down not more than six shells on certain features during the day for no apparent reason. These shellings were followed at night by an attack on them from a different direction than that of the shelling. This was presumed to be a method of target indication to infantry who were some miles from and in a totally different direction from the line of fire. Subsequent precautions against an impending attack were taken and were nearly always justified.

During these same operations in the Silchar Track area, the enemy only supported his numerous night attacks with artillery on three occasions. That might have been due to ammunition shortages yet, when attacking some particular features by day, there was very close mortar and gunfire, irrespective of casualties caused to his own troops.

In attack and defence, and on patrols, the enemy made use of grenades in greater profusion as the campaign went on. On many occasions the bulk of the attackers were armed with grenades only.

Japanese grenades were lighter than the British '36' grenade. After the war, while on operations in Cochin-China, a Japanese grenade was hurled at a passing convoy of Gurkha soldiers and landed in the truck ahead of the one I was travelling in. It hit one of the Gurkhas on the head and dropped on the floor of the truck. The man picked it up and threw it out before it exploded, taking no more notice of it than had it been a large and angry fly.

On another occasion a grenade was hurled at the vehicle I was in and exploded under it, causing no damage. The Gurkha driver stopped, jumped out and chased the man who had thrown it, brandishing his kukri. As he aimed to take the man's head off the man lunged forward and the blade cut off his right buttock.

Troops under attack knew that a Japanese withdrawal was likely when they saw a red Very light or a round of tracer fired.

It was most noticeable that the enemy directed his troops at points or villages clearly marked on the maps (which were all British reproductions). In none of his captured orders or plans was the original attack into new country directed on a feature or a place not so marked. The highest hill (no matter how steep or how much covered in jungle) was a magnet to Japanese planners.

Defence was often based on the highest piece of suitable ground in the area as the Japanese placed the greatest importance on such features, which were strengthened by extensive digging. First to be dug were 2-man trenches, usually undercut to give added protection from air attack, with head cover over part of them. Emplacements would then be constructed and, finally, all would be joined up with communication trenches that might well go right through the top of a hill leading to reverse slope positions.

Emplacements were sited in depth, mutually supporting, and often with automatic weapons. It was the all-round trench system that had been the most instrumental in beating off attacks.

Unlike British positions, Japanese defensive positions did not normally rely on patrols to warn them of impending attacks against them. Complete reliance was placed in sentries reinforced by tree snipers.

There were two methods of warning of movements against their positions. One was by orange lights facing the rear, well ahead of the defensive position and concealed from likely lines of approach. Signals were flashed back to the main position, backed up by links in the chain where there was no line of sight. Another method was merely by knocking two pieces of bamboo together.

Not much reliance was placed on obstacles and use of wire and *panjis* was negligible on many occasions. Greater reliance was placed on mutually supporting positions, sited also to deny open commanding ground by automatic fire. Infantry were not usually brought up until the threat of attack was imminent. One chance of success in attacking such a position was the silent elimination of the machine-guns, but that was acknowledged to be very difficult.

Japanese camouflage was good and extensive, except in strong defensive positions on the top of hills, when it was only the artillery that was well hidden. To cover a jungle hill path, a small slit trench was often dug from the path into the bank on the upper side just round a bend, with the spoil thrown down the slope of the hill on the lower side.

It was found that the Japanese went to ground for the preparatory shelling and bombing prior to an attack. They occupied their positions as soon as that had stopped. Even one aircraft flying overhead when the assault went in kept Japanese heads down.

Patrolling did not seem to be a strong point of the Japanese in any theatre. They relied on the locals for much of their information and, certainly in Burma, whenever small patrols were used (which was not often) they tried always to find local men to go in front.

When there were no locals, small patrols would operate at night, often in conjunction with a larger party of noisy patrols that tried to draw fire by shouting.

Fighting patrols, of about twenty men, were not very skilful. They liked to keep to paths and moved without precaution, often giving their presence away by soldiers talking. Their offensive battle drill when ambushed was always the same: holding the ambushers in front by fire, while carrying out a quick but often clumsy encircling movement on the flanks of the ambush. As a counter, ambushing the encircling troops was easy.

The Japanese made use of standing patrols, in villages wherever possible, relying on the locals for warning. Stand-to positions and defences were seldom prepared.

Many more Japanese patrols were commanded by officers than was the case in the troops opposing them. Passing of information about what was found on patrol was particularly poor and led to many more Japanese being killed than might have seemed possible. Lack of signal equipment, lack of instructions and apathy were the causes.

Tanks were boldly used, certainly when no threat of opposing armour was envisaged. They would be driven up to defended localities at night, close to 25-pounder gun positions, as much as to frighten as anything.

Some Japanese tank attacks were very difficult to deal with, especially when the tanks were manoeuvred at night, protected by infantry, into hull-down positions within 70 to 100 yards of the opposing defended localities. By daylight they would have established a series of mutually supported pillboxes which were very difficult to attack, and their 47mm gun was deadly at such short ranges. On two occasions such support was decisive in Japanese attacks being successful.

Tanks were not used for mopping-up or in a counter-attack role. When tanks were known to be in support of the troops being attacked, the Japanese were careful in the offensive use of their own tanks. Limited advances were made with close support of infantry and the maximum security of the tanks was assured by taking up good positions, either hull-down or specially dug-in as near as possible to the objective under attack, or in the closest co-operation with other weapons in any defended area.

Artillery in Japanese hands was well used and often deadly. To blast emplacements and wire, a gun or two would be brought up to within 600–800 yards. The Japanese seemed reluctant to use their guns at night, possibly because they did not want their positions to be given away by flashes. Attempts made to make them reveal their positions to flash-spotters were never successful.

Medium artillery was not boldly deployed, being kept well back and dispersed, but observation parties would be with the most advanced troops. By moving guns frequently from one position to another, it deceived observers and gave the impression of having greater artillery strength than was the case.

Japanese gunners were good at predicted shooting. Fire was accurate, especially when observed and, because first rounds were on target, not much ranging fire was needed. On the debit side, artillery communications appeared poor, long periods being required to bring down defensive fire.

In the New Guinea campaign it was the Australian artillery that the Japanese blamed for their defeat as much as any other weapon.

JAPANESE HINTS FOR THE SOLDIER

The Japanese produced a treatise, 'Hints for the Soldier' which fell into Allied hands in the Pacific theatre. It renewed emphasis on such matters as individual firing of small-calibre weapons, hand-to-hand combat and physical endurance. It recognized that the hostile forces had a 'superior number of weapons' and recommended measures to overcome this handicap. As it is of interest, it is reproduced here as it was to the Allied forces in January 1945.

1. Unfounded self-confidence arising from the tradition that 'we've always won' is of no great value. Confidence in victory should be based on superior physical endurance and thorough training. It is essential that a soldier be proficient in the use of firearms, in the use of cold steel and in marching.

2. With regard to shooting, large quantities of ammunition are seldom available at the front; therefore expert marksmanship must be developed during the training period. The principle, 'Get a man with every round', is very sound. This is particularly important with regard to heavy weapons. You must avoid random firing; aim your shots well.

Train yourself to fire rifles and light machine-guns from the hip, and to fire the grenade-discharger in a horizontal position. In this manner, you should be able to fire these weapons without conscious effort in case hostile forces make an unexpected attack. If we immediately take the initiative, the hostile forces will throw away their arms and flee; conversely, it is essential not to let the opposition take the initiative.

3. When fired upon unexpectedly by hostile artillery, deploy and lie prone without moving.

Go about your duties silently. Hostile forces will fire blindly in the direction from which they hear the sound of voices.

Never neglect to dig in whenever you make a halt; always remember that digging in is essential, whether you are going to attack or to be attacked.

Deploying and crawling will reduce casualties, and are the first steps toward victory. It should be known that if you deploy and conceal yourself there will be no casualties from hostile bombing or from rifle or artillery fire.

A soldier should never forget his camouflage.

No soldier should lose his direction. When assigned as a runner or on a patrol, mark your direction by breaking branches of trees or by making notches on the bark of trees as you go out.

4. You should engage in bayonet practice every day, with real weapons. Practise until the mind, the body, and the weapon are all co-ordinated in a perfect forward thrust. Drive the bayonet to the hilt and immediately tackle a second and third 'enemy'. Such practice is excellent for the morale.

Hand-to-hand combat is the deciding factor in an engagement and is most feared by the American and Australian forces.

5. Do not allow yourself to be captured, even if the alternative is death. Bear in mind that capture disgraces not only the Army but also your parents and family, who will never be able to hold up their heads again. Always save the last round for yourself.

Endure all hardships. Shortages of rations is a normal condition. The saying 'poverty dulls the wit' would not hold true for military men.

Left: *It was tough and unglamorous for the communicators. Line played a great part in most battles as it obviated the use of runners to a large degree and was relatively secure, though putting the stuff up made the linemen a target for snipers. Both laying and recovering it was a slow business. (Royal Signals Museum)*

Below: *Wireless set 19 (not 'radio' then!). Without the skill and dedication of the communicators, aerial resupply would have been frantically difficult. It was as a result of this resupply capability that the Allies obtained a 'horizontal' dimension to the war that had been absent from the Japanese planners, who had presumed that the British and Indian Army troops would not stand and fight. The Japanese believed their enemy's bloated commissariat would supplement any shortage of rations. By standing and fighting where they were, the British and Indian troops caused the Japanese to become surrounded. (Royal Signals Museum)*

4
Minor Tactics and Administration

If major tactics, the domain of the senior commander, can be likened to the wheels of an army as it progresses, then minor tactics, chiefly consisting of ambushes and patrols but also including sniping, can be likened to the lubricants inside the engine that keep these wheels turning. In this chapter, minor tactics at platoon level already described are considered no further.

The ambush is one of the oldest forms of skulduggery known to history. The patrol is equally old. Other than sentry duty, troops probably spend more of their operational time on these two measures than on any other and it is then that junior commanders can show much initiative. Ambushes and patrols are both recognized as military operations that need as much care taken over them as any other normally encountered. In Burma against the Japanese they were especially valuable. There was nothing new about them; all they needed was modification.

AMBUSHES

Ambushes, which always depend on surprise for success, were seen as being especially suitable for killing Japanese who could be curiously careless about how they moved along tracks. They often took no notice of how many of their numbers were killed along any one stretch, using it more than once with some of them being killed every time. Their advance would be too rapid for them to take proper precautions and they often moved with inadequate protection.

No one ambush will ever be like any other. The overriding principle of an ambush is surprise. Without that element no ambush can be successful. An ambush also has to have a reserve to take advantage of favourable opportunities and deal with the unexpected.

Japanese reaction to ambushes was stereotyped and therefore predictable. The leading elements of the Japanese force would get off the track and try to outflank the ambushers. As the enemy seldom moved without mortars, fire would be brought down and, often within five minutes, an attack would be made astride the track.

The enemy was often successful, too often for the comfort of our wounded. His own wounded would be recovered, not necessarily for medical treatment but to stop them from falling into our hands. In planning an ambush there was always a nice decision whether to stay and find out about the enemy or to abandon the position.

The relative strengths of the two groups, the ambush party and the reserve, needed careful consideration. If the aim was merely to cause confusion and then carry out the main fighting by the reserve, the actual ambushing party could be very small indeed, possibly only three men. However, the ambushing party had to be big enough to deal with the size of group or groups expected, otherwise it would·court disaster. In the Chin Hills the ambush reserve would make it their business to hunt for the mortar, about a thousand yards away in the direction that the Japanese had come from, as soon as the ambush had been sprung.

Useful experience was gained as the fighting swung more in favour of the British. The Japanese would lie doggo for long periods, feigning death. A bayonet or a bullet in a 'corpse' saved casualties to the ambushers. Likewise the use of *panjis* in the area from which it was expected the Japanese would counter-attack was often a good way of causing them more casualties.

Ground always plays a crucial part in the selection of an ambush site. Whether to have men on both sides of the track or only one, where to put the *panjis* and other points can never properly be decided until the characteristics of the area, especially of the chosen killing-ground, have been fully appreciated. This was found to be especially true in hilly country when tree snipers were useful in a re-entrant.

Footprints often gave notice that someone had been in the area and might still be there. Particular attention had to be paid to this aspect. Non-European troops used to enter the area barefooted. Even then, a good tracker could tell, by looking at the toes, whether the prints were made by normal wearers of shoes, so potentially hostile, or not. This is because the 'spread' of the toes of a normal wearer of shoes is not as splayed as that of a person who always walks barefooted. The latter is also more likely to have flat feet and the impression of a low instep is left on the ground – another 'give-away'.

Clear orders should always be given about opening fire. Ambushes often failed because each and every man in the ambush force had not fully understood this cardinal requirement.

Fighting following an ambush was normally confused and a rendezvous (RV) for the ambushers was essential. It often took several hours for all the troops to assemble at the RV, so the teaching was to use the reserve part of the ambush when confusion was at its greatest. Keeping one's nerve and acting boldly were prerequisites for staying alive. Private Lindo reinforced this point when he wrote to me in 1988.

> There is one thing that will cause panic in any body of even disciplined troops and that is being ambushed. One moment you are moving along, then all hell is let loose. Chaos prevails.
>
> In daylight this is a terrible thing to happen to you, but at 1 o'clock on a night as black as only a tropical night can be this is most terrifying. Coupled with all this, imagine this happening 150 miles behind the enemy lines and the enemy being cruel Japanese who were taking no Chindit prisoner and you will have some idea of what happened to 82 Column of the 1st Battalion, The King's Liverpool Regiment on the night of 20 May 1944 . . .
>
> . . . [On the way to relieve 'Blackpool' road-block] some of the column had crossed the road. We had yet to cross it when [we were ambushed and] all hell broke loose. Mules were dashing around throwing their loads, screaming in terror, grenades exploding, machine-gun and rifle fire, and the worst of all, the screams of the wounded and dying.

My platoon put in a bayonet charge onto the road, but it was a foolish and foolhardy effort. It was a pitch-black night, so we could not distinguish foe from friend.

I found myself completely on my own . . . with Japs all around. This was without doubt the most frightening night of my life. The orders were if anything stopped us from getting to the 'Blackpool' block, we were to make back to the last place we had stopped at before making for the road. I started out to go back not really knowing exactly where it was. I saw a figure in front of me and wondered if it was a Jap. I approached cautiously. I noticed his bush hat . . . it was a comrade [named] Webber . . .

He was as glad to see me as I was to see him. Being on one's own behind the Japanese lines was frightening. We started back . . . Before we tried to cross the road we stopped for a rest and Webber pulled out his cigarettes. I caught him just in time: 'You bloody fool,' I said, 'don't you realize the Japs are all around us.' He apologized for his stupidity.

Just then we saw a figure approaching. We lay in wait, then challenged him. He stopped and we saw he was a Burman. It turned out to be the guide who was to guide us into the 'Blackpool' block. He put his fingers to his mouth, meaning for us to be quiet. He beckoned us to follow him . . . and he took us to his . . . house [which was] on stilts . . . His family were huddled in a corner looking terrified as they obviously were. He made signs for us to sleep but sleep was out of the question.

During the night we heard a noise under the house and our bowels rumbled with fright. I looked at the Burman who smiled as if to say it was alright . . . It was a bullock tethered . . . and [it] had got to its feet to relieve itself. Sounds funny now but believe me it was far from funny then . . . God bless that Burmese guide . . . He gave us a dish of stew next morning, vegetables, chicken and a big lump of hairy pork.

He then took us back to the last stopping place, where we found more of our column who had made it back successfully . . . Yes! I do hope that Burman survived the war. He was a very brave man, a very loyal man to the British. I regret to say I did not thank him enough, such was the relief at meeting up with some of my column, such is youth.

PATROLLING

Patrolling is essential to victory. A report from a large operation in the Milne Bay area of New Guinea said that 'the side which wins the patrolling encounters wins the battle'. That has been borne out many times.

Patrolling is a wide term. In the Burmese jungle, where the lack of communication forced the use of smaller bodies of troops than in Europe, patrolling had a wider application than ever. It was, in effect, the technique of moving and fighting over long distances and for periods which might extend to ten days or more and distances of seventy miles were not unknown for bodies of troops of up to company size.

It was one method of dominating the jungle and making it unsafe for the Japanese to move about. The policy advocated in Burma was to use a patrol superior in strength than the expected Japanese opposition. This was seen essential to reconnaissance patrols remaining unmolested so as to be able to find out sufficient detailed information for successful future planning.

The person lying in wait, the ambusher, should always be at an advantage compared with the mover, the man on patrol. Patrols were exhorted to stay still as soon as they were contacted by the enemy – not an easy thing to do. The formation and the battle drills adopted by the patrol were of great importance.

Above: The bridgehead at Myinmu on the north bank of the Irrawaddy. Mules played an important part in the war, giving forward troops a flexibility that vehicular transport lacked. To ensure that their braying did not give their position away to the enemy, mules had to be 'de-voiced'. Some handlers would get attached to their charges, others never. (South East Asia Command)

British troops have a tendency to be noisy in the jungle. So have Americans. The Infantry Journal USA, in March 1943, published an article on Jungle War. This describes how and why a sergeant of Marines moved silently: 'I practise walking quietly over rocks, twigs, grass, leaves, vines and so forth . . . because I practise this is the reason I'm alive. Some of the other non-coms laughed at me . . . but they have stopped laughing because I have been on more patrols and am still alive.'

The selection of an RV that was known to everyone, and one that might have to be changed as distances from base became longer, was most important. RVs could be forward of the patrol, provided that the skill of the troops was up to the challenge. It was more often the case that the RV was behind the troops.

Patrols from two hours' to ten days' duration were planned by bounds and each bound had its own RV. This had to be unmistakable to be of any use. They were looked on as a movable ambush. It took much practice for men to find just that one place in thick country. It might be a stream junction, on the flank of a particular clearing or by a large fallen tree. It was often difficult to find a good spot. It was easy to forget that although a patrol commander had map and compass his men had neither.

It was always necessary to rest from time to time, but never near a village or a track. If the patrol were large enough a sentry could watch any track to see if it were being used while the rest of the patrol was well inside the jungle. Rests were never supposed to be for too long. Cooking or brewing were best finished a mile or so away from a night stop. Litter was tantamount to telling the Japanese that his enemy was somewhere about.

Use of tracks for patrols has always been debated. Patrols using tracks were always in danger of running into an ambush. The best defence against an ambush is not to move into it, yet to have to move through thick undergrowth is always slow and often a waste of effort. The opposing sides used footwear of different patterns, British forces using hobnailed boots and the Japanese rubber boots that had zigzag markings. It was easy to tell if tracks were fresh or not. It was not unknown for a patrol of one side to be followed by one of the other. One way out of that problem was to travel barefoot. Another was to leave the track altogether, but that gave indications as to the point of departure. Whatever action was taken 'track discipline' was vital.

One successful alternative was leaving the track walking backwards into the jungle with some of the force continuing walking forward then leaving the track into the jungle on the opposite side. With good trackers this was risky as the footprint of those walking backwards (when the toe imprint is greater) and those walking forwards (when the heel imprint is greater) are patently obvious. Nevertheless it was a ruse that was used successfully against the Japanese.

Adverse reaction on being surprised was minimized by well-tried and instinctive 'immediate action' drills. In some cases an immediate bayonet charge was the best way out of trouble. In others dispersal was the best alternative. However, dispersal at night was to be avoided at all costs, it being fatal. At night fire is unaimed and often to sit tight was the best answer. In that same issue of the American Infantry Journal an interesting sidelight on 'sitting tight' is given in the description of what one American soldier did when he became lost from a patrol and spent a night in a Japanese bivouac area. He wandered into the Japanese position and, rather than try to escape, pulled his hat over his eyes and sat, Japanese fashion, a little apart from the group. He kept his head down and held a hand-grenade, with the ring pulled, in his fist all night. The Japanese he said, did very little talking and assumed he was ill. About dawn, before it was light enough to distinguish his uniform, he escaped, only to lead another patrol back to the area to wipe out the Japanese the next day.

Japanese patrols were often of between 30 to 50 men in strength and had a mortar detachment. If one of our patrols was undertaking a reconnaissance mission maybe one leader and two men would be enough to do the task. When a small patrol bumped a much larger one, fading into the jungle was often the wisest course of action.

The strength of a patrol would, naturally, depend on its task, hence would its range and duration. To operate for two days in an area four days' walk away entailed being provisioned with ammunition, kit and food, for ten days. Often it was wise to set up a base which, in turn, needed men to protect it unless it was cached. A wireless set (a luxury to many patrols had it not been for the weight, the need to conserve batteries and difficulties of making contact against static interference) would be needed, as would be a medical orderly.

A member of the Burma Intelligence Corps was taken along with the patrol for liaison when local inhabitants were to be contacted.

Animals were also used to help move a strong patrol. Here, too, they posed their own problems of security and fodder. Mules were easier to administer than elephants as these large animals cannot march all day and need time off to collect their own fodder.

The success of any patrol was enhanced by the degree of planning, both operational and administrative, done before setting out. The advice given was to 'reduce clothing and equipment to an irreducible minimum and then reduce again'. Uniforms in the early days were still khaki and it was a good idea to dye part of men's clothing green to break up the outline. Rope- or rubber-soled shoes were recommended, with boots to be used only for very long distances.

Sometimes patrols went to an area known to contain the enemy, to try and capture one of them or a local inhabitant for interrogation. At other times patrols would be away from their main positions for a long time to observe, for instance, a particular stretch of river for enemy movement. These patrols would involve only a comparatively few men.

There were a variety of tasks for long-distance patrols: to discover the extent of a Japanese position and any gaps in it; to link up with a flank formation; to see if the enemy were in a particular area of country. It was in this last task that information given by locals, often with details of the terrain that were not obvious from the map, was at a premium. However, only certain ethnic groups in Burma were to be trusted and many units made sure that they never spoke to locals. The time-honoured points about patrols never returning by the same route as they left, or leaving camp at the same time every day, were as relevant under these circumstances as anywhere else.

Every patrol had to use jungle craft the better to do its job. I have come across some notes that an 'old Burma hand' gave to officers about to go on draft to the front from a reinforcement camp. Despite much common-sense advice, they have an old-fashioned ring about them and sound a trifle odd today. Some extracts deserve to be quoted:

> There are other aids which may be practicable in certain circumstances. A well-trained dog may be an efficient sentry or even messenger to camp. Carrier pigeons may be invaluable. Goats are silent active animals [not the ones that I have met!] that will follow through all sorts of country and carry 10lb of supplies each. They may be killed and eaten as a last resort.
>
> The woods are quiet and the children of the jungle know that there is grave danger from disorderly and inconsidered movement. Do not violate the sanctuary of the woods by unnecessary and clumsy movements.
>
> Jungle warfare should be regarded as a game, healthful, interesting and thrilling; the men should feel at home in the jungle and regard it as a friend. They must realize the absolute necessity for jungle training as a means to defeat the Japanese who come from one of the most highly industrialized countries in the world and have no natural advantages as jungle infantry.

After I had read those notes for the first time I realized that there has indeed been a social revolution in Britain since then. I also reckoned that the writer was of the 'cold-bath-every-morning' brigade. I had forgotten much of what I had been taught in preparation for the Burma campaign, but it had never sounded like that.

Private Lindo has his own patrol experience, which he remembers as though it had happened only a short while ago:

> Any Tommy will tell you that next to making a bayonet charge, the things he hates most are patrols.
>
> I took part in many patrols, but the one I will always remember was a listening patrol, just outside of Mogaung. On a listening patrol you are away from the main

body of troops, listening and noting any movement of enemy troops. On this occasion, there were just four of us lying by the Mogaung road.

It was pitch-black. Time was dragging. All we wanted to do was to get back to the main body of troops.

Suddenly there was a movement, a sound. The usual challenge was shouted, 'Halt, who goes there?' There was just a lot of muttering.

The password was shouted. More muttering. Then the Bren gunner opened up. Hand-grenades were thrown. One could not see a thing, just flashes of bursting hand-grenades.

We were all lying flat on the ground. Suddenly I got the urge to urinate. To stand up was out of the question. I could not hold on any longer, so I just lay there and pissed myself.

Next morning we found one dead Jap who had taken the full burst from a Bren gun magazine.

To the main body of troops it must have sounded like a big battle. How many Japs there had been I don't know. All we found was one dead one.

Perhaps he had wandered away from his own lines. Perhaps he too had wanted a piss. Perhaps he had been on patrol and was the unlucky one to be killed, the rest escaping.

That was the only listening patrol I did. One was enough.

Major Bickersteth went on a night patrol and was wounded:

May 3rd [1944]. . . . By 0200 hours . . . we reached a path at the head of one of the re-entrants near the top of the valley . . . The moon by this time had just set . . .

Then the anti-personnel bomb went off. I often wonder if I set it off myself. All I then remember is everyone rushing back down the hill, all the weapons on the far side of the wire opening up and myself getting hit on the side of the head behind my right ear . . . it knocked me over completely and destroyed my balance so that the world was first over then under me. I think I passed out for about thirty seconds but I do remember seizing my rifle tightly in one hand and my steel helmet which had fallen off in the other. When I came to and balance was restored I was in tall grass on a steep slope of the hill. The post, which I had realized was the Madrasi one (which we had tried to avoid), was still firing the sending up parachute flares. There was no sign of anyone else. However I was thankful to find I could think straight. I was also hit, I found, in my right thigh, which was bleeding profusely. I got out my 1st field dressing and tried to tie it up. Not very successfully. I was more afraid of the bleeding than the actual damage. I continued to slide down on my bottom to the path up which we had come. Llangol was still burning and this had enabled me to get my bearing. I thought I might come across the rest (or some) of the men here, as I had said if we bumped anything and got scattered the RV was 15 Platoon away back. I actually staggered along the path using my rifle as a crutch to see if I could find anyone, but the pain was too great, and I collapsed to the ground again pretty soon. Anyhow (as I thought might happen) DF [defensive fire] from our guns came down. Luckily I was still in dead ground from the post and so crawled close to the bank of the path and prayed hard the shells wouldn't come near enough to do damage though some were unpleasantly close. After that I decided to wait till the dawn came up before moving and then try and attract the attention of the Madrasis. I spent an agonizing two hours lying on the path watching the dawn over Llangol. I couldn't hear at all with my right ear and found I had been hit in my left calf and in my back on the right side. But as far as I could make out I had broken no bones and no bits had entered the vital organs. I waited actually till 0600 hours although it was light before then. I then crawled into a position where I could see the post and yelled at them. They were very suspicious, but at last after what seemed ages came out and brought me in . . .

SNIPING

The enemy sniper was normally a Japanese rifleman who had been detailed to find an advantageous position, such as a tree-top from which to fire at his enemy. The true Japanese sniper, skilfully camouflaged, supplied with concentrated rations and specially armed, was responsible for only a small amount of what was so often termed 'sniper fire'.

The nuisance and morale value of sniper fire was continually illustrated on all fronts. Snipers presented a constant problem in both front line and rear areas. On some occasions it was found necessary to employ patrols with the sole task of eliminating Japanese snipers who had infiltrated into our lines. There was nothing more disconcerting than to have a battalion, a regimental command post, line of supply or communications subjected to sporadic fire from a source unknown. Although, in most cases, this fire was extremely inaccurate and caused few casualties, the psychological factor involved was important.

Employment of our own snipers: it was useless employing a sniper who was not an excellent shot and fieldcraftsman. It was essential that the sniper was not used in a happy-go-lucky and 'what-can-we-give-him-to-do' manner. There had to be a clearcut aim, such as killing commanders and signals personnel, crews of machine-guns or individuals discriminately.

Other aspects of minor tactics include fire discipline, digging, wiring, observation, fieldcraft and the use of booby-traps. Deception must be mentioned: it was attained by battle cries, drawing bamboo bundles on long pieces of vine through the jungle, and the occasional shot, its aim being to draw fire on the easier lines of approach. Booby-traps attached to a wire were detonated in the required directions by throwing a long string or vine with a weight on the end across the wire and pulling from a covered position. Similarly, snipers rigged a line to a bush and pulled it to draw the enemy's attention, thus getting a standing rather than a moving target.

ADMINISTRATION

A subject that normally bores people, especially men of action, administration, nevertheless, is essential for any and every military undertaking. In Burma it had a tyrannical effect on all operational planning. To see how the 'Forgotten Army', fighting the first jungle warfare campaign ever undertaken against a first-class enemy, managed to survive when priorities were so low, especially viewed from the standpoint of the 'push-button' army of the 1980s, is instructive.

In a theatre so ill provided with communications of all sorts as the Eastern theatre of operations, the problem of administration was so difficult that it normally became the biggest factor in deciding the scope of operations.

In addition, L of C were unusually long and precarious, vulnerable to the vagaries of the weather if not the enemy. Every endeavour was made to build-up reserves of supplies, *matériel* and personnel as far forward as possible so that breaks in the L of C would have the minimum effect on operations. In order to relieve the burden on the L of C, conservation of supplies was imperative. The greater the care of arms, clothing and equipment and the more stringent the

Right: 4/10th Gurkha Rifles advance through Burma, May 1945. Guarding the temple is the Burmese lion, the chinthe. This was the name chosen by General Orde Wingate for his Long-Range Penetration forces. He misheard it and called it chindit, a name used ever since and one that will never be forgotten. (Gurkha Museum)

Right: Kalewa-Chindwin ferry bringing armour across the river, under the auspices of the Royal Army Service Corps. Many a tooth-arm soldier was apt to take Supplies and Transport for granted 'when the going was good' but they soon learnt how dependent they were on people in the rear when things went wrong. General Slim compared the tooth-arm troops with the hands of a watch, and the tasks of the administrators and 'the tail' as the vital pieces inside the watch, without which the hands would not keep turning. (Royal Corps of Transport Museum)

Right: Private Sutton of Blackburn on a raft, which carried up to 40 tons each, being towed by a DUKW on the River Irrawaddy. Travel by river could be dangerous because of enemy ambushes. It could also be hot and sticky, but at least it would be a change from being inside the jungle, especially when a breeze cooled one down in the early morning. (Royal Corps of Transport Museum)

control of ammunition expenditure, the less were operations dominated by administration and the transport situation.

Man Management: it has always struck civilians as strange that looking after soldiers should be called 'man management', as has the idea of calling tidying-up the place and mending socks 'interior economy'! But both were and still are of the greatest importance. As far as Man Management is concerned, it is a constant. Units where this aspect was bad always had trouble, sooner or later.

As far as the 'Forgotten Army' was concerned, making contact with the enemy was a far greater strain than in any other theatre of operations. This was due to the short range at which actions were fought in the jungle and the opportunities of surprise which low visibility provides. Troops in Burma and the Pacific in contact with the enemy in jungle were continuously strung up to a high pitch of alertness, which could not be maintained for long periods without rest and relaxation, otherwise not only loss of efficiency but also loss of morale were the inevitable result.

It was imperative that commanders arranged for frequent reliefs of forward units or brigades if the fighting qualities of the troops were to be kept at a high pitch. When and where possible relief of about one-third of a force to be in a rest area for two weeks in every six was the ideal to work to.

In the jungle suitable rest areas could be found within one day's march from the forward zone, so that those units in such areas were still within supporting distance. Use of troops in rest areas was the exception.

While in the rest area, the plan was that the men were carefully examined as to their physical and mental condition. It was recommended that those unfit were not to go back with their units, although this was seen as a one-way ticket for scroungers. Increased rations were issued and units were refitted and reorganized after taking casualties. It was a good period for reinforcements to become more fully integrated within their units. Morale was higher when men knew that their welfare was being cared for by resting them when conditions permitted.

Recreation facilities and mail arrangements were obviously of prime importance, as was a realistic drink ration and a cinema when possible.

Maintenance was always a great problem. Unlike most theatres of war, in the Eastern theatre it was frequently impossible to carry out operations astride existing roads, railways and waterways. It was then necessary to build roads suitable for motor transport behind the advance of the leading formations, developing the axis of advance from a pack track to take jeeps and trucks, and later to an all-weather standard suitable for heavy traffic.

The principles of maintenance remained unchanged but, like the tactics of the teeth arms, methods employed had to be modified considerably. With limited engineer resources it was unlikely that more than one road for each forward division was developed for more than one axis of advance. In consequence it was necessary to restrict the amount of transport using the road to the absolute minimum. This was only a success when all types of transport were pooled and redistributed where most required and where the terrain dictated.

There was a nice balance to be maintained between air and ground supply. Air supply to the forward units was an expensive business but could maintain the speed of advance, yet resupply by road was cheaper and heavier items could be more easily brought forward. By keeping the rear areas free from animal and motor transport the engineers were able to upgrade a road in the shortest possible time with the least interference.

In default of air supply, forward troops, companies and even battalions had to be maintained by porters (both civilian and military), mules, sampans as a forward echelon of transport while animals, 15cwt trucks, jeeps and country boats were required to bridge the intervening gap to the road head. Long communications in the jungle are particularly vulnerable to enemy interference and protection of daily maintenance convoys was sometimes beyond the protective resources available. This meant that some roads were only open at certain times.

The mules and their handlers had a tough time. In February 1944, defending the Ngakyedauk Box, it was especially grim, as the history of 5th Indian Division, *The Ball Of Fire* relates:

> . . . The rain poured down upon this jungle and its narrow tracks. The mud deepened, the branches dripped in melancholy rhythm, and progress towards the . . . Box was slowed down most seriously . . . Anxious and confused, men slithered on the slopes, sweated and swore as they struggled to drag their frightened, obstinate mules uphill. So slippery was the muddy surface of the tracks that even when mule loads had been taken off the saddles and laid in the slush, the mules still stumbled and kicked in their game efforts to mount the slope. Mule drivers fell to their knees and held on the saddle ropes to stop themselves from rolling down to the bottom . . .

At Imphal, too, it was a nightmare for mules and handlers:

> . . . so great were the distances they had to trudge, tugging their strings of mules from the valley up to the summit, from the crest of one hill along a wooded ridge to the top of another, and then down again to the valley and across the paddy fields on a rough track that was deep in dust when not surfaced with soft mud . . .

Staging-posts for animals, handlers, vehicles, drivers and porters had to be set up with the ensuing protective and administrative requirements every unit in the jungle had to have.

Ration scales were a problem in the Indian Army where some people only ate rice, others flour; some would not eat beef and others only ate goats and chickens. There were five ration scales for Indians, Gurkhas and British troops, more when Africans and Chinese had to be catered for. Quartermasters and staff officers had to have a greater understanding of such problems than normal. As the Indian Army never had any but volunteer soldiers and as victory without that army was never possible, regard of peculiar and particular ration scales was of the greatest importance.

Rations came in many forms; the compo pack, the 48-hour mess-tin ration, the light scale, emergency rations and reserve rations.

In New Guinea it was found that each Australian soldier required an average of six pounds delivered to him daily. This included ammunition and the hard ration – bully-beef, biscuits, tea and sugar. Ten pounds were required if the ration were other than hard tack. Native porters required two pounds a man daily. The average weight carried by the individual soldier averaged 50 pounds. This included normal fighting equipment, personal items, ammunition and reserve rations. The average weight carried by the native carrier was about 35 pounds. A battalion needed a minimum of 40 porters, but 60 were preferable.

94 Conventional Warfare – Minor Tactics and Administration

Ammunition supply was crucial. For limited periods the infantryman could be expected to carry extra:

.303in	100 rounds for each rifleman.
.303in	8 magazines for each Bren gun.
.45in	200 rounds for each submachine-gun.
2in Mortar	12 bombs for each mortar.
3in Mortar	24 bombs for each platoon
Grenades	Average of two for each man throughout the unit.

Intercommunication presents particular difficulties in the jungle, certainly with the generation of wireless sets then available. Sets had to be 'netted' and frequency changing was a laborious process. Apart from wireless, messages could be passed by line, runner – on motor cycles or on foot – and, as the training manual puts it, 'short pre-arranged messages can be transmitted by whistles, sirens, tom-toms or the firing of small bursts of machine-gun fire to indicate an alarm or to attract attention.' (Years later my bird- and monkey-call signals in the Malayan and Borneo jungles were so good that I would get answers from the real owner of the noises and my men often mistook the one for the other!)

One of the most important aspects of intercommunication affecting the safety of everybody is the correct challenging of sentries and the password and its counter-sign. The accurate passing of messages by soldiers always needs practice. 'Send reinforcements, I'm going to advance', being read as 'Send 3/4d, I'm going to a dance.' and, 'Camel ruptured. Am returning,' being read as, 'Rommel captured. Am returning' may be apocryphal, but more mundane mistakes were, regrettably, commonplace.

CSM Moore tells of one particular problem in a Chindit column, which always advanced in snake file:

> At times this would cover an area of up to two miles. To keep the column closed up was considered most essential and due to the difficulties in communication this led to a very amusing incident (not very amusing when it happened). We relied on verbal messages . . . On this particular occasion all hell broke loose as we were passing through an area of scrub jungle, urgent voices were shouting, 'Japs in the column.' After some semblance of order was restored and quite a few smiles, yes our verbal message had commenced with, 'Breaks in the column' to 'Gaps in the column' and, of course, the final message . . . Such is the character of the Tommy we all believed this was a deliberate mistake.

(In 1964, I was commandant of the Borneo Border Scouts, attached to the Malaysian police. Dick Noone, working covertly, had certain things to discuss with me when I returned to Kuching from Brunei where I had gone to attend an army conference. He was not in my mind when, working hard to produce a brief for a visiting minister from Britain, I was given an 'immediate' signal message which read, 'From the Inspector General of Police. For Superintendent Cross. MEET NO ONE IN BRUNEI AT 1100 HOURS ON TUESDAY.' That very day! That very minute! Something must be very amiss for me to have to hide. So I didn't go near the airport and missed Dick who looked everywhere for me. I justifiably earned a strong rebuke for lack of imagination! – for 'NO ONE' read 'NOONE'.)

So the war came to an end and, with an enormous corporate sigh of relief, the British Army turned away from the jungle – but not for long!

III
UNCONVENTIONAL
WARFARE IN
JUNGLE TERRAIN

Above: Helicopter medical evacuation (medevac) has become synonymous with the American war in Vietnam, but it was a vital skill which had been in practice much earlier, witness this dramatic rescue of a wounded man. (Popperfoto)

Left: An advance in 'open' country with the Coldstream Guards. (Popperfoto)

Previous page: The de Haviland Beaver, out of service at the end of 1988, operated for many years in a communications role. In Borneo one such aircraft of 11 Liaison Flight, Royal Corps of Transport, drops a parachute-load of supplies, from the cabin, to troops on the ground. (Museum of Army Flying)

5
The Post-1945 Scene

The Allies won the 1939–45 war, during which they expended much blood and treasure. Only the most prescient of the victors foresaw the welter of wars in Asia and Africa, and later Latin America (not then known as the 'Third World' nor their many countries as the 'non-aligned nations'), which have so disfigured the intervening years. The Devil must have laughed up his sleeve to see the once mighty whites as they lost their wars the second time round or gave away politically that which they had won militarily at such cost.

In Asia the Second World War was fought in countries where both participants were alien. After 1945 there was a political sea change which led to colonial countries becoming independent. Sometimes this came about peaceably, as in Ceylon and Burma, only to erupt later. Sometimes, despite all parties agreeing to transfer of power, it was the reverse, as in the Indian subcontinent where millions of people died.

Other countries were deemed not to be ready for the onerous task of ruling themselves (regardless of any residual commercial interests possibly slowing down the transfer of power). No longer were the inhabitants content with their colonial lot. Not all the indigenous population wanted to run affairs on their own, some apathetic, others – often ethnic minorities – apprehensive of how they would be treated by the ruling clique. Change comes about through the dissatisfied and in every country where there was a colonial government there were those who felt passionately that they wanted to run their own affairs without any foreign interference, however inefficient such an administration might be. This was the case in Indo-China, Dutch East-Indies (now Indonesia) and, to a certain degree, in Malaya, where an armed struggle seemed the only way forward.

COMMUNIST ASIAN VERSUS NON-COMMUNIST EUROPEAN
Since all the campaigns fought in Asian jungles have been in the tropical zone and against the Asian enemy, certain constraints on men and machinery have been inevitable. Having won the Japanese war, British jungle warfare thinking was geared to a conventional enemy fighting on exterior lines when the Malayan Emergency broke out in 1948. It took them some time to realize that the fight against the Communists was an unconventional war where the enemy had interior lines of communication. Communist revolutionary warfare, with its jungle-based army, its civilian support and its different philosophy, was not something the British were geared to thinking about. When a doctrine that could counter the threat was evolved, the machinery of a colonial government, staffed in many cases by men who had just emerged from being prisoners of war, was inadequate to

cope with the new stresses and strains that overtook their normal tempo of life and thought-patterns. It took a leadership crisis and the appointment of the 'benevolent dictator', General Sir Gerald Templer, who combined the posts of High Commissioner and Director of Operations, to revitalize the system and so ensure eventual victory.

COMMUNIST REVOLUTIONARY WARFARE (CRW)

In 1945 the rulers of these Asian colonial territories were still as alien as they had been before the war and during the fighting. The great difference now was that the new opposition was 'home-grown'. Any aspect about the strategy of the entrenched powers being global was political, not military (later on the 'domino theory' was a classic in this respect), and tactics spawned by those who wanted to run their own country themselves – 'guerrillas' to some, 'freedom fighters' to others – flummoxed those whose military fortune, if not their competence, had brought them victory in 1945. How was it that armies with no traditions and few support weapons managed to tie down well-organized, conventional armies for so long with such success?

For the first few years the pattern of fighting was not understood by the metropolitan armies of the European powers whose task it was to counter it. The anti-colonial uprisings were based on Communist principles of revolutionary warfare. For greater understanding (with hindsight) it is necessary to go into some little detail of its origins. It is not easy to tell when the Communists had finally worked out their revolutionary strategy and tactics; certainly the Chinese guerrilla leader and later Chairman of the Chinese Communist Party, Mao Zedong (Tse-tung), was working from proven principles of CRW during the 'Long March' of 1934–5.

Mao found himself unable to compete with Western armies when he tried his hand conventionally in Korea, and a plausible hypothesis is that, realizing an error had been made, he was determined not to get embroiled again. General Vo Nguyen Giap (the very successful North Vietnamese military commander, an ardent student of Napoleon and probably a better military brain than Ho Chi Minh) should have learned that lesson but, a gambler by nature and swayed by an 'advisory' Chinese general who had fought in Korea, allowed himself to engage superior French forces at least three times to his disadvantage before he was strong enough to succeed. He also made the same mistake in February 1968 against the Americans at Hué.

It is probably true to presume that the Western world did not appreciate that Mao had realized his mistake, and so made a further error of presuming that the only way to beat Asian Communists was in a Korea-type conflict. (The British Army Singapore Base was established to support two divisions in such a conventional role.) That this error has been rectified in a costly fashion was borne out by the casualty figures in Indo-China/Vietnam as well as by the plethora of such American 'non-army' units as Civil Action Teams, Rural Reconstruction Teams and Psychological Warfare Teams. In the 1940s I wondered if we knew our Asian enemies, or friends for that matter, well enough to ensure that our approach was correct and if not, did we know enough about them to be able to correct our approach? 'The scene changes but the music never' and I am still wondering forty-four years later.

I further believe that the Western world helped defeat itself by not realizing its weaknesses and weakened itself by not knowing its strengths. By eroding its standards it eroded others' trust in it, so still lives on borrowed time.

Any aspiring student of Asian-style CRW is advised to consult three notable works: *The Selected Works of Mao Tse-tung*; *Selected Writings of Mao Tse-tung*; and *People's War, People's Army* by Vo Nguyen Giap. Two proverbs reveal the mentality of these two Asian leaders: Chinese, *Feigning to be a pig he vanquishes tigers*, and Vietnamese, *The pitcher goes so often to the well that at last it breaks*. I see the significance of the Chinese proverb being that a strong person, giving a false impression of weakness, more easily has success than otherwise and that of the Vietnamese being that nothing fabricated lasts for ever – not even French colonialism.

The main points of difference between CRW and the warfare that we were used to are not given in any fixed order, nor are they in any priority, except the first which has been mentioned earlier but is made once more; it is social not territorial. This means that such warfare is concerned with people and politics rather than places. It involves all the populace and will not have succeeded until everybody (except the unborn, the dead and the demented) has been fully indoctrinated. Everything that the armed forces do militarily is subsumed by its political worth. This, in turn, means that, at every level, there are two men in charge, the military commander and the political commissar, the 'cadre' who is elder brother, stiffener and keeper of ideological purity for his charges, and the latter has the last word. During some of the heaviest fighting in Vietnam, the Americans often gained the initiative essential to winning that particular battle with the Vietnamese outnumbered and badly-wanted reinforcements not far away. They would not be committed to battle, however, until they had been fully indoctrinated, even though their arrival on the scene of action would have probably changed the course of events in their favour. Politics is always of paramount importance – a modern and very unholy Grail.

In Western countries the 'military' are often regarded in isolation from the rest of government policy. In Britain Parliament has to vote for the armed forces every year otherwise theoretically they would lapse into unconstitutional illegality. In Communist countries the 'military' are viewed as important a thread in the rope of rule as any other aspect of government, be it home affairs, foreign policy, economic, cultural or whatever, and are never considered in a vacuum.

After the French defeat at Dien Bien Phu, Giap said that North Vietnamese foreign policy had been directed to winning the support of the people throughout the world and particularly to influencing French public opinion against the war. Very successful he was, then and later, with the offensive carried on to the American campuses.

The West often 'shoots itself in its own foot' by **unbalanced media reporting**, wittingly or otherwise, and this is a bonus for the Communists. A classic example is given in the October 1972 issue of the UK-based 'Institute for the Study of Conflict'. This journal, which has the highest regard for objective reporting and writing, had four articles on 'North Vietnam's Blitzkrieg – An Interim Assessment'. It talked about the North's invasion of the South in 1971 and

> . . . then followed an act of calculated butchery unprecedented even in this conflict.
> Forward observers for the Communist artillery targeted the columns of desperate

refugees. They blasted them on the roads and in the fields, whether they travelled by truck, car, bicycle or on foot. On 9 May President Thieu claimed that NVA guns, during this horrifying 72-hour period, inflicted 25,000 civilian casualties, dead or wounded. Details escaped the Press because on the heels of the slaughter came the rout of the Third Division from Quang Tri city – a moment of frantic controversy that may never be fully clarified . . . The world's Press vibrated with hair-raising accounts of drunken Third Division troops . . . looting, burning and terrorizing as they went. Many reports were grossly exaggerated.

The BBC account, presenting a picture of imminent disaster, is credited by senior Americans with *actually triggering* the initial civilian stampede. Equally senior Vietnamese, believing the BBC to be scrupulously objective, overrode situation reports that field commanders forwarded. This led to panic-engendering orders being given to the troops and this spread to the civilian population. The powerful effect of the media should never be underestimated in modern warfare. As an aside, interrogation of prisoners disclosed the interesting fact that, when they had the choice, more North Vietnamese soldiers listened to the BBC news than to any other!

The military culture of the Western armies has led to positional and linear warfare being the norm until mobility is required for any particular offensive. CRW postulates a different concept, one embracing both mobile and guerrilla aspects. By the former I see that Mao advocated that his forces should never be in one place long enough for his enemies to mass enough forces to defeat them. Eventual victory could only be assured if his forces were never engaged by a superior force. Only if conditions permitted should his men be concentrated sufficiently to be superior to the enemy's in one particular place, at one particular time, for one particular task. As soon as that was finished dispersion had to be effected and, if the battle were obviously going against him, he must break off as expeditiously as possible.

Giap had this to say on mobile warfare: '. . . [it] is the fighting way of concentrating troops of the regular army, in which big forces operate on a vast battlefield, attacking the enemy where he is exposed with the aim of annihilating enemy man-power, advancing very deeply, then withdrawing very swiftly, possessing to the extreme dynamism, initiative, mobility and rapidity of decision in the face of new situations'.

One characteristic of this type of warfare is the large number of government security forces (troops and police) it ties down. To illustrate that this is not just an Asian phenomenon, figures for Central America in 1987 are germane: Guatemala's 43,000 armed forces were up against 3,000 guerrillas; El Salvador's 49,000 against 4,000; Honduras' 22,000 against 200; and Nicaragua's 75,000 against 18,000. No wonder that the governments of those countries wanted a political settlement and, equally, no wonder the guerrillas wanted to maintain the initiative. In stark contrast, in 1947 in North Vietnam the French had only 15,000 men to the North Vietnamese's 60,000 in an area of nearly 80,000 square miles, so they could never take any initiative other than locally.

'Guerrilla' used in this context means that non-main force troops and most of the civilian population join in the struggle according to the overall operational and political plan. Apart from bolstering the strength of the main forces when required, such tasks could be, for example, the gathering of information about enemy movements, strong-arm intimidation against those unwilling to throw in their lot with the Communists, provision of supplies, felling trees and digging holes in a road of known or expected security forces movement, sabotage, incendiarism and giving shelter to hard-pressed men.

Deception is another characteristic of CRW. Sun Zi had this to say about it:

> All warfare is based on deception. Hence, when able to attack, we must seem unable to do so; when using our forces, we must seem inactive; when we are near, we must make the enemy believe we are far away, and when far, we must make him think we are near. Hold out baits to entice him. Feign disorder, and crush him. If he is superior in strength, evade him. If he is taking his ease, give him no rest. If his forces are united, separate them. Attack him where he is unprepared, appear where you are not expected. These military devices leading to victory must not be divulged beforehand.

In the Malayan Emergency one of my platoon commanders, Lieutenant (QGO) Tulbahadur Rai, practised deception on a very modest scale by pretending that he was a Communist terrorist and demanded money from a group of rubber tappers. The one man who offered him some was a suspected sympathizer and was arrested. This was condemned by the brigade commander (an ex-sapper and a devout Christian) as being 'a *ruse de guerre* unbecoming to civilized warfare' and he told me that he would not put up with it. He obviously regarded deception as 'not quite the done thing, that it lets the British Army down'. I don't think he ever spoke to me after that little incident!

The requirement of the Communist forces not to be engaged conventionally before they are completely ready means that they need a sanctuary to go to. They stay there until it is expeditous to leave and where their enemies cannot penetrate without the grave risk of escalating the crisis to a new dimension. The concept of a sanctuary is as old as time itself. In Korea the sanctuary for the North Koreans was China, as it was for the Pathet Lao and North Vietnamese forces in northern Laos. It was safe for the Vietminh (or Vietcong as they were pejoratively known later) in South Vietnam, north of the demilitarized zone (DMZ) and Cambodia, except against American bombing. Southern Thailand provided a sanctuary for the Malayan Communist terrorists. Indonesian Borneo (Kalimantan Utara as the Indonesians know it) was thought of as a safe haven until the doctrine of 'hot pursuit' was evolved and made it unsafe for Indonesian troops within five or so miles of the border. Anti-Sandanista contra guerrillas use Honduras as a sanctuary.

It was disastrous for the Communists whenever they were engaged by superior forces at times and in places not of their choosing and when could not get to their sanctuary, especially as they never had any air force.

CRW embraces the entire population and divides the military effort into three. Apart from main force units, there are regional forces and village guerrillas. There could be about five to ten of this last category in each village: they operate near home, know the countryside like the back of their hands and normally are soldiers by night and civilians by day. They form a hard core but not more than two or three – the basic cell – will be dedicated Communists. They will be lightly armed, not very well trained and, apart from intelligence gathering, they can perform such tasks as assembling *panji* pits, maintaining simple ambushes, activating certain types of booby-trap and giving early warning of security force movement. They are adept at minor sabotage, arson, terrorism and murder, but they are probably not heavily politically indoctrinated. To identify them without informers is a most difficult task. To be an informer is a dangerous occupation.

Regional soldiers are more indoctrinated and better trained. They operate in one region and can expect to be soldiers for, say, six months of the year and civilians for the other six. Crops have to be sown and harvested, food supplies have to be built up. They can concentrate and disperse quickly. Such forces will be less well trained and more lightly armed than the full-time soldiers and, where possible, their arms will be the same as their enemies' so that replacement is easy. Even if they are of a different type it is of no serious consequence provided the ammunition of the enemy is of the required calibre.

These three different types of soldier may be blurred in reality, never being as neat on the ground as they are on paper. In Malaya the organization that equated with the militia, the *Min Yuen*, were not armed, nor were there main force units as there were in Indo-China. Nevertheless the principle is valid. A parallel form of civilian involvement that bolsters conventional Western armies as and when required are normal territorial and reserve forces.

One aspect of CRW that bears close scrutiny is the time it takes to prepare. In sharp contrast to the military emasculation that took place in Britain between the two world wars, and gave such a false impression of ability in the 'Fools' Peace' that lasted from the outbreak of war until the summer of 1940, CRW takes a long time to foment. There are three phases to be gone through before the revolutionary government can attain power: these are known as the passive, active and counter-offensive phases, with some military *gurus* preferring to divide the active phase into a lower and a higher intensity.

The passive phase consists of the penetration of such organizations as trades unions, local government, student unions, touring repertory groups, newspapers and broadcasting, and even government security forces. Governments try to foil this by use of their counter-intelligence agencies and police force, not by military means. In Malaya this phase can be said to have started in 1928, by which time Communist agents from China had established a South Seas Communist Party in Singapore, although the Malayan Communist Party (MCP) itself did not start up until 1930. Throughout the 1930s its main form of action was disruption of the two major industries of rubber and tin. As its aim had more of a personal sacrifice motive than one of personal gain it did not achieve much success but, helped by the conditions of the war against the Japanese, the Communists managed to forge links with the local villagers as well as with many townsfolk. Natural antipathy between the Malay – easy-going, lacking any great interest in commerce, but having some latent ability for organized work and in a position of political power – and the Chinese – very industrious, motivated by money but with no political power – had been exacerbated to a great extent by post-war conditions of near breakdown of the civil administration. These factors prompted the Communists to launch into the second of their revolutionary phases, the active phase, in the summer of 1948.

In French Indo-China this passive phase lasted from 1930 until 1945. Activities during this time were not fundamentally different from what happened in Malaya although the basic antipathy against the French and the militant unrest that marred the inter-war years were pointers to a less tractable and potentially more explosive situation.

I fully subscribe to what Archimedes L. A. Patti writes in *Why Vietnam? Prelude to America's Albatross* about the situation in 1945: '. . . if national independence could assure a Vietnamese of survival, he saw the Vietminh as the answer. It mattered not to him whether the medium was democratic, socialistic or communistic. The question was to be free from want, to enjoy the fruits of one's labours, and to exist unmolested.' As regards Laos, 'the hyphen between Indo and China', a cynical American described French policy there to me as 'giving only enough food to keep them hungry and putting just enough salt in their water to keep them thirsty'.

As its name implies, the active phase is when the revolutionaries take more militant and open action to increase their influence by guerrilla activity, with this being countered by the security forces at a corresponding level of military activity by the government under threat. In Malaya this consisted of such actions as raiding police stations for weapons, coercion, intimidation, acts of banditry, burning buses, burning or mutilating identity cards, sabotage by slashing rubber trees to weaken the economy and generally making life uncomfortable if not dangerous for those who did not submit to these pressures. At such times it becomes impossible for government forces to give the protection necessary for the ordinary citizen to go about his business undisturbed because the Communists have the initiative. Recruits are gathered, numbers swell and elementary training is given to militant activists. The type of person attracted by a spirit of adventure joined, so did many criminals 'on the run' from the police. The other two classes of person consist of those whose wives, mothers or sisters have been threatened if their man did not join the cause and, lastly, the genuine zealot who, though few and far between, is the most deadly of them all. Such a situation provides the 'sea of people' for the Communist 'fish' to swim in. Detection is very hard, as the French discovered in the Indo-China conflict (where this phase lasted from 1945 to 1953) and the Americans later when that sad, torn and tormented territory was known as North and South Vietnam.

In Malaya the active phase lasted from 1948 until 1960 – known as '*ulu* [Malay for 'headwaters of a stream'] bashing' to British soldiers – and it showed that the Communists had overestimated themselves. The party had to revert to phase one until they were ready to restart the second phase. There never was a third phase.

Like the widening ripples from a stone thrown into a pond, the influence of the Communists would spread to swathes of territory, which would then be taken over and become 'liberated zones' in which the government had no influence except when it sent in large numbers of troops. The theory is that, as these liberated zones increase in size and numbers, so the time becomes ripe for the third phase of CRW, the counter-offensive phase (so called, presumably, because by then the Communists are in a position to counter the government's security forces successfully). The Communists will be in a position to topple the government by defeating it militarily with their main force units and take over responsibility for the running of the country. It is then that conventional tactics and encounter battles occur on a large scale.

In Indo-China/Vietnam this is what happened and the Communists won; in Malaya it only happened once and then was of no consequence. Indeed, very few of us 'at ground level' even heard about it then. It took place in a remote area of Kelantan, a state in the north-east of the country, where there was an isolated Chinese settlement. Visited by the Communist guerrillas, the villagers were told that they were the only ones in the whole of Malaya yet to be liberated. They were given weapons and told to dig and man trenches. Some Royal Malay Regiment soldiers drove the guerrillas away a week later and the situation returned to normal.

The guerrilla situation in Thailand, the centre of the moribund South East Asia Treaty Organization (SEATO), never left the active phase. A grumbling and potentially dangerous Communist threat that claimed many lives was seen, at one time, to be the next domino to fall after Indo-China. In 1971 the Royal Thai Army invited me to be their overall adviser on jungle warfare on the ground. In the event I was posted to Laos as the defence attaché. (In 1971 there were three times as many recorded sightings of armed and uniformed guerrillas in peninsula Malaysia than there were in Thailand, and I was asked by a representative of the Chief of the [Malaysian] General Staff to recommend measures to end the trouble. This I did but the Malays are past masters at equivocation, so, of course, this was never officially announced.) The end of China and Vietnam's quarrel, rather than any other policy, seems to have been the reason for the guerrilla problem in Thailand being declared over in 1984, although it was not until 1987 that significant surrenders took place.

INDONESIAN INTERLUDE: 1945

CRW took some time to spread and one of the first bouts of post-war fighting, in Indonesia, was not CRW although it was unconventional. The Japanese had summoned the anti-Dutch leader of the Indonesian Nationalist Movement (a hitherto little-supported group) from the island of Java to Saigon, two days before they capitulated. He was instructed to form a government and to proclaim the establishment of the Indonesian Republic before the Dutch in particular or the Allies in general could return. A deliberate campaign of virulent propaganda against the Netherlands and of ill use, brutality and oppression against the unfortunate women and children in the internment camps was started. All Dutch men and boys were seized and imprisoned, leaving the women and children to the mercies of rough and lawless extremists.

Only later were British and Indian troops able to reach Java and release the captives, regain superiority and restore the situation. A conference was arranged between the British – Colonel Pugh – and the Indonesians and, as the history of 5th Indian Division, _The Ball of Fire_, puts it:

> The place was in a ferment. Road-blocks covered by muzzles protruding from nearby houses obstructed the streets. At every halt a horde of excitable youths, armed to the teeth, pressed round the car in which Colonel Pugh was being escorted to the conference. Rifles were thrust through the windows; bayonets all but impaled the occupants of the car; and it was obvious that many fingers trembled on the triggers and that the use of the safety-catch was unknown.

Military action was on a low level but nastily sharp enough for fatal casualties to be inflicted and decorations for bravery to be won. There is an interesting account of the fighting, written by a distinguished regimental soldier, Lieutenant-Colonel H. C. Gregory, who was a company commander in 3/10th Gurkha Rifles. Although the countryside was not jungle by some definitions, it was thick enough to require a modification of open warfare tactics.

We were ordered to move from Tampin in Malaya to the capital of Java, then known as Batavia, in HMS *Glen Royal*. On the afternoon of 16th October we arrived in Batavia harbour but instead of landing were ordered to go without delay to Sematang on the north coast of the island, a serious situation having developed there as a result of Javanese rebels arming themselves with surrendered Japanese weapons. They were attacking large camps that still contained mainly Dutch women and children.

At 0745 hours on 19th October the two leading companies, I commanding one of them, were lowered away and landed unopposed although firing could be heard in the town. The camps were on the far side of the town, so we moved on two parallel lines towards them as rapidly as possible, not knowing quite what to expect.

The rear platoon was attacked by a Japanese patrol which had evidently taken the Gurkhas as Javanese. Shots were fired and three Japanese soldiers were killed, the only other casualty being the Dutch doctor accompanying the rear platoon. He was wounded in the arm and took it calmly, remarking that he found the gunshot wound 'clinically quite interesting'.

Gregory saw a Japanese flag farther down the road.

I went in that direction hoping to find a command post of some kind, which I did and I expressed regret for the loss of life that had just occurred due to lack of information, and explained our mission. The two Japanese officers were not unfriendly and thanked me for what I was able to tell them, promising to pass on the information about our role in Semarang as soon as possible to other units.

The Gurkhas got to the Dutch family camp.

When we reached it shots were being exchanged between Japanese soldiers guarding the camp and some Javanese trying to break into it. All was soon quiet and we were given an unforgettable reception by the hundreds of women and children who had been hoping and praying for our arrival.

The next move was to Magelang, in the middle of the island, not far from Jogjakarta. There was a good deal of fighting around both places and on the road connecting them to each other and to Semarang. It was mostly road clearing, dealing with ambushes and snipers, and preventing access to camps and hospitals.

There was an interesting episode during this period. This was the re-arming of Japanese soldiers under a Captain Yamata and employing them under command.

They seemed extremely pleased with the arrangement and did very well. The company commander called on the commanding officer of 3/10th Gurkha Rifles to express his appreciation of the honour done to him and his men and his thanks for being entrusted with such excellent British weapons (No. 5 rifle and Bren gun). So what was done out of sheer necessity, because of our small numbers and the immensity of our task, turned out a very happy arrangement.

The Japanese company in 3/10th Gurkha Rifles operated a little differently from other companies. Tactical battle drills, devised for use in jungle or fairly thick cover, were second nature to us by this time and orders were reduced to a minimum in consequence. The Japanese company commander, on the other hand, gave very detailed orders and so did his platoon and section commanders. When operating with our B Company (Major Philip Dunkley) on one occasion, to clear a road, they were given the task of eliminating snipers from a two-storied building at the side of the road. Orders were taking a long time and Philip Dunkley, an excellent and very experienced leader, impatiently requested action. He was courteously asked to wait just a little longer as it was necessary for each man to know exactly what he had to do. Then suddenly the Japanese soldiers deployed and only moments later, as it seemed, there were bursts of small-arms fire and then Japanese helmets began to appear at all the windows. If orders had been slow the action that followed was rapid indeed – altogether an impressive demonstration.

Although Java was open country on the whole, the lush growth of tropical shrubs and small trees had created patches of excellent cover and these were naturally made full use of, especially where they occurred near a cutting or defile to lay ambushes. We continued to rely on our well-rehearsed tactical battle drill to deal with these, but casualties were inevitably quite heavy – about a hundred killed and wounded during the few months we spent in Java.

EARLY DAYS IN INDO-CHINA

The other fighting around that time was, however, CRW – in Cochin-China. In Indo-China, as it was in 1945, the French were doomed from the very start: this is not said from the comfort and safety of a non-combatant's chair, nor with the benefit of hindsight. I was in Cochin-China from early October 1945 to the end of January 1946 with 1/1st Gurkha Rifles, as part of 20th Indian Infantry Division. We went there to take the Japanese surrender, having disarmed them and, when we were prevented from doing both by Vietminh activity, we had to take prophylactic action. With the atomic explosions of a few weeks before still metaphorically ringing in our ears, it was risible, yet indicative of this new type of warfare, that the first weapons we captured were bows and arrows.

The Russians were meddling in the area even then – indeed, in 1983, when working in the university in Kathmandu, I heard them boast about it. In Calcutta in early 1948, meeting as 'The World Federation of Democratic Youth' and the 'International Union of Students', the Russians laid plans to rid these three countries of their colonial occupation by Communist methods and replace their governments by Soviet-inspired ones.

Even before then there was evidence of involvement. We were sent north from Saigon to disarm the Japanese but the Vietminh actively resisted us. There were not enough of our troops to keep the Vietminh at arm's length and disarm the Japanese at the same time. Accordingly two Japanese battalions, untarnished by any atrocities committed against the Allies, were detailed to help 100 Brigade out. Both of them, *Yamagishi Butai* and *Takahashi Butai*, came under command of 1/1st Gurkha Rifles at separate times. The commanding officer had to report to us once every 24 hours. As the intelligence officer I helped my commanding officer, Lieutenant-Colonel C. E. Jarvis, with these reports.

One day they announced that they had captured a Russian. 'Shall we kill him or bring him to you?', Major Takahashi asked through his interpreter.

'Bring him to us tomorrow. How do you know that he is a Russian?' Jarvis countered.

'Because of his uniform and because he is carrying a jar of coffee.'

The information was given with the quiet dignity of one who talks from a position of strength because what he says is true. We did not follow the logic of the coffee, but when the Russian appeared on the morrow he had clasped to his bosom a large glass jar full of roasted coffee beans. He was red-haired and stocky, was wearing khaki drill, with a yellow hammer and sickle emblem on a red background on each lapel, with a similar badge stuck in his khaki forage cap. He was sent south to Saigon on the next convoy; we never heard of him again.

I myself was in command of a Japanese battalion, the *Yamagishi Butai*, in action against the Vietminh when we contacted a stay-behind party with one man hidden in a dry ditch, under dead leaves, with two wounded – one a youth armed with a catapult – as decoy. This was in an overgrown rubber plantation.

The hidden man was only discovered because, as the wounded were being examined, some Japanese soldiers urinated on to the leaves and they saw a hand emerge and wave about. I turned to see some Japanese gesticulating wildly as they stood on the ridge above the ditch. I asked the interpreter to find out why. He returned, bowed gravely and said, 'Respected sir, they are afraid.'

'Why?'

'They have seen a hand,' came the enigmatic reply.

I went to see what it was all about. Sure enough, a skinny brown arm was waving about, palm upwards, not unlike an oriental Excalibur looking for his sword.

'Pull it,' I ordered callously. 'They are afraid to,' replied the interpreter.

My temper snapped and, sensing valour the better part of discretion, I quickly ordered the soldiers to pull the hand. One man, braver than the rest, bent down ready to grasp it. A second caught him round the waist and a third man the second likewise. In one movement the leading soldier grasped the hand and all three pulled. I watched, fascinated, as a small, stark-naked man, with the Star of Tonkin tattooed on his left shoulder, emerged carrying a brand-new machine-gun of curious design. He looked up at the sky and suddenly seemed to go berserk. He wriggled free of his captors, crouched low and, just as I noticed that the gun was loaded with a tray-like magazine, he bent both sides down, jamming the gun. The Japanese were on him in a flash and he jumped up and down, shrieking as he did, trying to get away.

Only then did I understand why the man had looked up at the sky when he was pulled out and became hopping mad when he saw that the sky was cloudless. On feeling the sudden surge of liquid wetting him he had put his hand out to see how heavily it was raining! In future years, when I gave South Vietnamese army students lectures at the British Army Jungle Warfare School, I used this incident as an example both of the need for constant vigilance when engaged on this type of operation and of the fact that secret weapons need not always be modern!

I saw French behaviour, their attitude to the local population and the van-quished Japanese on a number of occasions and was grieved. I was struck forcibly by their complete lack of empathy with and their intolerance of 'the natives' – who were regarded as expendable – which contrasted drastically with the way the British treated such people. Militarily they gave the impression of adversely over-reacting to any particular situation, so suffering needless casualties. In general terms, once we had handed over to them, they took as many casualties every few days as we had taken in the three months we had been there and we all said that it was only a question of time before the French were no longer in the country.

In retrospect, the British have been blamed for going to Indo-China. Those laying the blame, as is so often the case, were not in the dreadful position of having to make the decision, there and then, according to the available evidence at that time. We were not as unpopular as some historians have made out, nor as Vietnamese I have spoken to since would have us believe. In October 1945 leaflets appeared where the battalion was billeted in a girls' school compound. The message started: 'To our friends the British' and went on to say that there would soon be an armed struggle against the French and that the Annamites, as they were known, did not want to hurt us. It finished: 'Be prudent and never ramble around with the French', which none of us ever did!

In 1963 the Royal Marines were asked to go to Laos to fight, but this was turned down on the excuse that the British were fighting their own war in Borneo. Even had British forces been committed against the North Vietnamese, there is no question in my mind that the eventual result would have been any different – delayed, maybe, but different, no. What the British did was to run courses for South Vietnamese students at their Jungle Warfare School in Malaya (later Malaysia). From 1964 to 1970, 1,693 Vietnamese students were trained in jungle warfare and, on occasions, visual tracking. (During the same period, 210 Thai, 34 Filipino and 21 South Korean students were also trained.) In Vietnam itself some aid was provided; for instance the Protector of Aborigines in Malaya, Mr Dick Noone, went to advise on ethnic minorities and the Secretary for Defence in the Federation of Malaya, the ex-Chindit and jungle warfare expert, Sir Robert Thompson, was often there.

The French fought a war based on the mobility of armies, whereas the Vietnamese based their fighting on the mobility of the individual. The French tried to hold a fortress barrier, but failed because they did not control the surrounding jungle and the North Vietnamese had the inestimable advantage of being able to use China as a sanctuary and having time on their side. The French then tried to match Vietnamese mobility on foot with mechanical mobility but the Vietnamese used the jungle to nullify such action. In the final analysis, the French lost because they did not have the full backing of the government at home for a campaign of higher intensity, did not have troops on the ground in sufficient strength to defeat the Vietnamese (although they did have enough not to lose) and, supremely, they did not have the support of the people. They were not wanted; they never had been; they never would be.

In the case of the Americans, when there were two Vietnams (as opposed to the political geography of Tonkin, Annam and Cochin-China of French colonial days), the overriding factor of their defeat was that the strength of the political base in the south which they were supporting was not equal to that of the north, which they were opposing. The Americans produced many mechanical aids that the Vietnamese could not match, such as 'people sniffers' (see page 148) and helicopter gunships, ploughs to obliterate the jungle, starlight-scopes to aim weapons at night and much electronic gear. None of these prevailed sufficiently for eventual political victory although they probably slowed down the inevitable collapse.

The many battles and fire-fights that the Americans did win should not be forgotten, nor indeed should the extraordinary sacrifices made by them. It was not militarily that the Americans lost the war, despite the self-imposed constraints of not invading North Vietnam, of having bombing pauses that allowed the North Vietnamese to reinforce and resupply without fear of reprisals from air action, and of not bombing Hanoi on the scale that the British bombed Dresden during the Second World War. The Americans had many material advantages, but because they had no popular 'cause' or belief that transcended that of the North Vietnamese, and were ineffably naïve, they lost the war politically: on the campuses ('Hey, Hey, LBJ; how many kids have you killed today?') and in Congress, resulting in a loss of national will. On another level they lost it in the composition of their army, as it had too many conscripts, many of whom were not of higher-educational calibre and who could not keep away from enervating pastimes when not fighting. Their biggest military disadvantage was that they were fighting a different war from that which the Vietnamese were fighting, with an army which could never win, despite all the individual dedication shown, the collective spirit engendered, the modifications it sustained and the adjuncts it fostered.

The North Vietnamese soldiers were altogether different people from those found in the type of 'non-political' and 'non-religious' army the Western world espouses. They had belief in a cause few South Vietnamese and fewer Americans could match; they had self-discipline on a scale that bewildered other nations; they were masters of guerrilla warfare; they accepted casualties that Western armies would never have been allowed by their governments at home; they used fear and the unexpected as weapons; they were completely unscrupulous. As a minute example of this, Vietminh guerrillas took a dog and, having slit it open, inserted a time bomb in its innards then stitched it up. The dog was abandoned near an American camp where it was rescued and made comfortable. A number of soldiers were wounded when the wretched creature exploded.

The introduction of a new element into guerrilla warfare, engineer commandos (Dac Cong), produced ingenuity and bravery – in the jungle, the villages and even the main towns – that were heroic even by North Vietnamese standards.

I went back to Vietnam almost exactly thirty years after my first visit. I saw training, both South Vietnamese and American special forces, and visited operational units, comparing British and American techniques. The story going the rounds concerned the Republic of Korea (ROK) army contingent, who were the only 'Free World' troops alleged to use fear as a weapon to the same extent as the North Vietnamese. After losing men to the enemy, they captured a Vietminh guerrilla and cut him up into cubic chunks of flesh, gristle and bone, then took these grisly remains round to all the villages in their area. True or false, the result was that that area became the only one where it was safe to walk both by day and by night.

MALAYA AND BORNEO

It was only in Malaya (1948–60) that the Communists have ever lost in jungle territory of their own choosing. One of the fundamental reasons was that the political base which the British had created was strong enough to withstand an ideology that was and still is contrary to Malay thinking. The Communists were never strong enough to take the country over, but in the crucial days of 1948 they were not far from it. In the event it took twelve years to reduce the Communist threat sufficiently for it not to impinge on the body politic, although a Communist presence was maintained in the Malay-Thai border area for many years after.

Across the water, in British Borneo before it became the eastern half of Malaysia, 'Confrontation' by Indonesia against that new state (1963–66) saw a sterner jungle struggle than had been the case in the Malayan Emergency. Not directed by Communist-inspired ideology, it was its own expansionist attempt disguised in a mantle of 'anti-neo-colonialism'. Without British and Australian support I personally doubt if victory for the Malaysian Government would either have been so swift or so complete, if it had come about at all. Although the incorporation of Borneo within Malaysia was politically unpopular among certain sections of the indigenous population, the change was made without any undue commotion. The native Ibans have since shown their centuries-old dislike of the peninsula Malays, with hushed-up incidents involving both ethnic groups and resulting in scores of fatalities. On the military front, the intelligence skills of the SAS and jungle skills and tenacity of the Gurkhas in particular, and the provision of helicopters in general, combined with making the border people feel they were involved in their own border security by the raising of the Border Scouts to help the security forces, prevented an Indonesian takeover.

INDIA'S INTERNAL INCUBUS

In the north-eastern corner of India lies country that is thickly covered by forests, much of it bamboo. Part of it is inhabited by Mizos. Unsophisticated, yet having taken part in the Burma war, serving then – as now – in the Assam Regiment, many of them have been to Delhi and some as far afield as London. British policy in that region was to do nothing that would disturb the Chinese to the north and, apart from some map-making in the late 1940s, they were similarly neglected by both state (Assam) and central governments after independence.

Once every forty years a certain bamboo flowers and this causes a plague of rats that engenders famine. In the mid-1960s there was a particularly severe situation and Mizo leaders asked for help. None was given and a separatist situation arose. The central government responded by sending in units of the army and, for five years from 1966, conventional operations were mounted against an 'enemy', including some bombing. I gather that there was also considerable brutality; adults were killed and the children told to fend for themselves. As these unfortunates grew up they fostered a deep grudge. By 1971 the situation was worse than it had been five years before. China was supplying weapons but the Mizo problem was never a Communist one.

The Indian military authorities realized that they were making serious mistakes so changed from conventional to unconventional tactics, using the Burma campaign as their model. Five years later the situation was no better, so in 1976, counter-insurgency measures, as they were called, were introduced. Another ten years were needed to reach a settlement and it was a political, not a military, solution that was reached.

From 1976 to 1986 the accent was on trying to win over the Mizos, who were then no longer regarded as 'enemies'. Selected officers and men would be given instruction in tactics required (chiefly patrolling, ambushing, cordon and search of villages and 'combing' an area of jungle with beaters and stops). Psychological warfare was introduced and every intelligence-gathering organization extant was involved, military and civil. There was no police 'Special Branch' as such, but the Criminal Investigation Department (CID), the Central Bureau of Investigation (CBI), the Intelligence Bureau (IB) and Research and Analysis (RA) all came in on the act.

Five Golden Rules were introduced for all those taking part in operations:
1 Never interfere with Mizo religion, customs or traditions.
2 Never interfere with Mizo women.
3 Always apologize when mistakes have been made.
4 Always behave as soldiers.
5 Mix around and join in with the Mizos.

Point 3 was explained to me like this: when we had beaten up a suspected insurgent and found he was innocent, we apologized and, as he would have been given very little food for some time, we would give him a good meal. If a person's house had been ransacked in the search of arms but none found, the senior commander had to apologize for making a mistake, that he was only doing his duty and even offer to help to tidy the place up. Point 5 was one of the most telling points and, as my informant told me, 'we won by love and friendship'.

The Gurkhas who were involved during these years felt that it was not war, which it was not when compared to fighting against Pakistan and China; yet, in its way, it was as big a problem as either of the others.

Other campaigns that had a jungle dimension have not produced any particular new aspect of this esoteric branch of warfare: in this I am thinking about the crisis in Kenya in the early 1950s, Che Guevara and Fidel Castro in Latin America in the late 1950s and the desultory Indonesian adventure in Timor in the mid-1970s. As regards Kenya, only one-fifth of the population and one-sixteenth of the landmass was involved, with the breakthrough coming from the urban area of Nairobi providing the intelligence for Operation 'Anvil' to defeat the Kikuyu tribe in their reserves, using tactics proven in the Malayan Emergency. Che Guevara had decisive ideas of his own about guerrilla warfare as opposed to jungle warfare (known as the *foco insurrectional* theory) that, in fact, was never as successful as it was claimed. (For the record, the theory had three parts: people's power that could topple governments; the countryside was the critical battleground; and a small band of guerrillas could act as the 'focus' – hence the name of the theory – for revolution.)

Despite most military planners now, in the 1980s, having to worry about far more sensitive areas of the world than those covered by jungle, the sensible ones realize the folly of leaving this aspect out of training curricula entirely. Hard-won military knowledge can ill afford to be neglected or lost, as it was in danger of so being after the Burma campaign, then after the Malayan Emergency and, wonderful to relate, once more after the Borneo emergency. Restricted budgets and inward-looking politicians are no recipe for an 'all-weather' army! If jungle warfare is to be engaged in again, in any guise, at least the appalling mistakes of the past should not be repeated.

Left: This excellent shot of the dropping zone after the event shows the parachutes dispersed on the ground, but close to their intended mark, identified by the letter 'B' carved into the open area near this Malayan river bank. (Popperfoto)

Below: The jungle is always there and soldiers in it are always wet with sweat, rain or river crossing. The mind changes gear and discomfort becomes something that is always with the jungle soldier. (Popperfoto)

6
The Malayan Emergency: 1948–51

The Communist enemy in Malaya during the Emergency was neither of the calibre of the North Vietnamese ('lacquered bamboo' as they have been described), nor of, say, the tribesmen of the North-West Frontier of British India, now Pakistan. That was just as well, as the forces that they were against were in a parlous state, as was government machinery. The overwhelming initial Japanese victory against the Western powers had shown the frailty of the colonial masters who gave an impression of being an easier target than eventually turned out to be the case. Yet, although the Communists could be brutally cruel, callously unsympathetic and doggedly determined, they never seemed to have that 'fire in the belly' which gives staying power when it is most needed.

During the Second World War British clandestine stay-behind parties had mustered a force of Chinese Communists to fight against the Japanese. This was known as the Malayan People's Anti-Japanese Army (MPAJA) and numbered about 7,000 when hostilities ended, from a population of more than five millions. After the Japanese surrender those strange bedfellows, Chinese Communists and British imperialists, got out from opposite sides and started chasing each other once again, but this time not for reasons of courtship. It was about then that the 'J' for Japanese, whom the Communists' armed forces were anti, changed to 'B' for British before changing yet again to the Malayan Races Liberation Army (MRLA).

This force, the armed wing of the MCP rather than an 'army' in its own right, followed the British pattern of regiments, battalions, companies and platoons, some of which operated independently. It consisted of ten regiments, numbered accordingly, deployed country-wide, based in deep jungle camps cleverly sited and well hidden, with the approaches carefully guarded. Strengths of units varied considerably. The government called them 'bandits' until it was discovered that that term had adverse nationalist Chinese connotations, when they were officially designated 'Communist Terrorists' or 'CT' for short. There were no support units (sappers and signallers), no support weapons and no intrinsic logistical support.

There was a civilian side to the MRLA called the *Min Yuen* (Masses Movement) who were outwardly ordinary citizens. Their task was to provide the guerrillas with food and information. Their method of obtaining food was to take it from others, without payment and often by the use of threats of severe punishment for non-compliance. This effectively made the MRLA's supply system one from front to rear rather than the-rear-to front movement of orthodox armies. As regards information, such people as rubber-tappers, shopkeepers and Public Works Department labourers were used as 'screens' to report security forces' movements. Without the *Min Yuen* the MRLA would have been very severely restricted. As time passed, people with transistor radios would use them to tune in to the low-grade radio traffic between the troops in the jungle and their headquarters.

When the MCP made its decision to start the active phase of CRW there was a shortage of troops in Malaya. There were three British battalions, two in Singapore and the other on the island of Penang, and a gunner regiment in Tampin – used as infantry initially – about 160 miles north of Singapore. There were two battalions of the Royal Malay Regiment (a third was raised in 1949 and, later, many others) and, in round numbers, 10,000 police officers and (Malay) constables. Against such meagre opposition even the poor quality of the Malayan guerrillas would have made some headway. It was the addition of six of the eight understrength Gurkha battalions that had recently joined the British Army (all suffering from severe 'teething' problems) that proved to be crucial. Even with eleven battalions there were only about 4,000 fighters available to be deployed on operations. At maximum strength there were 24 battalions' worth of soldiers.

As a sidelight, when the decision to upgrade the struggle was made by the Communists, the factor of the Gurkhas' presence in Malaya as part of the garrison seems to have been overlooked initially, then hurried measures were taken to prevent their arrival. I passed through Delhi in December 1947 and was told by the British commander that he had been approached by a senior Indian official with the incredibly naïve suggestion that the Gurkhas destined to serve the British Army in Malaya, Singapore and Hong Kong should all stay in India for another year so that their accommodation could be made ready for them. Hardly a coincidence! Had that happened either the Communists would have been successful or it would have taken more than the twelve years it did to defeat them.

As the Malayan Emergency was a guerrilla-orientated campaign the traditional four phases of war played no part. Except for when an enemy jungle base was found and attacked, operations consisted of patrolling, ambushing and more patrolling – a grotesque and deadly form of hide-and-seek. There were no fixed lines, stable fronts or firm boundaries in the accepted military sense, as the enemy were all internal, less a few who came over the Thai and Singapore borders, and from Sumatra. The campaign was conducted in support of an established government, so the all-important political stability was never seriously threatened, unlike in Vietnam especially during the American involvement. After 1949 the MRLA rarely took any form of offensive action against the army and so had to be sought out by relentless cunning and time-consuming and patience-testing efforts at all levels. However, success did not essentially depend upon high command once correct policy was formulated. It was the man on the spot, in the jungle or rubber estates, whose initiative, resourcefulness, self-reliance, sustained courage, stamina and instantaneously correct reaction to a situation could be, and often was, decisive. Thus it was ultimately the junior leaders and riflemen, seldom above company level, more often at platoon strength, who slogged it out and bore the brunt of it all. This was a testing call to the best-trained troops under normal circumstances. Many of the troops were not well trained nor were circumstances normal.

Right: Eighteen months into the Malayan campaign the Army began intensifying its jungle sweeps and patrols in search of the elusive Communist foe. Here, a soldier from the Coldstream Guards is given advice on how to cross a mountainous torrent by his Sergeant who is already safely over. (Popperfoto)

Right: These men have paused for a 'brew-up' on their way to winkle out bandits; the troops have honed their jungle skills based on experience and instruction found against the Japanese. After this quick meal the men will move quietly on, destroying their camp in the process and expertly removing all traces of troops having been in the vicinity. (Popperfoto)

In the early stages there was no policy at the top. The threat was not taken seriously. When asked his reaction to the reports that were sent to the authorities by the planting community, the senior general replied that he took the last figure off and acted accordingly. 'I can tell you,' he said to one press conference, 'this is by far the easiest problem I have ever tackled . . .' 'It'll be over by Christmas,' were words eaten by more than one general.

To try and tap experience gained during the war, a unit called 'Force Ferret' was formed in mid-1948 to act as its title suggests in the jungle against the guerrillas. It was composed of civilian Europeans, British, Gurkha and Malay troops, backed up by Chinese liaison officers and Dyak and Iban trackers from Sarawak. Each group would be split into four sections, commanded overall by a European who knew the area well and, more often than not, had a fund of invaluable local knowledge, sometimes even of jungle lore. It discovered twelve permanent guerrilla camps and showed what even a scratch force could do and what was needed. However, units that contributed to it were understrength. The force was expensive in manpower and, in any case, no long-term solution; its slackness in and general careless approach to essential points of military detail so provoked its overall commander, Lieutenant-Colonel W. C. Walker, that he made it clear that he was highly dissatisfied.

As would be expected, his attitude was resented by the Europeans, but a very senior army officer visited the force during one of the more acrimonious discussions and the upshot was that Walker was told to set up a jungle warfare training establishment, later called the Jungle Warfare School. 'Force Ferret' was disbanded and serious training began. A Civil Liaison Corps was formed of such people as Chinese interpreters for the security forces. One, Goh Ah Hok, won the British Empire Medal twice.

One major weakness was that there was no supreme commander to co-ordinate military, police and various other organs of government. This meant that troops were called out, often at short notice, too late and on spurious grounds. Initially operations were confined to searching villages, patrolling rubber estates, guarding vital points in towns against expected guerrilla attacks and escorting the two nightly mail trains. The air force also found the jungle difficult. The first time they supported troops I was with, it was we who were strafed. Helicopters were very few and far between and were not a factor in planning operations. Supply dropping was not considered for some months.

The Communist guerrillas kept mostly to the jungle, coming out from time to time to commit atrocities. Food was then no problem; the main sources of supply were the *Min Yuen*-dominated 'squatters' and estate labourers. The 60,000 odd squatters were illegal Chinese immigrants who had settled in remote areas without land title. Over the years the government had done nothing about them, if only because it could not cope with the immensity of the problem. Despite guerrilla effort forcibly to dissuade the European tin-miners and planters from staying at their work, there was no wholesale evacuation from mining areas or plantations, which the MCP had optimistically forecast. So, from the very beginning, the Communists failed to achieve the disruption of the economy that was essential for success. They also operated in units too large at that time for the accepted methods of guerrilla warfare. Contrary to guerrilla tactics, by pressing on indiscriminately with their policy of terrorism, arson and murder, they failed to 'swim in the water' of the local people, polluting it instead.

THE CRITICAL YEARS

One example of what it was like trying to cope with problems on the ground concerned countering a guerrilla gang that operated in the squatter area behind a village called Sepang, in the state of Selangor, near the Straits of Malacca. Banditry, intimidation and clandestine activities had been worsening in the early part of the year. Headed by the 'Killer', the 'Extortioner' and the 'Drill Master', who was reputed to exercise his charges in weapon training and drill, even summoning them on parade by bugle, the gang was feared by the locals and the ten Europeans of the planting fraternity. Something had to be done about it.

In August 1948 I was sent for and told to take a platoon to the area for a week (later extended). To bolster morale we were to show ourselves to as many people as possible and to look for the guerrillas – incompatible aims.

Sepang was a typical village – a couple of streets, an assistant district office, a post office, a police station (all the staff were Malays except for the Chinese detective) and a few shops, all owned by Chinese. There were coconut and rubber estates on three sides (with some Sumatran labour) and on the fourth, the coastal side, were Malay fishing villages. Between the plantations and the jungle lived the Chinese squatters, tight-lipped and clan-conscious to a degree that made penetration by outsiders impossible. The squatter area was a patchwork of tangled scrub, tapioca plots, vegetable gardens, scattered dwellings and swamp. The jungle, with its foreboding, unbroken canopy, stood proud, extending to the north while, to the south, lay the tidier patches of rubber and coconut estates. My 20-odd men could be there for years and never get a smell of the guerrillas, but we did hear a bugle call and firing on a range in the direction of the jungle.

On a follow-up we found, hidden in some undergrowth, a sack containing a large tin brimming with packets of documents, weapon-training pamphlets, histories of Communism complete with pictures of Karl Marx and lists of monies. Although everything was written in Chinese, the pictures, diagrams and columns of figures were, to me, positive proof that we had stumbled into the home ground of the guerrillas.

I split my force into two. Having no radio I told the senior man of the other group that I would maintain contact by making periodical noises like a cuckoo. Some time later the ground rose and at the top of a hillock we found an empty sentry post with a kettle simmering on the hob. An alarm device had been rigged up outside. Inside the hut were some army blankets and a wooden bugle. I 'cuckooed' to the others to join me. As we were checking the area we heard a bird call from the jungle that lay, dark and sinister, a hundred feet below us. A short while later there was an answering call. Ten minutes after that, farther away and fainter, came two more calls, one answering the other and, even more faintly, another two calls ten minutes later still. I knew they were men, not birds, as the call each was using was of a bird that only ever called at dawn and dusk. It was not for some years that I, in my turn, realized that, as there are no cuckoos in Malaya, my signals must have alerted the guerrillas! On my way back to Sepang I mentally equated my wooden bugle as only one better than a wooden spoon.

Left: These Coldstream Guardsmen are mooring their Sampan on the river bank prior to disembarking, having just effected a river crossing with local help. (Popperfoto)

Left: Logging areas are criss-crossed with old paths, so making patrolling difficult and tracking a problem. Buttresses near the base of large trees are good cover from view. (Popperfoto)

A small guerrilla post was found and fatalities ensued. As I was in command when Malayan citizens were killed, I was told that, as the laws of the land stood, I would have to stand trial for murder. The charges were quietly dropped. There was no more trouble in the Sepang area for six months when the Chinese police interpreter was murdered.

Not long afterwards another murder charge was dropped against a corporal in 1/6th Gurkha Rifles operating in the deep jungle in the north of Malaya. His patrol captured a guerrilla and took his head off with a kukri. Thinking that that was not enough to identify the man, he cut the hands off as well. On arrival in Alor Star, the state capital, the corporal took his package – now not at its freshest – to the house of the head of the Criminal Investigation Department, Mr W. Carbinell.

It was 3 o'clock on a holiday and Carbinell had to go and fetch the official photographer. He put the head and the hands in the refrigerator and left the house. His wife was having a siesta in the bedroom.

While he was away his wife woke up and, wanting a cold drink, went downstairs to get one from the fridge. On seeing the grisly remains she fell into a dead faint. Her husband found her unconscious and took her upstairs before getting rid of skull and hands. When his wife awoke and asked about those dreadful things in the fridge, her husband could not believe such a story. He took her downstairs and showed her that there was nothing untoward in the fridge at all. She had been the victim of a horrible nightmare.

Military reinforcements, including the Brigade of Guards, were sent to Malaya soon after the Emergency was declared and extra police were enlisted. The Guards found that their training for bayonet charges when ambushed was expensive in casualties as their headstones still bear mute witness. Often headstrong bravery was not the whole answer to any one situation. Crucial changes to government agencies (propaganda and intelligence, for instance), however, were yet to be thought out.

By 1950 the Communist terrorists were becoming more daring in their methods as they learnt from mistakes they had made and as they probably underestimated the security forces' potential that was masked by weaknesses that were only slowly being overcome. Units were still thinking along Second World War lines. In the north of the country 1st King's Own Yorkshire Light Infantry, losing 35 men from 1949 to 1951, thought in terms of a 'hot' war with 'front lines' as some of their very experienced company commanders relied on tactics they had used successfully against the Japanese when now the battalion's task was to prevent enemy movement between Thailand and Malaya. There was no lack of keenness among the men (the farmers liked the jungle but soldiers from the cities hated it), but there was a lack of jungle craft. British soldiers are apt to be noisy and some find it hard to sustain a high standard of alertness when there is no action. Lieutenant-Colonel George Styles, the George Cross bomb-disposal hero, recalls that it was only after Dyak trackers arrived from Sarawak that standards improved. One night the Dyak with whom he worked woke him up to listen to a curious whining sound and explained that it was a cloud of mosquitoes following a tiger.

Training for operating at night was put in hand. To help aim, decaying phosphorescent twigs were tied to the foresights of weapons. Winking fireflies were often mistaken for a man using a torch. Whatever the merits of this idea, it was abandoned after a week as men found it too hot and too noisy to sleep by day. In my experience, any group that wants to move through the jungle without leaving tell-tale signs will not move at night.

There is no doubt that battalions enlisting its soldiers from the countryside found that their results compared more than favourably with other battalions whose soldiers came from the towns. The Suffolk Regiment was often cited as having the best British battalion in Malaya. Other battalions had their own characteristics. I think that the Fijian Regiment was of a standard few others could match. Hobbled by an inadequate logistical system and a lack of administrative awareness (weapons would be chucked into a store and forgotten once they had fouled up and didn't shoot any more), the Fijians were superbly fit. More than once were guerrillas who were stupid enough to fire on the Fijians chased and, ammunition expended, clubbed to death when caught. African regiments, 1st (Nyasa) and 3rd (Kenya) King's African Rifles, with later (the one I knew best) the 1st Rhodesian African Rifles, were normally only as good as their heavy complement of white NCOs.

The war-time concept of special forces was re-introduced when it was decided to raise the Malayan Scouts (Special Air Services). These were meant to be hand-picked British troops capable of living for protracted spells in deep jungle and beating the guerrillas at their own game. In theory the idea was excellent; in practice many commanding officers regarded it as a useful way of getting rid of difficult material. So unpopular did this organization become that when its founder suffered a social reverse, bill-boards all over the country shrilled his misfortune. The Rhodesian squadron came in for much unpopularity. In Tony Geraghty's *Who Dares Wins*, the details are carefully given and judiciously balanced. These I can vouch for, having been a puzzled and disinterested spectator co-located with the force during its birth pangs. I personally could see little merit in raising such a force, especially when such dubious material needed so much effort to reach the standard required.

One constant difficulty for British battalions was that of maintaining standards of fighting efficiency and jungle skills with a National Service element. In one 3-year tour one battalion had 73 officers and 1,646 soldiers, the equivalent of two complete change-overs.

A major weakness during this period was that there was no proper joint planning between the police, who had their ear to the ground but lacked the ability to take enough advantage from it, and the military who were in the reverse situation. Another was a wrong appreciation of the long-term gravity of the Communist threat which resulted in only short-term, essentially military measures being taken to combat it.

Nevertheless, the government did make two important decisions during the first part of 1949, although putting them into effect took a long time and much effort, with lack of experience and inadequate staff hampering easy or early results. These were registration of the population and putting those at risk of exposure to guerrilla pressure (the Chinese squatters) under some sort of organized protection (the 'Briggs' plan) in what were known as New Villages, a name that was easy to translate into Chinese as it had no political or party undertones. Later each had its own Home Guard. This concept was bitterly opposed by the guerrillas who saw their grip over that part of the population they regarded as essential for success being eroded. For the security forces it was the start of a two-pronged campaign – military action to wipe out the guerrillas and administrative action to protect the population – which was the basis of eventual victory.

The guerrillas discovered that weapons could be captured from ambushing military and police vehicles and this led to armoured lorries, scout cars and strict convoy discipline being introduced. Some senior police officers were against putting policemen into protected vehicles as it was considered to have a detrimental effect on their bravery. This was only rectified after many needless casualties.

Large-scale operations appreciably increased, as did the use of airlifts to transport men and aerial resupply to keep them operational once deployed.

Locating and destroying guerrilla camps was the aim of company commanders yet such a manoeuvre was seldom successful. Camps were hard to pinpoint from the air, harder to take by surprise on the ground. Enemy sentries a distance from the camp too often gave the alert before a close reconnaissance could be completed and, even if such were achieved, the actual surrounding of the camp site by troops close enough to prevent guerrillas escaping, let alone a surprise attack by the assaulting troops, was always fraught. The danger that the assault troops' fire might cause casualties to the cut-off troops always worried commanders.

IN THE BALANCE

Two years after the Emergency started matters hung in the balance. Guerrillas were being eliminated at a rate that outnumbered military casualties, but the police were losing more than the guerrillas were. Over a hundred civilians were being killed (often by torture) each month.

The realization by authority that planning at all levels was needed led to the formation of War Executive Committees at state (SWEC) and district (DWEC) level. It was here that the administration, police and military were appropriately represented. This was essential if efforts were not to be frittered away by lack of co-ordination; Special Branch intelligence-gathering, psychological warfare, food-denial operations, New Village defence and a host of other problems could not be the concern of only one element of government.

Company bases started to be a feature of battalion life. These were defended outposts, sometimes fifty miles from battalion headquarters, where a company, sometimes with an armoured car troop and a gunner detachment, was given its own area of territorial responsibility. Based in buildings on a rubber estate, with the soldiers under canvas or in portable shelters, they allowed a much greater and more intimate knowledge of the terrain and of the pattern of guerrilla movement to be acquired, besides allowing time for members of the local DWEC to get to know and trust one another. Also it made the planting fraternity much more settled to have their own 'tame' soldiers nearby. Operations at company level became known as 'framework' as they took place within the framework of DWEC's plans.

Some areas of Malaya had more Communist activity than others. Johore in the south of the country was probably the toughest state if only because of the proximity of Singapore with its teeming Chinese population. On 5 January 1951 the guerrillas (7 Company, MRLA) ambushed a train in the north of the state but extensive follow-up operations failed to locate them. Information then came to Special Branch as to the gang's whereabouts.

A message was sent to 'B' Company, 1/2nd Gurkha Rifles, in the small hours of 22 January and the men left at dawn. The combination of being roused from a deep sleep and a bad telephone line meant that the company commander (Major Peter Richardson, tall, shy and adored by his men) failed to get the message accurately and did not go to the spot mentioned. As it turned out, the place mentioned by Special Branch was not where the gang was and the place where 'B' Company went by mistake was; the ensuing action turned out to be the most successful of the whole Malayan Emergency. Even then it was not fought in deep jungle but in terrain that was an area of rubber plantations, swamp and paddy, with all visibility being severely restricted by thick ground mist.

As there was still a shortage of senior ranks in Gurkha battalions the two platoons Richardson took were commanded by corporals – the most important rank in the army for this type of operation once the correct decisions have been taken and adequate support for the task has been provided. Richardson was in the centre, advancing with a platoon on each flank. There was soon an exchange of fire when the two sides saw each other, with the Gurkhas killing four guerrillas. Richardson and a Chinese fired at each other and both missed! There was then a blood-curdling shriek as a terrorist slashed a Gurkha with a heavy knife, a *parang*, in the head and neck.

Meanwhile the other guerrillas tried to break contact but were prevented from so doing by a deft flanking movement by the company sergeant-major, WOII Bhimbahadur Pun, who had taken over the platoon when the trouble started. The mist had lifted by this time and the enemy were forced into an area of swamp and paddy between the two platoons. The slaughter was swift and bloody.

After the battle had died down the killing-ground was searched. Twelve bodies and some weapons were recovered. As the ground was swampy other bodies and weapons could have remained hidden. Several months later it was learnt that 35 guerrillas had either been killed or mortally wounded, including the commander of 7 Company.

Later on in the year a platoon of the Royal West Kents were ambushed when they were in three vehicles on a rubber estate. The company commander was travelling with that group of trucks and was killed, as were three sentries who were standing in an open vehicle. The third vehicle was also forced to stop and the scout car's guns jammed. The situation was desperate and only the bravery of two soldiers (Lance-Corporal Martin and Private Pannell) prevented a rout. Eleven of the battalion and three Iban trackers were killed and five soldiers were badly wounded. The guerrilla losses were four dead. Many lessons that the battalion should have known were, in my estimation, disregarded and the guerrillas, having watched such conduct often, took the opportunity of hitting where it hurt a lot.

Apart from rifles and Bren guns, flame-throwers were introduced in 1949 but were normally considered too bulky and temperamental for extensive use. Refuelling in the jungle caused logistical problems and the occasions when effective use of them could be made were very few. The British version of the Patchet submachine-gun, called the Sterling, was popular among some. Certainly there was a misconception about using silent ammunition with machine-guns, the working parts of the weapon giving its presence away!

As regards artillery and mortars, 5.5in guns were the most feared by the enemy, whereas we soon learnt that they liked 25-pounders. This was because they did relatively little damage and the guerrillas knew that they could move freely during any firing as there would be no security forces to bother them. Indeed, later on during the Emergency guerrillas would use the cover of 25-pounder fire to walk out and surrender knowing that they stood virtually no chance of being killed as they did. Besides 2in mortars, 4.2in mortars were used.

The RAF used flying-boats and the Royal Navy coastal patrols to try and keep reinforcements away, but the steady trickle of Sumatrans (more war-like than Malays) was not stopped by these methods which were ineffective at night.

Some time in 1951 a new, world strategy was put into action by the Communists. As far as Asia was concerned priority was given to attracting and making use of nationalist sentiments to build up a Communist-neutralist bloc against the Western powers. For the secretary-general of the MCP, Chin Peng, this changed his policy from inculcating fear to that of 'non-inconvenience'. Troops and police were still to be legitimate targets, but more effort was to be made on the political front for legal penetration of important parts of society. This is what Mao Zedong (Tse-tung) meant by the struggle being conducted on two fronts. If the Communists changed, so should the government. Sir Robert Thompson is reported to have said that it was all very well having bombers, masses of helicopters and tremendous firepower, but none of those would eliminate a Communist cell in a high school which was producing fifty recruits annually.

Details of the new policy only slowly seeped down to the guerrilla in the jungle during which time there were many sharp skirmishes, both sides showing bravery. During one of these a Gurkha of 2/7th Gurkha Rifles, Rifleman Harkabahadur Rai, used a kukri when ammunition ran low, severing a guerrilla's arm with it. Such close combat was rare during the Emergency.

The guerrillas tried to disrupt labour relations on the rubber estates. Their sympathizers demanded military protection. This had a double purpose; while the economy was being sabotaged, the troops were kept out of the jungle.

Soon after that General Sir Gerald Templer was sent from England to combine the post of Director of Operations and High Commissioner. On his arrival he was displeased with what he found: morale was low, complacency in high places rampant and the plan to resettle the squatters delayed in its full implementation. With a determination and a vigour that the sleepy administration had never experienced before, nor which it believed could be sustained, Templer managed drastically to change the situation so much for the better that, within 32 months, there was no more need for a 'benevolent and paternal dictator'. Those who served under him, certainly at company commander level, were in complete awe of and had absolute trust in him.

Templer brought the message that the British Government would declare its intention to grant Malaya independence, but he had to convince people at all levels that it was in their own interest to work to this end by helping the government and not the Communists. In pursuance of this policy he coined the famous phrase about the battle being won in the 'hearts and minds' of the people.

The ratio of kills to contacts was not as high as it should have been and Templer ordered that every occasion when the security forces met the enemy on patrol or in ambush, all was to be analysed. To this end a form called 'ZZ' was produced and the lessons learnt from this were very valuable.

General Templer also said that Malaya was an intelligence war; 'You can never beat Communism with troops alone.' The Special Branch was increased and, for a time, pressure by curfew was imposed on communities that were either rabidly pro-Communist or who lived in mortal terror of reprisals by the Communists. Within weeks of 38 arrests being made after one 22-hour curfew, some 3,500 men volunteered to join the Home Guard.

He was responsible for arranging that new helicopters and support aircraft came to aid the ground troops. In all there were eighteen different types of aircraft in 20 subsidiary roles. These included:

*Offensive air support to kill the guerrillas, to disrupt their command and organization, to lower their morale by inducing a sense of insecurity and fear of attack in every one of their hide-outs wherever located. This included a procedure known as 'Smash Hit' for when the security forces found a camp, did not attack it but inflated a marker balloon nearby and retreated. The camp was then bombed.

*Reconnaissance, photographic and visual, and crop-spraying.

*Transport aircraft for supply-drops to forts and for airborne forces, including tree-drops.

*Helicopters for troop lifts and evacuation of wounded or sick soldiers.

Major-General R. L. Clutterbuck, who was on the staff in Malaya from 1956–58, wrote in the *United States Military Revue* of 1965:

The real crisis in Malaya occurred between 1948 and 1951, when the guerrillas operated in bands of 100 or even 300, numbers which enabled them to overwhelm any small village police post – maybe a sergeant and ten men – and to murder all government officials and known supporters in the village. It was vital that these police posts should hold out or, if overrun, be replaced; it was important that they had sufficient confidence not to succumb to the Communist offers of a 'live and let live' deal. The call for platoons to bolster up every village police post had to be resisted. The solution was to position the infantry in company-sized camps from which they could respond for help . . . patrol the jungle fringes . . . react to raids . . . [make it hard for] large bands of guerrillas . . . to withdraw quickly enough to avoid casualties. These big bands suffered a constant drain [and] gradually split up into small groups, twenty or thirty strong [against whom] the village post could hold out with confidence.

7
The Malayan Emergency: 1952–62

1952–56: RESURGENCE OF HOPE

During these years the Communist quarry became more and more elusive as the security forces gained the upper hand militarily and the political goal of independence robbed those who were against the government of the main plank of their platform. These years coincided with most of my time as a rifle company commander.

Food denial operations became a constant. By mid-1953 a new pattern of operations could be observed. The guerrillas had been forced, either because of military pressure or by their own Politburo decision, to keep away from areas of civilization and to move into deep jungle. Once there they had to become more reliant on their own efforts to maintain themselves and so a number of cultivations or vegetable gardens were hacked out of the jungle. Simultaneously government introduced stringent food denial operations which were designed to prevent such commodities as rice, sugar and salt, as well as normal espistolary contacts, from reaching the comrades in the jungle.

Part of our task was to try and destroy these cultivations. In August 1953, on Operation 'Boxer' (no operation was ever complete without its own code-name!), for the first time ever the whole battalion was flown in to deep jungle landing sites (LS) by helicopter. This saved days in wearisome approach marches and eating into our rations, so lengthening the time left for the actual operation.

It was a problem to know how to despoil the cultivations without any chemicals. Burning undergrowth merely produced wood ash which acted as a fertilizer, and uprooting crops, tedious and effective only in the short term, helped to keep the place weeded.

In retrospect, much of what we did has merged into a tangled, confused memory of the jungle; the weight of the pack, the heat, the discomfort, the frustrations, the occasional adrenalin-heavy pounding of the heart and the comradeship of the Gurkha soldier without whom many officers with decent records would never have survived. It was not easy, as a company commander, always to find the appropriate type of target or terrain to deploy a company of between sixty and eighty men. But I quailed at the idea of commanding some of the world's finest soldiers from my office desk and I would do as much in the patrolling line as many another soul.

One night I had a dream that the air-drop for next day contained no rice. I laughingly told my platoon commanders who stoutly upheld the commissariat organization by asserting that such a thing would never happen. But it did – and added insult to injury by dropping two packs, marked 'African Rations' containing bully-beef, taboo to all self-respecting Hindus, and mixing the sugar with the salt. An Auster aircraft was mobilized with a supplementary drop of rice. The pilot saw smoke curling up out of the trees and thought it was our signal. That his map showed us ten miles farther north did not then bother him, for he dropped his load and returned for the second lot. Two hours later he was over the same area but failed to raise any smoke. He then flew north and saw the large dropping-zone, capable of holding three helicopters, where we had taken our air-drop. We spoke together on our radio.

'Here is the rest of your rice.'

'We haven't had any yet, what do you mean by the rest?'

'Wasn't that a platoon of yours at . . .?' and he gave the grid reference. I denied having been anywhere else that day. 'What troops are there to your south?' was his next question, asked with a trace of anxiety.

'None,' was my terse answer.

'Oh Lord! I've gone and dropped two sacks of rice on the bandits.'

So much for food denial and cultivation destroying.

It took us three days to walk out. During the last 2,000 yards to the jungle edge our maps had shown no streams whatsoever, but we nearly lost two men drowned in two river crossings. The men's comments about the surveyors were caustic.

Other food denial operations that were planned in and around the Seremban area (where we were based) bore the stamp of what was by now the accepted fact of 'war by executive committee'. One such operation was to be called Operation 'Key'. I suppose it was meant to be symbolic of opening up or unlocking the door to something not connected with guerrillas. However, all the leaflets that were to be dropped over the jungle had the inexplicable English word 'Quay' written over them, so the code-name was changed to an equally inexplicable 'Pibroch'. It also coincided with municipal elections and, as this was a very new departure, a voice aircraft was used to inform the citizens of Seremban that they were all now supposed to learn how to vote for their own representatives. Simultaneously it was decided to utilize the aircraft to overfly the surrounding jungles and warn the guerrillas that they had better surrender before they were starved out. Much of the effectiveness of this measure was lost when the tapes which had these messages recorded upon them were wrongly loaded. The surprised citizens of Seremban were indignant at being abjured to surrender, while the guerrillas were complacent on being advised to vote for town councillors.

Yet another food denial operation, this time code-named 'Chapman', was commented upon by the guerrillas:

1. *Determination.* All the comrades were full of fight and ready to attack the Red-Haired Imperialists, or the pawns whom they hold in their hands. We thus determined to kill the Malay policemen who went daily from Durian Tipus for rations in Simpang Pertang.

2. *The Plan.* Our leader divided us into seven parties consisting of:

    a. Front Intercepting Unit. It was their task to fell a tree across the road in front of the police truck.

    b. Covering Fire Squad. This was to intercept the police as they fled from their vehicle into the jungle on either side of the road.

    c. Another Covering Squad. Same as above but on the other side of the road.

d. Leader and Sentry Group. This group was to watch the road and give the signal to fire.

e. Light Machine Gun Group. This group was armed with two Bren guns and was to shoot up the vehicle when it stopped.

f. Charging Unit. This unit was to attack the vehicle with hand-grenades.

g. Rear Intercepting Unit. This was to block the road behind the vehicle and prevent escape.

3. The whole ambush position was to extend three hundred yards along the road, where it bent around a spur.

4. *Execution.* We waited from dawn to dusk and saw the police truck go south for rations, but we waited to attack it as it returned, so that we should get some rations too. Presently a powerful military convoy of armoured vehicles passed, travelling north, and at 14.15 hours it returned the other way. There was no other traffic.

5. At 14.30 hours the ration truck returned with a Chinese 'running dog' inspector sitting by the driver. Fierce fire was opened. Many of the comrades' bullets did not fire. The shooting also was inaccurate, through insufficient training due to ammunition shortage. The police truck was wrecked. Several policemen were seen to have been killed. Our leader decided to withdraw and gave the signal.

6. Our casualties were none.

Recognition of friend and foe was a constant problem, as were operational boundaries. I was once under command of another battalion, during one of those operations when food control and 'swamping an area' seemed a good idea to the planners.

I had taken a patrol of four men, moving on a bearing of 10 degrees away from the patrols on either side of me, to explore up to our operational boundary. We came across a large enemy camp, empty, but well laid out with strong defences and primitive facilities for repairing weapons. Eighty to a hundred men could have been accommodated there.

A little farther on at the top of a small rise we all heard a noise from the north, on the far side of a swamp that now appeared below us. Opinion was divided: I thought it man-made, the Gurkhas a bird. A few minutes later we heard it again, much nearer this time – and definitely man-made. I looked at my map. My boundary was still half-a-mile away to the north, so the noise had to be made by the guerrillas.

There was little chance, so I thought, that the enemy would cross the swamp, so I decided to take my men over it and see what we could find on the far side. It was about thirty yards wide, little more than a water-logged creek full of a type of very tall cactus that had barbed edges and which made a great noise when brushed against. We went down the bank and very, very cautiously started to cross.

Halfway over there was a noise like a tin being pierced, then the unmistakable clink of a water-bottle stopper hitting the side as it dangled. We heard muffled Chinese tones and, before we had a chance of moving on, the gang slid into the swamp and came towards us. We froze as we stood, lifted our weapons to our shoulders, took aim and waited.

It was mid-afternoon but in the swamp it was gloomily dark. One, two, three men came into sight. a dozen yards away, across our front, dressed like soldiers but with a red emblem in their hats – no recognition sign any of us knew – seven, eight. I whispered an order to open fire when I did and tensed myself.

Left: These Royal Australian Regiment troops, armed with an assortment of weaponry, are wading through a damp stretch of jungle in Kola Tinggi, Malaya, some 40 miles north-east of Singapore. From here, these Assault Pioneers from the Support Company of the Third Battalion will move northwards for operations against the Communists. (Popperfoto)

Below: Security forces testing their Owen sub-machine guns before going out on patrol. (Popperfoto)

As if on a sudden impulse they turned and saw five men facing them, all in the aim position. They instantaneously brought their weapons to their shoulders, ready to open fire. The man on my right turned to me and urged me not to shoot, hissing out the name of the battalion whose command we were under.

For a dreadful, loaded second, thirteen men stood poised. I was in an agony of doubt. In a flash I saw that there might be a mistake and the men facing me in the gloom might just somehow be Gurkhas with a guerrilla hat sign, rather than Chinese in security-force uniform and captured equipment, as had been known in the past. Yet, to avoid anything remotely like this, I had checked the boundary with the other battalion the very night before and been given a reply about paying attention to orders when given and why check again. No, I couldn't be wrong. And yet the cold worm of doubt was working overtime in my bowels. If I shouted 'Don't shoot!' in Chinese and they were Gurkhas, they were much more likely to shoot and not to miss than if they were Chinese and I shouted 'Don't shoot!' in Nepali. I chose the former, took my hat off so they could see my face, lowered my weapon and moved forward.

They were Gurkhas. They were from the battalion to the north (our sister battalion) and the signs they wore on their hats were intended to mislead, as indeed some years back the guerrillas has misled them by using their crossed kukri motif on stolen jungle hats.

The tense atmosphere relaxed and mutual recrimination set in until we realized that neither of us had strayed – the operational commander had given us different boundaries that overlapped, despite my request for verification and his dusty answer. (Two weeks earlier The Queen's Regiment had killed six of each other in a similar situation.) The noise we had heard was the patrol finding sealed tins of rice which they had slashed with their kukris so that the rice would become uneatable and it so happened that the Chinese-sounding voice was the patrol commander's, whose vile accent had earned him the battalion nickname of 'Chinaman'.

Back in our jungle base I switched on the radio, having learned that there had been three other instances of our patrols clashing. The operational commander came on set and I started my transmission with '. . . by the grace of God you have just been saved the responsibility of many Gurkhas' unnecessary deaths . . .'

That evening I called over the soldier who had been on my right in the swamp and asked him why he had urged me not to open fire.

Came the devastating reply, 'Because I recognized my brother.'

But whether the operations were food denial, framework or anything else, the common denominator was the jungle. During this period it became harder and harder to contact the guerrillas until I seem to remember that it took a million man-hours of combined effort for twenty seconds' contact. Searching for the enemy took up more time than evading his fire in an ambush or attack, so it was movement that became all important, to avoid one's own tracks being spotted by the guerrillas.

It was always difficult to convince the planners that movement was slow. Many of our senior officers were fashioned on experience in Africa and Europe, not in Burma. These men almost always made an error in all their time and space problems as they simply could not envisage the laboriously slow conditions the jungle demanded. It had been reported that the Malayan Politburo had been building a concrete headquarters on the top of a large feature in the Cameron Highlands called Gunong Plata. Shades of Russians with snow on their boots were evoked by reports of men, including Gurkhas, carrying bags of cement up into the jungle! Accordingly an operation was laid on and three rifle companies were to surround Gunong Plata and assault it, soon after a bombing attack had gone in. The argument that has been going on for half a century about the efficacy of air power in relation to ground power received a jolt in this instance. At 7 o'clock in the morning the feature, some 7,000 feet high, was bombed, but so difficult was the country that it took two and half a days for the first rifle company to get to the top. The concrete, unlike the snow on the Russians' boots, had melted away to leave no trace whatsoever. Sensible country fellows never go to a waterless, cold, outcropped peak when fertile valleys offer good crops, easier living and rivers plentiful of fish.

Movement through the jungle was normally restricted to about a thousand yards an hour, while in swamp it could be as slow as a hundred. At that speed it was possible to read the signs on the jungle floor. Some of the tracking skills I saw used by the Gurkhas thrilled and baffled me. Once we were following some guerrillas through jungle; they were tired and hungry, while we were fresh. They moved slowly but carefully, covering their tracks professionally. We were catching them up. During the day we had heard a tiger roaring, probably uneasy at the smell of men. Next morning we continued following the tired enemy but soon lost their tracks. The platoon commander (Gurkha Lieutenant Tulbahadur Rai who 'deceived') had gone forward to try and pick them up again. I was sent for and moved cautiously up the column. 'Look here,' the Gurkha said, pointing to the ground. I saw the jungle floor, dead leaves in profusion and a lot of undergrowth but no detail. 'Would you have thought that the tiger was going in the direction we are coming from? That's what the lead scout thought.'

He looked up for confirmation that what was obvious to him had been obvious to me. I made a non-committal reply and the platoon commander continued to show me his find. I saw, more by a commitment of the imagination than a conscious act of the naked eye, the vague outline of a tiger's paw. I sympathized with the lead scout! The almost invisible paw mark had been facing away from the direction the 'tiger' was moving; the end man was turning round and making paw marks but, as he was facing his rear, his 'tiger' was also shown as walking backwards. The platoon commander returned to his correct place in the column and we continued tracking the enemy. That evening we were so close to them that we smelt the smoke of their fires. This caused great excitement and we deployed, using our noses as guide. At one place we actually saw the smoke come curling around a spur – a resounding success at last! We were dumbfounded at finding nothing; no tracks, no camp, no signs made by humans, only the jungle rapidly growing darker. Next morning we found out that we had been searching diametrically away from where the guerrillas had been as some quirk of nature had blown the smoke in a semi-circle, clinging to the dampness of the jungle undergrowth.

Guerrilla movement could be of a very high standard, since their lives often depended on an unbroken twig whereas if we broke a twig all that that might mean could be a missed contact. Patrols (of my 'A' and 'D' Companies) came across each other, in a rubber estate, with a guerrilla in the middle. The guerrilla surrendered his weapon to one patrol but was called over by the other. He went and they claimed him. It took months before the two companies were on speaking terms again! Even so the prize eluded both companies as the guerrilla platoon commander was hiding in a stream all the while, watching what was happening with only his head above the water. He was only two yards, so he said later, from a couple of soldiers who came to fill their water-bottles and who missed him. He escaped after dark and later surrendered. He showed us how he could walk through thick ferns without leaving any traces. A yard in half an hour, his deftness as he passed through was as nimble-fingered as any Chinese artistry.

Tracking is an art in itself. There are so many points that can be looked for that can give a clue to someone else having moved through the area – although there are no visible boot marks or bootprints – a sudden change in the colour of the foliage, or foliage bending against the grain, dampness in dry surroundings and dryness in damp, traces of mud, scuffed roots of trees, the bole of a tree 'wounded' with sap forming for no apparent reason, disturbed insect life, broken spiders' webs, muddy water in a stream, birds flying towards the trackers, incautious animal movement and anything with a straight edge. Nature very seldom produces straight edges and, unthinkingly, a person can pluck a leaf, fold it then drop it, thereby giving an important clue to those who know what to look for. Telling how long since anything has been cut is one method of gauging a time frame.

Long-term infiltration of the guerrilla movement was practised but seldom heard about. One agent so placed rose to the position of propaganda-cum-political adviser in a regional committee. He gradually shaped plans to lead the whole of the committee into an ambush. Communications with authority were tenuous and spasmodic in the extreme, involving a few trusted men, all working under great stress and danger. In this instance it was hoped to eliminate 32 guerrillas and the plan was based on the enemy coming down from the hilly country where they were hiding to the rubber fringe, then along the estate road by foot to the area of a manager's bungalow, now deserted, and collecting supplies. It seemed foolproof, but the one cause for concern was the agent's safety. He was to join up with the security forces during the operation and be taken away, unhurt, being announced for public consumption, as dead.

The night was carefully chosen. One company of troops crawled into position with such an armoury that surely none could escape. All knew that the agent would wear a white shirt, as would the 'guide' who was bringing the guerrilla group to the collecting-point. There would be plenty of time because the food dumped for the guerrillas had to be broken down into man-loads and then taken away. Suspense grew as the hours slowly passed.

The task of my company was to pursue any remnant and to attack the camp whence they had come as another forty odd guerrillas were believed to be there, including seven wounded. I had to take two Chinese with me (a police inspector and a Malay Film Unit photographer), two aboriginal trackers, a British soldier dog-handler and his dog. I was sorry for the photographer as, hapless man, he had just returned from his honeymoon and was in no fit state for any type of jungle operation. My task was to pick up the agent after his 'escape' from the ambush and he would lead us back to his camp.

Before midnight we heard firing in the distance and made our way to the ambush site. There I learnt that only one man had been killed and one captured on being wounded. All the rest had got away. Apparently at the last moment the guerrilla military commander had baulked at all his men being used for the foodlift so the other half were either still at the jungle edge or in camp. Those who did ferry the food did so with impunity as, somehow or other, white flour sacks had been provided for the ferrying and, in the dark, a man carrying a large white sack on his back could not be distinguished from a man wearing a white shirt. Sensibly fire was not to be opened until the agent had indicated that he was out of the danger area. He did not move into safe territory to give the signal to spring the ambush for some time because, unexpectedly, at the last moment he had been given an escort who had to be disposed of first. He proved a very tough customer when the time came, causing even more of a delay. It was not surprising that the slickness of the operation was thrown out of kilter.

At 2 a.m. I was introduced to the agent, who was having his meal and a glass of brandy. Reaction had just set in and he was dazed. Yet, despite the obvious dangers inherent in his return to the jungle, he signified his willingness to go with me, along with two of his friends – police or guerrilla, I never knew.

I took them outside into the night and moved off into the rubber estate, thereby losing what little light there had been. Movement became very, very slow and the soldiers, already tired, were growing frustrated. I decided to halt for an hour till dawn, have a quick brew of tea and then move fast. My six 'foreigners' were mighty slow movers.

I had a fair idea of where the guerrilla camp was, so made with all speed up into the hills to an area from where we could start surrounding it. It was there that I had a big disappointment: the agent was so lost that he had no idea where he was. Only later did I learn that the Communist hierarchy relied entirely on their underlings for local knowledge and that this policy was encouraged to prevent defections. It meant, in this case, that I would be unable to pinpoint the camp. This was entirely in the guerrillas' favour.

I had hoped to be fighting a battle by 8 o'clock; it was cold comfort to be searching their empty camp at half-past one. We found a radio, armourer's tools, documents, sugar and salt, but all the occupants had left during the morning. We tracked them sedulously and when the tracks split up I feared we had lost them. This proved to be the case and as it was getting late in the afternoon I decided to let the soldiers have their first meal of the day. The 'hangers-on' were hardly able to move, so tired were they and not one was of any use – not even the nice dog.

We never did catch up with the other guerrillas so, after a week's thrashing around, we dispersed to our various base camps, marvelling at the satanically good luck of our opponents in escaping virtually scot-free, from a very tricky situation. Things seldom worked out as planned – as I found out in another context when I had to send an amending signal to headquarters after we had been

Above: *RAF Sycamore helicopters were in use between the Malayan Emergency and Borneo Confrontation. They were not designed for the tasks they had to perform and were not easy to handle. Nevertheless, they were an essential ingredient for communications work and were invaluable in helping to suppress the efforts of the Chinese guerrillas to inculcate Communism in the north Malayan jungle communities – for the first time since during the Second World War – by saving a 50-mile approach march. (Museum of Army Flying)*

Right: *A supply drop in Malaya. Soldiers from the Special Air Service secure the landing zone while other men jump out to join them; the Sikorsky 55 Helicopter hovers because the ground is unsuitable for landing. The use of such air power allows regiments like the SAS to conduct a 'pounce and strike' campaign behind the enemy's lines with troops either parachuting into virgin jungle or clambering down ropes to a selected clearing. (Popperfoto)*

so proud of ourselves in capturing a quantity of gun powder: 'For gun powder, read ink powder.'

Special Branch was, however, the key to many successes. One particularly fruitful operation started when a tip-off was received that a cycle courier would be passing through a town at a certain time. A random, snap police road-block and search was organized and the suspect was duly brought in. At last, after every item of the man's clothing had been shredded and every component of the bicycle had been dismantled, the vital rolled slips of paper were found. They were in the man's shoes, stuck along the inside edge and covered by a glued-down inner sole. The result was a spectacular success.

However regimental histories (of which my definition is 'tall stories, hot air and quick-drying ink') depict their time in the jungle, the vast majority of our time and effort was uninspiring, uninteresting, monotonous and, we felt, taken for granted by many of those above us. If it was bad for us it must have been infinitely worse for the guerrillas, who were, in the main, heavily outnumbered, having to live on their wits, off the land and by courtesy of local loyalties.

I remember the day Mr Churchill resigned as prime minister. We were due to search for the 'North Johore Regional Committee' or two sections of their No. 23 platoon in a large area of featureless swampy terrain. Three helicopters arrived and quickly shuttled us into a patch of drier country ten or so miles away. I had had a discussion with the pilot as to our destination and his ability to fly us there. He was working off a quarter-inch-to-the-mile map while I was better equipped for jungle navigation with the standard inch-to-the-mile map. He expressed his complete confidence in his navigational ability.

As soon as we deplaned I sent off patrols to establish our true position but, as is often the case, each estimate differed a little. I had to move north-east and search a thin ridge of hills which was where the guerrilla hide-out was believed to be. Taking advantage of the remaining daylight, I forged on and made camp for the night by the first stream we met. It provided a fix, but even so I had a feeling that either the map was inaccurate (as one of the soldiers said, 'the survey party must have had a hang-over when they made this sheet') or that we had been dropped in the wrong place. Doubt assailed me for three days, and yet the streams we crossed were never so grossly inaccurate either to confirm or deny the feeling of being off course. They all flowed in a similar direction, the distance between them was as shown, and the intervening countryside was flat jungle with no obvious or separate characteristics.

On the fourth day the line of hills was reached and I sent out patrols to confirm our position. It was here that I could at last confirm that we had been put down in the wrong place; the ridge line was not just one thin hill feature, but contained the foothills of a much larger feature well to the north.

I reported this fact and asked for a 'fix' the following day. This too had complications because Austers were having trouble with their propellers falling off and were heavily restricted in their flying hours. Also, as I had made no contact and seen no signs of the guerrillas, I had been ordered out by helicopter from another clearing the very next day.

When eventually the Auster arrived over where we had thought we were, we were too far apart either for us properly to distinguish the noise of its engine or the pilot to see our smoke signal. We spoke to each other by radio and then we were pinpointed, not a few hundred yards north or south of where we had believed we were, but 4,000 yards to the north. And not only that; the helicopters were scheduled to pick us up, starting from 10 o'clock. I told the Auster pilot to tell the helicopters that we would be ready to be picked up by half-past one that afternoon, the time then being just after 9 o'clock. We had about 5,000 yards to move over an infuriatingly difficult bearing of 127 degrees, difficult because only one degree's difference either side would have sent us past the pick-up point and much time would be wasted in searching for it. Were it a round number of degrees the compass dial would have been easier to watch. I put my best navigator in front, he of tiger-tracking repute, and away we went. During our march the helicopters had been heard droning far away and I had fired a Very pistol. They saw it, flew over us and, so I learnt later, told the commanding officer that we could not possibly arrive until the following day.

However, I had said (more in bravado than in confidence) that I would be at the appointed LS by half-past one so the helicopters were refuelled to meet us there then. My delight can well be imagined when we got there by 29 minutes past. The commanding officer flew in with the first sortie and was reproachful about my map-reading. Also the brigadier had threatened to bomb 4,000 yards to the north of where I was supposed to have been (why I never knew) and the commanding officer had the utmost difficulty in restraining him. I was very glad he had managed to!

We were quickly given more rations and sent back into a fresh area. This time we had to walk in and, as it was from a known location, we did not get lost. It is one of the most difficult tasks to locate a position accurately in featureless country when the point of entry is wrong.

Senior airmen regarded as very poor the infantry's kill-to-contact ratio when surrounding an occupied enemy camp. The policy of 'Smash Hit' referred to earlier was their attempt to improve upon it. In March 1956 1st South Wales Borderers and Special Branch located the notorious Goh Peng Tua and Lincolns of RAAF and Canberras of RAF dropped a hundred bombs which killed most of the guerrilla force. In fact it was a fluke because the enemy had moved before the bombing, but as the bombers dropped their bombs on where the guerrillas had gone and not where they were meant to be the end result was the same! However, use of 'Smash Hit' became mandatory whenever an occupied enemy camp was located.

My own experience did not end so happily. I had been on patrol and heard sawing and talking. It was the guerrillas making a camp. I reported it and was ordered to go forward and fly a marker balloon. As I was doing this with two men we all clearly heard sounds of guerrilla activity.

Either the enemy found the balloon's cord and freed it or I tied the knot badly, but the spotter aircraft did not see it. Even so the bombers came over and bombed where I had said the suspected camp was (despite the map being white and marked as 'unsurveyed'). It was unsuccessful because the bombs were dropped without their fuzes. We were furious and disappointed and my anger and disdain rubbed off to my detriment when I was called to talk to senior RAF officers about it.

I never did like bombing. Another small example of how it could go wrong was when the whereabouts were established of as high-ranking a group of guerrillas as had ever been found in the past or were likely to be ever again. Troops were sent in but, three weeks after the operation started it was decided to bomb suspected hide-outs. Intention of this was given over Radio Malaya; somewhat naturally the guerrillas moved. Maximum air effort for three nights and two days was deployed, but the only bodies we found after intense searching were three dead monkeys and a dead pig.

On the political front the British Government had promised to let Malaya govern itself once the militant Communist threat had been seen to have abated sufficiently that Communist victory was no longer possible and its military defeat not far off. To start the independence process preparatory elections were held for an executive council. This body, formed chiefly of the newly constituted Alliance Party, felt it politically expedient to declare an amnesty for all guerrillas who had committed offences before a certain date. In 1955 peace talks took place between the newly elected Chief Minister, Tenku Abdul Rahman, and the Secretary-General of the MCP up in the north of the country at Baling.

Many millions of leaflets were dropped over the jungle and voice aircraft also played a large part in disseminating the amnesty conditions. We were plagued by

Left: *During the Malayan Emergency (1948–60) air operations played an increasingly large part. Most of the air effort was on the supply side, but much aerial reconnaissance (visual and photographic) and some interdiction were achieved. It was a great art to be able to spot a guerrilla camp from the air, pinpoint it and not let the inmates know that they* had been found. Here 656 Squadron, Army Air Corps, the RAF and 1st Somerset Light Infantry are shown attacking a camp in the area of Kuala Kubu Bahru in the north of Malaya, in September 1954. This was the 'Smash Hit' procedure. (Museum of Army Flying)

Below left: *Without a follow-up much value was lost. Here a Royal Navy helicopter is lifting the point section of the follow-up troops into a clearing nearby. Some commanders considered it risky to fly into an area that had so recently been bombed because of the possibility of falling trees. (Museum of Army Flying)*

Below: *An aircraft flies over a smoke-marked clearing; this could be produced by a fire or a flare, and would be used to attract aircraft attention, request a lift-out or fix a position for an air drop or an air strike. (Museum of Army Flying)*

restrictions and were given reams of propaganda material to leave about the jungle, a gross parody of a paperchase. These surrender leaflets were of interest and had photographs of contented men, the theme being, 'You too can lead an easy life if you give up.' Some of them had little scenes depicting, in strip cartoon fashion, the return of the prodigal son. Father rushes out and falls on the neck of his returning and once-errant offspring who shakes father's hand and they all live happily ever after. It was clear that this was the work of a European ill-versed in the Chinese etiquette. No such parental joy would be expressed in public nor such carefree filial bad manners be entertained. These leaflets must have nullified much patient good work by those who knew what they were doing but could not advertise it.

Those of us at ground level felt that the amnesty was a mistake; it had a touch of ingenuousness and complacency about it that boded ill. It gave us the impression that the new leaders did not fully understand the threat of the realities of CRW. The talk at the time was that, with the British no longer part of the political scene for much longer, Malaya's own politicians would be able to solve the remaining problems politically now that militarily no major threat was posed.

Sure enough, the Communists, with an eye for the main chance, utterly ignored the government's initiative and took the situation as being a golden opportunity to build up their supplies and, certainly in Johore, to increase their own offensive. Exactly the same pattern was seen later in Vietnam when pauses from US bombing allowed the Communists to regain much lost ground.

At about this time we were suddenly ordered over a hundred miles away from our base. None of us knew that plans to end the amnesty had been made or that a very important meeting of high-ranking Communist terrorists (including the number two under Chin Peng, one called Yeong Kwoh, later killed by the Rifle Brigade) was scheduled to be held near the small village of Simpang Pertang. It was on this gathering that news of proposed bombing was put out on Radio Malaya and that I found no traces of humans during my follow-up. (I gather that the news was given because the amnesty was still technically in force.) Before the bombing the guerrillas split up into two parties. One man of one party was killed as he tried to cross a road that was ambushed. The party fled back into the jungle. The other party also searched for a place to cross and discovered that there were two 'rings' of troops, an inner one in the jungle and an outer one ambushing the roads that flanked the area. The road ambush had scout cars and searchlights – and bored troops. Despite artillery shelling and mortaring the guerrillas escaped harm because they hid near obvious military camps. They had the luck of the devil. One night they came to the road and saw the silhouette of a British soldier standing in the cupola of his scout car. They watched him for some time and thought he might be asleep. So they sent a few men across the road to see what would happen. Nothing did. The soldier was asleep and the rest of the group, with all the high-ranking Communists, got away.

This emerged when one of the guerrillas gave himself up soon afterwards. He was the chief propaganda merchant for them all. I was only told about him by the brigadier after his background had been discovered, but my instant reply was: 'I'll bet he was a Sumatran who came over with the fishing fleet in August 1948.' He was. I never did hear if the man who slept was discovered, let alone disciplined. In all probability he never was the wiser of the results of his incredibly bad soldiering. If ever there was a good illustration of the old tag '. . . all for the want of a nail', this was it.

The guerrillas did not always have the good luck. We were in deep jungle and one morning I awoke with gut ache. I therefore countermanded the order for an early start and decreed a 10 o'clock move after eating. I ordered double sentries to be put out and, as they were moving into position, two guerrillas walked into them. There was some confusion as some of my men were in the line of fire and the smoke from the cordite hung over a stream where the shooting had taken place. Only one guerrilla was killed but both packs were recovered, full of magazines and some papers rolled into spills. The lurid covers of the magazines made me think they were all routine propaganda from a clandestine press. As they were bulky I nearly dumped them but decided not to, however uninteresting they were sure to be, not like those canny little spills of paper – or so I thought.

As it was impossible to take the corpse to the police for recognition, I photographed him instead and took his fingerprints. I had him buried and then moved off to a helicopter pad. It was a dreadful journey as we had to help a sick soldier along, but I held on to the documents and gave them to the pilot, together with the reel of photographs and the fingerprints.

It so happened that the spills of paper contained only low-grade information, but there was something about the text in the magazines that intrigued Special Branch at district, circle and finally at state level. Only at state level did they manage to decipher the code they felt was somewhere concealed in the otherwise straightforward text: this was that every fourth word made up another text that was too important to be published *en clair* so to speak. Once the magazines were in sequence a remarkable discovery was made: a new policy from the central committee was being promulgated down to all branches, urging much more subversion than before, and giving party members not living in the jungle detailed instructions about urban targets, especially schools. Singapore was included. I gather that the government ignored the warning and there were nasty incidents in the schools and the university, with acid being thrown in people's faces and other atrocities that law-abiding folk could have done without. It was almost as if the MCP had decided to revert to the first, passive phase of CRW.

Malaya was lucky to be forewarned. Mind you, none of us would have been any the wiser if I had thrown those wretched magazines away – or not had a gut ache!

1956–62: THE FINAL SLOG

As the menace of CRW receded from any one area, it was declared 'white'. That meant all restrictions were lifted and people were free to live normal lives. This had the added advantage of allowing troops to go to 'black' areas where more pressure against the remaining guerrillas could be exerted. Nine years after the Emergency started there were comparatively few areas not yet designated as 'white'. Emphasis was still on food denial, which included checking at the gates of new villages, to prevent food being smuggled out to the rubber estates, many of which were now operating at full production for the first time since 1941. The flavour of these checks was captured by the diarist of 2/10th Gurkha Rifles when he wrote: '. . . pre-dawn to locked and barbed village gates where arc lamps throw a sickly white light on to the straggly groups of men and women, buckets and bicycles gathering to go out and collect latex, the arrival of the police in an armoured vehicle, the search, of people by the police, of bicycles, tins and bottles by the soldiers, and finally the opening of the gates and the release of the flood, tins clanking, bicycles bounding over ruts in the road, coloured scarves flying in the pearl-grey half-light. And then the weary searching throughout the day, of all who pass. A distasteful and soul-destroying task, but one in which the Gurkha soldiers' thoroughness, fairness and manners earn him the respect of all, and make the job worthwhile.'

Security forces relied more and more on the Special Branch for information. Sometimes troops were on stand-by for only a day or so, other times for as many as a month, expecting maybe twenty enemy who had deliberately kept their time and numbers vague. More often than not, only a handful would turn up.

Post-Independence there was still work for the British Army as well as Malaya's own forces. One company of Gurkhas was on operations continuously for 58 days. Another ambush waited for guerrillas to come down a track about which Special Branch had given information. In this instance the killing-ground was in a swamp and that is where men of 2/2nd Gurkha Rifles had to be. After 25 days of waiting their commanding officer reckoned that they had passed the point of endurance for them to remain efficient. On the very next day three guerrillas walked along the track and were disposed of. The Gurkhas were then allowed back to base.

Even after the Emergency was over officially (almost 12,000 lives were lost in twelve years), a rifle company was deployed on the Malay–Thai border in an effort to prevent guerrilla movement southwards. Twenty years after Spencer Chapman was instrumental in helping to set up the MPAJA in 1942, there were still 36 guerrillas on the police 'wanted list' in the border area. These men were regarded by the Malayan Government as the rump of a once-powerful organization; they regarded themselves as the advance party of the next Communist push from their sanctuary in Yala Province, Thailand. Spasmodic efforts had been made by Special Branch to get to grips with this remnant – by Australians, New Zealanders, British, Malays and Gurkhas, to say nothing of 'Q'-type operations involving 'surrendered enemy personnel' and a force of aboriginal Temiar (one of the ten or so aboriginal groups found in Malaya, mostly in the north of the country), who roughly equated to Home Guard – and none had had any success.

The guerrillas had maintained their presence in north Malaya by being friendly with the aborigines, treating them well, at times intermarrying with them and speaking their various languages. The aborigines acted as a screen between the Communists and the security forces, thereby having prevented any contact, when I arrived on the scene in 1961, for five years. The Malays had always been distant, if not disdainful, in their relationships with the aborigines and this was reciprocated. My task was to wean them from the guerrillas, win them over and then get them to accept Malay authority – a tricky operation in that the Malay is a proud person and, having won independence, the British should no longer have been a factor in this equation.

In the event the tactical requirements of operating in deep jungle for months at a time, without recourse to supplies, hiding up and living like guerrillas ourselves (never more than ten of us), demanded all the skill, cunning and patience we were capable of. I laid down rules for movement:

*Never tread on what you can step over.

*Never cut what you can break naturally.

*Never break naturally what you can bend.

*Never bend what you can move.

*Never move that which you can get through without moving.

*Never step on soft ground when you can tread on something hard.

*Tread in water; get wet feet.

*Where possible move backwards through soft ground.

*Never do anything needlessly.

Even so, success would not have been achieved without learning the aborigines' language and using it as a tactical weapon to the extent that, once out of months of hiding, the children loved me so much that the senior headman (himself originally elected by the Communists) asked me to live in his house with his family as the children took more notice of me than they did of him. In this instance, success was not in body counts (there were none to be counted!), but by managing to transfer the loyalty of the aborigines from the guerrillas to the security forces, even though it was a matter of individual personalities rather than an amorphous cause. I felt I was stealing a leaf from Mao Zedong's book – well, sort of!

What little that has come to light of the way the security forces of Malaysia carried out operations in their border region with Thailand from 1962 onwards – newspaper articles that could have described the situation pertaining at any time in the 1950s and 1960s – did little to encourage the thought that their standard was high enough to cope with the situation, however quiescent it was most of the time. It was, therefore, of more than passing interest to learn, in late December 1987, that during the year the Thais successfully concluded negotiations with some of the Communist guerrillas operating in the border area contiguous with the Malay peninsula. In March they persuaded the whole of 8 Regiment MRLA to surrender, in all 114 persons bringing 286 weapons and 30,000 rounds of ammunition with them. In April 539 Communist guerrillas from 12 Regiment surrendered, bringing 527 weapons, 132,000 rounds of ammunition, 119 hand-grenades and 9,000 anti-personnel mines. In December negotiations were continuing with 10 Regiment, the hard-core faction, led by Chin Peng. Ah So Chai, the man I chased for so long in the early 1960s, was reported alive and well.

Each surrendered guerrilla family was given fifteen *rais* of land (37.5 acres) and settled in groups, also having an allowance of eighteen *bahts* (equal to ±US$0.50 at mid-December 1987 prices) every day for their first year. This equated with what other guerrillas of the Communist Party of Thailand were allowed. In all this, the Malay hierarchy were dubious about the Thai plan and played little part. The Thais were trying to persuade the Malaysian Government to be more flexible, and to take back the 172 members of 12 Regiment who were of Malay stock. The other guerrillas, being Chinese, felt happier and safer in Thailand.

So, forty years after the Emergency started, it was politics that resolved the situation – but only after the Communists had been unsuccessful militarily.

8
French Indo-China/Vietnam 1952–60

T he war in what was first known as French Indo-China then as Vietnam is a horrifyingly difficult one to understand impartially or in depth, as anyone who has read *Vietnam, a History* by Stanley Karnow, will known. He brilliantly shows that it is a classic example of a struggle that was waged in two dimensions by opposing cultures; European colonialism, followed by American 'world-policing' against a nationalism harnessed to Communist principles.

The jungle itself was not the scene of the final outcome, yet during parts of the earlier stages it was of immense, if not vital, importance. The course of the war is a complex one to follow and, in a framework of jungle warfare, much of it is extraneous as it was tropical warfare fought only sometimes in the jungle. In 1945 it was reckoned that 86 per cent of the country was covered in 'dense spontaneous growth' and that at least 47 per cent with 'outright jungle'. The same question must have plagued the French and the Americans as it does the historian – When is jungle warfare not jungle warfare?

It is apposite, nevertheless, to go into some details that lie outside the strict meaning of jungle warfare as a study of methods of guerrilla warfare, and their counter, employed from 1945 to 1974 is needed for a better perspective of the whole and for analysing similar problems.

THE FRENCH IN INDO-CHINA

The French had an impossible task in Indo-China for a number of reasons, chiefly political, military and psychological. Bernard Fall in *Street Without Joy* gives cogent details about the first two aspects. The war became politically deadlocked in 1948; it became strategically hopeless when the Communist Chinese arrived on North Vietnam's northern borders in 1949, so providing that all-important sanctuary; it was lost tactically when the French were beaten back from the northern border region in the three battles of Cap Bang, Dong Khe and Lang Son; and it was lost strategically in 1953 after the cease-fire in Korea allowed concentration of the whole of the Asian Communist (and some Soviet) war effort on the Indo-Chinese theatre.

One of the political platforms that the 'League for the Revolution and Independence of Vietnam', shortened to Vietminh, made much of was the Atlantic Charter, produced by the Allies in 1941 and which stated *the right of all people to choose the form of government under which they will live and to see sovereign rights and self-government restored to those who have been forcibly deprived of them.* It is also a fact that, although the French did not see their treatment of the native population as being out of kilter with the times, the native population did, as I know from personal observation. The French wanted to keep Indo-China as a part of France and this feeling was not reciprocated. There was, therefore, no bedrock of mutual trust at national level as there was in Malaya, although it must be said that, individually, there were Frenchmen who had a deep and genuine love for the country and the people, and there was some intermarriage. Nevertheless, France's 'outrageous over-estimation of their own worth' was a cardinal error.

The French could not believe that the Vietnamese could beat them so they were continually surprised (in a military sense) when, however hard they, the French, tried to hold the initiative or wrest it from the Vietnamese, they failed to produce a stable situation. As has been said before, the French never had enough troops to win the war but did have enough not to lose it. Even so, when, in 1951, Giap attacked French forts in the north of the country with full field formations, including heavy mortars, artillery battalions, recoilless rifles and 105mm howitzers (many of them captured American weapons), he inflicted 'the heaviest defeat the French had suffered since Montcalm died at Quebec'. The Vietnamese in the north were meticulous in their planning, using sand-table models of ground they were to operate over.

Five centuries earlier, the Vietnamese leader Le Loi waged an 8-year struggle against Chinese invaders (1418–26) who left their garrisons only by day and built fortified towers along main routes. Similarly, the French initially tried to hold a fortress barrier in North Vietnam, but that failed because they did not make use of or control the surrounding jungle, or take advantage of it as the Japanese had so spectacularly done in Malaya in 1941 and 1942.

In 1859, when the French captured Saigon, they were plagued by Vietnamese guerrillas who employed tactics very similar to those used ninety years later. On both occasions the Vietnamese were not strong enough to protect places and the French not strong enough to hold them. In 1924 when in Moscow, Ho Chi Minh learned Lenin's key dictum: *revolution must be launched under favourable conditions*. As the Vietnamese waited for a situation to develop to their advantage in their post-war struggles, they based all their tactics on the mobility of the individual soldier, using the jungle and jungle craft to conceal them. This led to them enduring conditions on a scale that Western armies would shudder from and probably not attempt except when forced to. The French believed in the mobility of military formations, so were tied to the few roads or open areas. When the French transport, armoured or otherwise, arrived with troops at a jungle area for a specific operation, news from locals or noise from vehicles frequently resulted in only partial success at best. The Vietnamese melted into the jungle and so were no longer targets. Such mechanical mobility would have been useful only against an enemy similarly equipped.

This lack of battle security often resulted in French troops being led into traps and hit hard, except for the few occasions when they did manage to win battles to their own advantage. How much of that was the battle being lost by the Vietnamese rather than being won by the French depends on whether one is the winner or the loser. It is of no concern to the clinical and disinterested observer.

The French reckoned that they had the best balance of forces in a *groupement mobile* (GM), or regimental task force. Some of the heroism shown on both sides, to say nothing of the grossnesses, show a measure of ferocity that is only generated when utter belief in a cause meets similar belief in intrinsic superiority. Casualties on both sides were horrendous – for instance, GM 100 had 3,498 men in it to start with but only 107 at the end. Yet neither small nor large units ever really got the full measure of the incredibly versatile Vietnamese and their audacious tactics, nor blunted their resolve to win the war despite such heavy losses. The risk of annihilation was preferable to capitulation.

Giap had his own ideas as to the necessary stages of the war he was waging against the French. Stage one was when he saw that the French were not interested in giving the Vietnamese independence; he had to go to a place where he could train his men, militarily and politically, away from French interference. Here the sanctuary in China and the remotenesses of his own country gave him cover to do this. The second stage was to enhance his position when the French found that they could no longer maintain an offensive and had to go on to the defensive, and, thirdly, when the French were driven from the country. That third phase started with a general counter-offensive, with the aim of total destruction of the French forces. In 1951 the Vietnamese over-extended themselves when they tried to move from the active to the counter-offensive phase of CRW and were beaten by the French. They accordingly reverted to the second, the active phase, until conditions were ripe for another attempt at phase three.

The conditions for this to be successful were also threefold: Giap had to have superiority of forces; international opinion had to be in favour [an unusual criterion for those in the Western world not used to such a condition]; and the military situation had to be favourable. During this phase guerrilla warfare, that had played such a key part to date, became of secondary consideration, while mobile warfare – having enough men at the right place at the right time to win that particular battle – became the main consideration.

Giap is quoted as saying this about the political aspect during this phase: 'To rely on foreign aid without taking into account our own capabilities is to show proof of subjectivism and of lack of political conscience . . .' Most, if not all, non-Communist soldiers would take no notice of this esoteric utterance. The French, and later the Americans, showed that they had never understood its true significance.

Some French and Vietnamese forces were to be found permanently behind each other's lines. One task of a French long-range commando group was to threaten Vietnamese depots near the Chinese border sufficiently for them to withdraw nearer to their supplies. Sometimes the French were near to success and Vietnamese main force units would have to be repositioned. French troops would return to normal duties but the unit would remain behind in enemy-held territory where, by mid-1954, there were 15,000 French forces needing 300 tons of airborne resupply every month. As with many such specialized units, it was a good way to get rid of troublemakers. It was a long and tedious business to train a man to go behind the lines. There were mountain dialects to learn, there was a difficult climate to get used to without the convenience normally associated with soldiering in a modern army, but above all there was the correct frame of mind required for any chance of survival, whether physical in the short term or mental in the long.

Behind the French lines the Vietnamese 42 Independent Infantry Regiment used dense vegetation, caves and holes, bomb- and napalm-proof where possible.

Above: The head of a French patrol stops for a while during the advance of a battalion of Paratroops to the north of Dien Bien Phu. This type of jungle and bush made for heavy going. (Popperfoto) *Below:* This relief column is trying desperately to make its way through dense jungle in order to reach Dien Bien Phu before it falls. Operation 'Condor' left Muong-Sai and headed through wild jungle in Northern Laos attempting to create a diversion; the country proved to be impenetrable and the efforts required, plus the constant harassment from Viet-Minh and their Laotian sympathizers, meant the French only got to Ben-Mdijei, 20 miles from Dien Bien Phu, when the fortress fell. They then had to fight their way back to headquarters, objective unattained. (Popperfoto)

Above: *French troops, having emerged from the jungle, are here engaged in a shoot-out with the Vietminh in a village in Tonkin. The French are using a bamboo fence to shield themselves from enemy fire, or at least to prevent themselves from attracting attention. (Popperfoto)*

Below: *This is Colonel Goddart's column en route to relieve Dien Bien Phu, having here discovered a hiding-place thought to contain enemy guerrillas. The French troops riddled the hole with machine-gun bullets in order to kill anyone that might be inside. (Popperfoto)*

Like all other units, they excelled at road ambushes, using dense cover for surprise. All Vietnamese troops regarded good personal camouflage as paramount. Wearing palm-leaf helmets that had wire mesh over them, they changed their camouflage whenever the foliage of the countryside altered.

Difficulties of resupply can be imagined for a Vietminh regiment, normally spread over an area of 17,000 square metres and needing a minimum of three tons of stores a day with no 'fixed' system of replenishment. It was believed that a ready reckoner was: coolie, 55 lb; bicycle, 150 lb; horse, 470 lb; ox cart, 1,770 lb; truck, 5,000 plus lb and sampan, 10,000 plus lb. A regiment needed 40,000 porters to maintain its supplies.

The French found themselves in the constant military dilemma of conventional forces (however modified for specific conditions they had become) fighting unconventional ones. Should they try and penetrate deeply, causing destruction and hitting hard where it hurt, for a short time, or achieve shallow penetration for a long time? Overall control was tight because the diversity, speed and logistical requirements of French forces only allowed tactical initiative for local ground battles. The Vietnamese, on the other hand, gave their field commanders a much greater measure of operational freedom, letting each unit decide which task was the most important. The nearest other armies came to this, but in a much lower key, was 'framework' operations in Malaya.

Casualty evacuation among the French forces was never easy. Carrying a stretcher over mountainous jungle tracks, being jolted as the bearers slithered in the mud, never knowing when another ambush would be sprung, was always a problem. There were a number of instances when the Vietnamese did not allow French doctors to give first aid to their own casualties but shot them and the doctors instead. Very rarely was the reverse true. Wounded Vietnamese soldiers were scared of falling into their opponents' hands.

The classic place for Vietnamese concealment was in their villages. Here they used ponds and wells with imagination. Water surrounded hide-outs and the siphon-and-vent principle was used, that is to say, the person hiding had to dive through the water that hid the hole to be entered and this, in turn, kept water out by having a kink in it. For ventilation holes were dug and hidden by undergrowth. As *Street Without Joy* puts it, 'to find a Vietnamese hide-out or depot, sheer luck or torture' was needed.

The Vietnamese used tunnels to conceal large headquarters and hospitals. Some of these tunnels that the Americans found later had been in existence for a score of years. One puzzle that has yet to be solved is where the spoil excavated during the construction of such formidable earthworks was hidden and, if it was not hidden, why was it never noticed? And if similar signs were observed today, would they be recognized and would that prevent another similar type of situation from erupting?

Fear played its part: the Vietnamese took off the heads of soldiers they killed and exhibited them on poles stuck into the ground. Villagers and, in the jungles, the tribesmen, feared the network of Communist spies, informers and agents. They were in the awkward position of the weak: stay rigid and break or bend and survive. In the former context, the result could very well be death or mutilation, in the latter, self-respect and standing in the community would be in jeopardy. The Communists were organized, indoctrinated, motivated, disciplined and xenophobic in their intensity – for them it was almost a holy war.

The final battle of Dien Bien Phu, that costly and doom-laden fight, began in November 1953. By January the French position had deteriorated because of a lack of national will to win, a reluctance to meet Indo-Chinese demands for true independence and the refusal to train indigenous personnel for military leadership. The war in Indo-China finished so tragically for the French over the octave of Easter, 1954; all white men in Asia were the poorer for the way the French had behaved before they lost the war, but all were the richer by their display of gallantry and dogged determination as they were losing it.

That having been said, there is another factor that is pertinent to French defeat, namely that the French Army simply did not have a philosophy or coherent training doctrine during the Indo-China war. '. . . and that was part of the problem,' writes an officer of my regiment, Lieutenant-Colonel R. C. Eyres, a noted linguist of both Asian and European languages and who has served and studied with the French military forces. In my quest for details I was advised that he 'avoided the use of the word "philosophy" as this would be quite likely to put French academic types on to the wrong tack altogether'. Colonel Richard Eyres continued:

> I have to confess, reluctantly, that I am no wiser . . . [and] in two years at the Ecole Supérieure de Guerre in Paris, the topic was never once mentioned, in either a historic or a contemporary context. Even when we conducted 'exercises' planning a brush-fire war/restoration of law and order in Martinique, no attention was given to the problems of acclimatization, equipment or specialist training for the troops who would be sent from France.
>
> Similarly, we visited the 2nd Battalion of the Legion in Corsica, shortly before they made their dramatic jump into Kalwezi in 1978, and I did not get any impression that this élite unit, with a spearhead intervention role worldwide, regarded the jungle as an element requiring any particular modification to the training programme.

THE AMERICANS IN VIETNAM

The Americans badly burnt their fingers when they became involved in South Vietnam where they found themselves trying to contain Communism, thereby defending continental United States (CONUS) on the mainland of Asia. Whereas the French had seen the war in a colonial light, the Americans saw it in a global one. The eventual result was humiliating and never expected, especially when their anti-Communist crusade had started with such high hopes. As far back as 1947, Ho Chi Minh confided to an American agent that he would welcome 'a million American soldiers . . . but no French'; in 1950 a US State Department official had said, 'whether we like the French or not, independence is coming to Indo-China. Why, therefore, do we tie ourselves to the tail of their battered kite?' Why indeed? One answer is that, by the middle 1960s, the prevailing American view was that mainland Asia was the best place to contain Communism. History will probably record a verdict of 'the wrong war in the wrong place'.

At least the Americans proved that Communism was not monolithic but only the most successful – and dangerous – confidence trick in modern history. Be that as it may, there were many instances of American and 'Free World' bravery, with the Australians winning two Victoria Crosses and in *A Soldier Reports,*

General William C. Westmoreland quotes one American who had seven wounds and 29 decorations and another who had 28. (As one Frenchman is quoted as saying, '. . . the Americans are brave soldiers but they are stupid soldiers. They are too brave. If the French, the British or the Germans were fighting this war, they would only suffer half the casualties.')

American proclivity for mechanical and electronic devices to supplement the physical side of human endeavour, their quest for perfection in such matters, along with an industrial base strong enough to put ideas into action, has all shown in its military thinking as well as in such remarkable exploits as reaching the moon. (It is interesting to note that when the moon-walk became common knowledge, Vietnamese morale took a tumble as they felt that now there really was no stopping the Americans on the battlefield.) It was this ability for putting mechanical ideas into action and producing tactics to use with them that marked the difference between American and French jungle operations, to say nothing of the shoe-string British in Malaya and, later on, Borneo. One invention was known as a 'people sniffer' and this was installed in an aircraft and flown over the jungle. It was designed to detect where people had been by urine fumes, which could also give an idea of how many men were involved. It was not possible, however, to tell whether it was animals or people who were being sniffed.

Reliance on machinery, over-reliance in many cases, a draft army that needed a mass training system, luxurious logistics (what campaign against dedicated Communists could be won by troops permanently supplied with so many of Mao Zedong's 'sugar-coated bullets' – vast quantities of beer, chocolate bars, talcum powder, cigarettes, shaving cream and condoms? – as overheard in the Korean war: 'What? No icecream for three whole days? Man, this is total war!') and an open society back home that demanded instant war nightly in its sitting-rooms were all features that affected planning and execution more than military common sense could have warranted.

Much American effort went into helping the Army of the Republic of Vietnam (ARVN) by training and equipping them. 'Hearts and minds' took the form of pacification and Vietnamization. The remark I heard when I was in Vietnam, 'drag them along by the balls and the hearts and minds will follow!', showed frustration rather than anything else. Much American effort was wasted as the South Vietnamese political, judicial and administrative systems were not integrated with their American counterparts as was in the case of French and British colonies; much the Americans wanted to do themselves had to be delegated or transferred to the Vietnamese and many decisions that were speedily wanted for tactical reasons were either slow or not forthcoming. In any case, with economic corruption rampant, no leader having an ideology to counter the Communists' and no popular mandate with a positive cause, Saigon's political base was too weak to survive for long on its own and was further weakened by reliance on the USA. American corpuscles in Vietnamese blood were, in the end, rejected.

The Americans tried to avoid the jungle by using it as little as possible, and tried to deny its use to the enemy by destroying it as much as they could. Defoliants were extensively used. (I am told that the best ever defoliant was when troops advanced against one another in the Biafran War of 1967–70. There was so much firing in the air that none of the trees was left with any leaves on at all – but I cannot personally vouch for the total accuracy of this allegation!)

Very many American infantrymen found that the war was much less glamorous than they had imagined and much lonelier – this the result of the draft system not allowing battalions to become closely knit. They feared and mistrusted the Vietnamese, never knowing who was their enemy, and loathed the mentality that planted so many deadly and outrageous booby-traps. With no front line they could be killed from any direction at any time. Three million Americans served in Vietnam and, for the majority, survival and counting the days before getting back home were all-important. Towards the end 'fragging' of officers by men (lobbing grenades into rooms where officers were sitting together) was a vindictive feature (as indeed it was in certain African battalions in Burma); it was reckoned that one-third of the Americans in Vietnam were taking hard drugs (opium and heroin); and race relations deteriorated. For a view from soldier level, *Dispatches* by Michael Herr makes scabrous and vivid reading.

American use of armour and air were characteristics of jungle fighting not previously seen on such a scale, as was their use of heavily fortified bases on hilltops cleared of vegetation. The framwork for operations against the North Vietnamese and the Vietminh guerrillas had three distinct phases: 'search and destroy' (later changed to 'sweeping operations' or 'reconnaissance in force' to try and overcome the stigma attached to the word 'destroy'); clearing operations to drive the enemy from populated regions so that pacification programmes could be initiated; securing those regions to protect the pacification teams, eliminate local guerrillas and uproot the enemy's secret political structure. Infantry tactics based on attack and defence, along with patrolling and ambush requirements were a constant, modified according to target and terrain.

Armour was used where possible. The Americans thought that the French use of armour was a tragic failure and efforts were made not to repeat mistakes. Vietnam is not an ideal locale for armour, but armour can make valuable contributions. As Lieutenant-Colonel R. B. Battreal, points out, 'Armor is not the medium tank or any other specific machine. It is a concept of mobility, firepower and shock effect on the battlefield. The need for this is an inherent part of warfare.' Parallels were made with earlier examples of this – light, swift horsemen, heavily armed and armoured knights, chariots and elephants.

Vietnam can be divided into four territorial regions: the delta of the River Mekong, the coastal plain, the central plateau and the rugged, jungle-covered mountains, in the northern two-thirds of the country. The central plateau is the only place for armour.

Armoured cars are road bound, except on the central plateau and, during the dry season, parts of the coastal plain. They are ideal for highway security and convoy escort as they discourage ambushes. By 1966, the V100 'Commando' was the only modern US car that was available in reasonable quantities.

Tanks cannot ford water obstacles nor can they swim and as there were no bridges, their use was limited. The main battle tank was the M113 Armoured Personnel Carrier. It was the backbone of armour in Vietnam 'for one simple and overriding reason, it can move!' The M41A3 had a 76mm gun and the M48 was armed with a 90mm gun. To counter the American armoured threat, the Vietnamese used a 'shaped-charge' type of anti-tank weapon.

As an example of casualties caused by using armour, from 11 June to 30 September 1962, 502 of the enemy were killed and 184 captured, as against US losses of four killed and nine wounded.

Locally modified .50 machine-guns were installed and, in each troop, three vehicles mounted 81mm mortars and two carried 57mm recoilless rifles. The Vietnamese had 57mm and 75mm recoilless rifles, 3.5in rocket-launchers and 82mm Chinese 'panzerfaust' mortars.

The main uses of armour were for reconnaissance, as a strike force, for encircling an area, for security and for sweeps. And, as was noted, if the enemy hid from armour, he was not doing his job!

Air operations played a very large part in all American activity, not only strategically by interdiction of supply routes and raids on various military installations – which were in no way as effective as the planners had thought – but also tactically in support of ground troops. The idea of using helicopters as an airborne 'cavalry division' was a particularly bold concept, 'vertical attack' becoming almost the norm.

Initiative is of paramount importance and the Vietnamese Communist leaders possessed that timeless advantage of the guerrilla – the choice, with infinite care, of the time and place of action. As in all CRW, without intelligence of all kinds, success was impossible.

Success in combat for the security forces, especially against guerrillas fighting on their own soil, depends on wresting the overall initiative from them. Without this at tactical level, there can be no foundation for winning the strategic campaign with all its political, economic, sociological and psychological implications.

Finding guerrillas in sufficient strength and in a situation that is disadvantageous to them is a time-consuming task. Not until guerrillas mount an attack do they disclose themselves and so allow security force action to be taken.

Airborne vertical counter-attack required a force of helicopters always to be available at short notice, an airborne strategic reserve. This was known as an Instant Ready Force. Communications were all-important. AD-6 Skyraider – 'close air' machines – and L-19 director Mosquito aircraft were used for this task.

For all airmobile operations the orders had to include a number of requirements: task, organization, fire support, the aviation element, the landing areas and the objective.

One difference between such operations and anything remotely similar in other countries was the American penchant for being resupplied once infiltration had been achieved. There are many stories of men being dumped in the jungle and having to have rations and water, to say nothing of extra ammunition, flown in daily. The noise this produced and the deceptive tactics employed to prevent the enemy from making a contact on his terms required considerable effort. Such raids could last up to four days and the extraction zone had to be secured before it was safe to lift the troops out. To my mind this caused needless casualties and I could not understand why the British method of taking in enough ammunition and rations for a period of days was never developed for the ordinary soldier. Special forces were more self-contained.

The C-47 aircraft was turned into a gunship with floodlights and rapid-firing Gatling-type 'miniguns' (firing 18,000 rounds a minute) and became known as

'Spooky' or 'Puff, the Magic Dragon'. It was a common sight – and sound – over night-time Saigon.

Air power on such a scale was expensive. In 1968, the Americans' worst year, five aircraft were lost every day, many of them by accident. One million tons of explosive ordnance was dropped from March 1965 until November 1968. Estimates put US damage to Vietnam as $300 million, with 100,000 civilians dead (let alone the estimated half-million casualties in Cambodia), while more than 700 aircraft were lost at about $900 million, out of a total cost of about $120 billion. Such sacrifices may have delayed the inevitable end but, without escalating the war further, could never have won it.

The extraction and evacuation of casualties, sick and wounded, by air was brought to a fine art and was greatly instrumental for American morale in Vietnam being as high as it was. Extraction of men from thick jungle when the helicopter could not land was effected by a web strap, 200-feet long, being dropped through the trees. The rescued man would sit in a loop of the strap and clinging for dear life as the helicopter rose vertically, its precious cargo dangling helplessly below it. Many lives were saved in this way. I had a trial run and was scared stiff!

173 Airborne Brigade was reputed to be one of the most effective airborne forces. 1st Air Cavalry Division had 424 helicopters integral to its units and everyone who owned a helicopter was expected to fly it himself.

TRAINERS AND ADVISERS

Training teams were of both American and Australian composition. Brigadier O. D. Jackson, who commanded the Australian team, wrote about being stationed in Ban Me Thuot, an area renowned for the finest tiger, elephant and crocodile hunting in Asia. Duties of the team were as advisers, trainers and commanders for ARVN and in certain special duties.

Australian officers and warrant officers participated in the training and administration of ethnic groups with US special forces, including command on patrol, and for company and battalion operations. Their tasks were to locate and destroy guerrilla cadres and infrastructure in contested hamlets and villages and to restore them to government security. There was a constant need to win the conflict at all important grass roots levels in villages, hamlets and towns by freeing ordinary people from the fear of North Vietnam's guerrillas.

At the Duc My Ranger Centre a training place was established on the lines of the Jungle Training Centre, at Canungra, in Australia.

There were also a number of American advisers. One of their tasks was to train the South Vietnamese in conventional fighting. Advisers from the 'Green Beret' special forces were seen as the 'cutting edge' of COIN; they concentrated on training Montagnards and Khmers – who were outside the main steam of official Vietnamese thinking and who, in any case, neither liked nor trusted the Vietnamese – at the expense of work among Vietnamese villagers. This was seen as a waste of skills.

(The Australian and New Zealand contingents in Vietnam based their tactics on methods of jungle warfare of which they had had operational experience in Malaya, enhanced by US air support. In any case they seemed to operate south in the Mekong delta region for much of the time and their jungle warfare training input for the British Army was peripheral.)

US Special Forces have a reputation for operating like the British Army's SAS. Certain functions of both units may indeed overlap, but one role of the 'Green Berets' is to train certain units in foreign armies in counter-insurgency operations, that is to say, operations against the Communists during the active phase of CRW. I have had the opportunity of observing training methods for Thais and Vietnamese in their own countries, including live firing and the use of booby-traps. At one special forces camp in Thailand I was shown a 'Lao house', modelled on the one my American guide, a tall man, had lived in when an adviser in that country. I told him he was lucky to be alive as it was obviously used by a tall foreigner. He was surprised that I should have guessed correctly and asked me how I knew and why he had been at risk. There were two reasons: he had had a bamboo stool constructed, something that the Lao would never sit on, and it was so high that it had to be for a man of unusual height – a foreigner and who else, under those circumstances, but an American?

I was the last British Defence Attaché in Laos, serving there from the end of 1972, before the cease-fire, until early in 1976, after the Communists had emerged from their hide-outs, the king deposed. Two episodes (of very many) remain in my mind and are germane to how the Communists won that war.

The first took place on 16 April 1975, two weeks before Saigon fell, at a strategic road junction in the north of the country, around which was a detachment of the Royal Lao Army, mainly an infantry battalion but there were also a sprinkling of armoured cars, a few pieces of light artillery and the local queen of the battlefield, a piece of medium artillery. It pointed towards the enemy, was the pride and joy of its crew and the main reason why the Americans thought it unlikely that the enemy would attack the place. It was superbly camouflaged, so well that to a casual observer its presence was a secret. The Lao colonel also hoped that enemy spies and agents were similarly in the dark. It was, unfortunately, unserviceable and had been so for an embarrassingly long time.

I flew to the camp with the American who was in charge of the funds that were paying for the Royal Lao Army. He asked the commander when the previously given advice about having the gun either changed or repaired was going to be followed – the general situation was deteriorating.

The astonishing reply was that the garrison commander was loth to disturb the camouflage around the gun 'as the enemy might then know that we had it, be angry with us and punish us by attacking the position which we would then lose, and then headquarters would also be angry with me. It is much better and easier to leave things as they are.'

His visitor then asked the colonel about his strength and was told that although some men were away working at a second job, there was a platoon's worth of soldiers defending the road junction. The Laos' minds were brought back to more interesting things by being given a quart bottle of whisky and several issues of Playboy magazine, complete with pull-out pin-ups. Having made his contribution to help stabilize the situation, we left a huddled, excited group of officers sitting round a wooden ration box that served as a table. As soon as we got airborne we heard the forward troops request supporting fire because they were being attacked by the Pathet Lao and the North Vietnamese Army. There was none available.

The second incident took place at Pakse, in the 'Panhandle' of Laos. The Communists had taken over by then, but the Royal Lao Army commander of Military Region 4 was still there. He had asked me to visit him to advise him whether he should escape or not. I flew down in the embassy Beaver. While talking to the general he turned and, with infinite sadness, told me why the war had gone on so long and all the American effort had failed. It was because most of the supplies given to the Royal Lao Army were sold to the Pathet Lao who gave them to the North Vietnamese. 'Nobody wanted to give up the chance of making money and those who were making it were not involved in combat.' I breathed a silent amen.

I then accepted as true that which I had heard but had been unwilling to believe – the reason why the Americans had flown such quantities of artillery, arms and ammunition into the Khmer Republic, even to the very end. President Lon Nol's men were selling significant quantities of all three commodities to the Khmers Rouges and getting equally significant amounts of US dollars in payment. So much for 'Free World' effort!

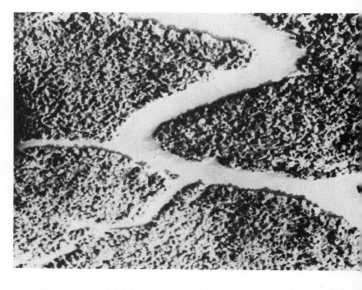

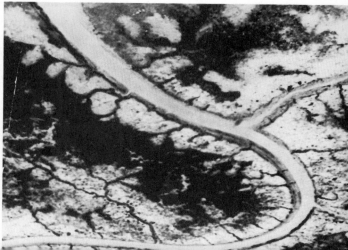

Right: *This aerial image starkly reveals the effects of US defoliants on the countryside in Vietnam. The American strategy for fighting in the jungle evolved into a simple maxim of 'remove the jungle!' This mangrove forest sixty miles from Saigon (above), was turned into the dry barren landscape below after chemical warfare had taken its toll on plant life. The long-term effects on both the ecology and man were and are still unquantifiable.* (Popperfoto)

Left: Knee-deep in water, a patrol of the Royal Ulster Rifles check their position on a map while moving through a jungle swamp in Borneo. (Popperfoto)

Left: Limbang, Brunei 1962. Hundreds of rebels were rounded up by security forces, the main prison was overcrowded and all the inmates had to be interrogated for intelligence purposes. Except for a few dedicated hard-core guerrillas, all the others wanted to do was go home. (Popperfoto)

Left: A routine river patrol in the Borneo jungle. Men of the 1st Battalion, The Royal Ulster Rifles are using a native long boat fitted with an outboard motor to search a creek leading off the main river. (Popperfoto)

9
Confrontation in Borneo
1963–66

B ritain's disentanglement from empire and the consequent political pressures in territories which then had to look after themselves often resulted in upheavals and bloodshed. After Malaya had become independent in 1957 there were still three countries in Asia (apart from Hong Kong) for which Britain had some residual measure of control and responsibility. These were in the northern part of Borneo, the world's third largest island, and were Sarawak, Brunei and British North Borneo (later to be known as Sabah). The main parts of the island had belonged to the Dutch and were handed over to the Indonesians after the Second World War. They knew it as Kalimantan (and the northern part Kalimantan Utara). The tidiest way of getting rid of the three British territories without upheaval and bloodshed seemed to be to unite them with peninsula Malaya and Singapore to form a new country called Malaysia. This would entail a land border between Malaysia and Indonesia, but it was not expected to produce any problems – had not the border peoples either side got on well enough over the years?

This idea ran counter to another, more expansive but less realistic, in the mind of the President of Indonesia, Sukarno, which was to form a state to be called Maphilindo and made up of *Mala*ya, the *Phili*ppines and *Indo*nesia, which he felt could rival any other power bloc in the world. Neither idea came to fruition as originally envisaged, but Malaysia did become an entity, never with Brunei and with Singapore for only two years, whereas Maphilindo was stillborn. Nevertheless, in an effort to prevent Malaysia from happening at all, Sukarno waged war against it, the so-called Confrontation, which was preceded by a rebellion in Brunei – an oil-rich sultanate on the north coast of the island.

The rebellion was only loosely linked with later events and was ill-prepared, poorly led and not conducted with sufficient skill for success. 1/2nd Gurkha Rifles, quickly followed by the 1st Battalion, Queen's Own Highlanders, went to the rescue and stabilized the situation. The Scots had to be airlanded on an unreconnoitred grass strip held by the enemy – something that no self-respecting air force likes doing. To clear such a danger is the role of paratroops and it was this operation that showed up the need to have a parachute unit always on hand. Rather than denude the Home Base of such troops, it was decided to raise a small parachute force from theatre resources and the Gurkha Independent Parachute Company was raised on 1 January 1963.

The peoples of Borneo have been subjected to a number of external influences over the last seven centuries: Chinese, Javanese, Hindu, Muslim and European. The Muslim incursions led to the establishment of Brunei as an Islamic sultanate in the 15th century which influenced the whole island. The Portuguese also arrived then, followed by the Spanish two hundred years later, then the Dutch and finally the British. These last two divided the territories up, with Sarawak being ruled by the Brooke family (known as the 'White Rajah'), Brunei by its sultan and North Borneo by a trading company of that name, based in Hong Kong. The northern island, Labuan, ceded from Brunei, was a Crown Colony. The border between British and Dutch Borneo was so ill-defined that it was a cartographer's folly, with as much or as little importance or concern as anyone wanted to invest in it – not that it mattered then. When I made an inspection of the border I found that it had as little significance to most natives as a child in England going to school across the parish boundary would have to its parents. The Japanese occupation left the whole country in chaos.

Administratively Sarawak was divided into five divisions and Sabah into four residencies. Along the border I came across 29 different dialects and languages making the country a linguist's paradise but an interpreter's nightmare. In the First Division alone, not counting Malay, English or Chinese, there are five main languages. Between the two extremities of Borneo is as great a diversity of language, climate, dress, religion and custom as is found anywhere.

Much of Borneo is covered by dense, mountainous, tropical rain forest, which forms an almost unbroken canopy a hundred or so feet above the ground. Apart from the people who live near the larger waterways and the coast (where the largest and most developed centres of population are to be found), it is sparsely inhabited, especially in Sarawak. In the 1960s towns were not joined up by roads. The numerous large and small rivers and a few jungle trails are the only means of travel between coast and hinterland. This was where 'space can be sold for time' militarily; where it cannot be sold is in the First and Second Divisions as the country there is narrow, with the border marching near villages, and relatively heavily populated.

The war in Borneo was for territory and people. Unlike the Malayan and Indo-China/Vietnam conflicts, the attacking forces were not Communist, although the Communists in Indonesia did have a certain amount of influence with Sukarno. His defence minister, General Abdul Haris Nasution, decided to wage his war on guerrilla concepts. In a book he wrote he postulated that British Borneo could be for the taking; guerrillas would operate from safe bases inside Kalimantan and cross the border at will. They would stir up revolution and be supported by the Indonesian regular army to such an extent that Malays and British would become exhausted and demoralized to the point of submission. In the event the brave General's contention had all the characteristics of a damp squib. It did underline, however, the importance the Indonesians attached to those who lived in the border areas, who were also a major factor in all planning by the Malaysian and British authorities. 'Hearts and minds' was no mere cliché, but of campaign-winning importance.

One of the features of life in Borneo is the widespread custom of having what amounts to whole villages under one roof, built like a long house, hence the continual references to 'longhouses'. The longest of these houses I knew of was half-a-mile in length. The population is a conglomeration of many races – Land Dyaks, Ibans, Malays, Muruts, Kelabits, Kayans, Kenyahs, Punans and Dusans, to name but some of the bewildering complex jumble of people, known officially, and in no way derogatorily, as Natives. The most famous and the largest indigenous group are the Ibans, known and feared for being headhunters. It is a popular misconception that all Ibans are brave and expert trackers, although all are colourful, mercurial and earthy. They were particularly difficult people to deal with if they felt that they were being treated the wrong way. Infinite patience and human understanding were needed, as well as tact and courtesy.

All the Natives were very pro-British having been decently and kindly administered by 'prototype' Britons – men who were unorthodox, eccentric, devoted to duty and characters in their own right. As well as an 'official' administration, the country was divided up by missionaries who converted with zeal if not with discretion. Headhunting was discouraged by these men of God and by those of government – but neither had succeeded in obliterating the practice.

THE VALUE OF INTELLIGENCE

It was not until after the Brunei rebellion had been quashed and any danger of its disrupting the process towards the creation of Malaysia had disappeared that the Indonesians turned their attention to Sarawak. Here were two main methods of exerting pressure on the administration; from across the frontier, to the south, and in the Chinese populated areas, in the north, infiltrated by agents already in position and reinforced by others who arrived in small boats from round the coast. However important a factor this second threat was, it did not concern the

Below: Jungle and rubber come down to the water's edge at Brunei town. It was such country that allowed the rebels, in December 1962, to advance to the town unobserved and capture it. The rebellion fizzled out soon after it started. Even in the village on the water the jungle is never far away. (General Sir Walter Walker)

jungle as such except peripherally and then there were no differences in tactics from any other similar situation.

In the jungle areas, on the other hand, the Indonesians proved a tough and courageous enemy, able to bring down artillery fire and use booby-traps in a professional manner. For low-grade work they employed guerrillas, called by our security forces Indonesian Border Terrorists (IBT), who were hardy and used to rough conditions but, like all similar organizations, were only of limited value.

Sarawak had no military forces of its own that were capable of taking any action. Dyaks who served in the Malayan Emergency were part of the Sarawak Rangers, only much later expanded to become the Malaysian Rangers. The government in Kuala Lumpur had always been uncertain as to the temper of the Dyaks and Ibans enlisted at tracker level (because they had never had much respect for Malays) and so was most unwilling to give them automatic weapons. In fact, the two sources of unrest were among the Chinese in the coastal towns and Indonesian labour in the timber trade on the southern border of Sabah, nowhere near where the Rangers lived when they were not embodied. In other words, they were not then a factor in the equation.

Major-General W. C. Walker – a battalion and brigade commander of great experience during the Malayan Emergency – was now the Director of Borneo Operations and he laid down five ingredients for success against the menace of Confrontation. They were: unified operations; timely and accurate information requiring a first-class intelligence organization; speed, mobility and flexibility; security of all bases wherever and whatever they might be (an airfield, a headquarters, a patrol base, etc.); and domination of the jungle. As the maps were bad, a major survey effort was initiated.

The area to be covered by the security forces was vast, and domination of the jungle and battlefield mobility were only possible by timely and correct positioning of troops. This, in turn, needed helicopters, which were never in plentiful supply. To get early warning of any threat was, therefore, even more important than usual. Opportune acquisition of information being paramount, General Walker ensured that intelligence-gathering resources were upgraded and that the passing of that precious commodity was speeded up by setting up a series of re-broadcasting stations on the high and lonely mountain tops where required.

As there was very little crime in Sarawak, there was only a small police force and an even smaller Special Branch. Its expansion was therefore given immediate priority. It takes time, patience and much good will both to build any network that relies on other people telling it of any future activity and to have the skill and experience to know when reports are genuine or deliberately false. Apart from the type of intelligence that Special Branch could produce there was a great need of military intelligence, especially on the border with Indonesia.

The main source of this commodity was the SAS, whose primary task was to provide an early-warning system of any incursion, intended or actual. Small detachments of SAS were dropped off by helicopter and, using their talent, radioed back reports which were acted on, when necessary, by the infantry. For a most vivid account and one where British stamina and resourcefulness is at its best, the late Peter Dickens' book, *SAS; The Jungle Frontier*, makes compelling reading.

There was a third, unique, force for gathering and reporting information that had its genesis at the start of the Brunei rebellion. News of this new menace was sent upriver by traditional red feather to warn the upland tribes that revolutionaries might try to escape southwards through their territory and that, possibly, the help of these upland people would be needed in the troubled area itself. So swift was the response to this call to arms that the whole problem of border surveillance almost naturally fell into perspective. A force of Natives was raised for this task; enlisted as auxiliary policemen and known as the Border Scouts, I was sent for to command them. I got the impression that such a novel and esoteric concept as the Border Scouts initially confused, if not frightened, the police and the administration who would never have had the political will to allow the border dwellers to be so associated with their own security. Their basic training was run by the SAS and, until they had their own leaders, men of the Gurkha Para Company acted as section commanders. It was hard to remember that only the older Natives had even seen British troops before and none had seen Gurkhas.

Spread along the frontier, sometimes with an army unit but often as satellite to a remote longhouse, using a language that did not come easily to him – if it came at all – the Gurkha found it a lonely, uncomfortable, primitive and strange command, not without danger. He did not trust his men; his charges were frightened by the possibility of an armed enemy attack and were unused to Gurkha-type discipline. I knew of cases when, sent out on a 4-day ambush (a task for which the Scouts had not been trained) by the unit under whose operational command they came, the Gurkha in charge did not take his boots off or sleep at all. Overall results achieved and steadfastness shown by most of the section commanders were most gratifying. Sometimes the literal turn of mind of the Gurkha rifleman showed itself to the man's disadvantage. One night in a Royal Marine camp a Marine corporal was giving orders to the Gurkha rifleman in charge of the Border Scouts section and I overheard:

'I want four hands on watch at 8 o'clock.'

There was a pause as this strange request was digested, the Gurkha looking intently at the timepiece in his hand. Then the acknowledgement came: 'My watch has two hands at 8 o'clock.'

THE FIRST PHASE OF CONFRONTATION

In the first phase of Confrontation the security forces were primarily on the defensive. As the British Army supplied most of the troops, any action but the minimum required to repel border incursions was politically sensitive to and personally resented by the ruling Malays. (Just how hard the Malays tried to impress their smaller part of Malaysia on the people of greater Borneo was clear when they produced a pictorial map of the new country with the peninsula, Malaya as was, drawn to a larger scale than 'eastern Malaysia', Borneo as was. As copies were sent to every longhouse and displayed on the walls – which were never empty, the British Royal Family having held pride of place for many years – a cleverly erroneous impression of greatness was fostered in simple minds which believed in size equating to strength. When I pointed this out to Malay officials over in Sarawak they refused to believe the evidence of their own eyes and their government-issue rulers.)

A defensive stance managed to repel the attacks against Royal Marine positions in the First Division without too much difficulty and coped with shallow incursions against the Gurkhas in the Second Division. However, it got a nasty jolt in August 1963 when the first deep (thirty miles) incursion took place. Made by about sixty men with the aim of capturing the riverine town of Song in the Third Division, the raiders thought that the local population would rise up and join them. They had been launched without maps, compasses or rations. This showed that the Indonesian assessment of the situation was wildly inaccurate or that their military planning and organization were woefully bad. It was later thought that the raiders were used as an act of publicity and defiance to coincide with two United Nations teams, one a fact-finding team which visited Sarawak in that month to ascertain whether Malaysia had popular support or not, and the other an observer team to see that the Indonesians already in Borneo left. In the event the creation of Malaysia was confirmed by the United Nations and came into being on 16 September 1963.

For the first two weeks of that month there was no legal country or government, Sarawak and British North Borneo having stopped being separate entities on 31 August! Then came the observer team to see that the invaders left the country. Composed of Thais, it went to the small town of Tebakang on the border, where the first overt Indonesian raid had taken place. In front of the Thais a line of Indonesian soldiers walked out of the jungle and, having been checked, moved across the border into their own country. It was represented that they had been in Sarawak for some time but all their uniforms were clean and pressed so smartly that they could not have been operating in the jungle. The troops that so proudly marched into Indonesia had only left that country a short while before. Special Branch knew this but the observers, having seen a charade they chose to believe, departed by helicopter to Kuching where a reception was held to celebrate their helping to stabilize the situation while those Indonesian troops that had infiltrated into Sarawak stayed there. I had never been so near to international decision-making before and in no way was I impressed by the august body the team represented.

AIR POWER

By then there was an unusual feature of military land operations: helicopters from the Fleet Air Arm, normally based on HMS *Albion* or *Bulwark*, were based far inland and significantly bolstered the helicopter support provided by the RAF.

Air aspects, as seen by the RAF themselves, were more affected by the climate than in many other places. 'In the wet season it rains all day and in the dry season it rains every day.' That is certainly true in the Borneo Uplands where a thick mist lasts until 10 o'clock. The weather clears for flying until early afternoon during which time there is a gradual build-up of what is known in the jargon as convection cloud. This develops into massive cumulo-nimbus thunder-heads that are a great hazard to all flying. The mountains, as in New Guinea, make their own weather, causing turbulence even during fair conditions and downdrafts also constitute a flying hazard. Deficiencies in mapping and survey meant that pilots had to 'fly by the seat of their pants'. Local knowledge was often a crucial element of navigation as the many valleys and ridges, all with their

Right: Scout helicopters played a great part during Confrontation with Indonesia. Very often it was only this machine that could maintain the lonely radio re-broadcast stations at the top of a mountain. Each post would have its own Landing Site, made to allow as flat an approach as possible. Scouts from 11 Liaison Flight, Army Air Corps, had a range of 200 nautical miles and a cruise speed of 100 knots. They could carry four soldiers with their kit.

One radio re-broadcast station was at the top of Gunong (mountain) Lundu, to the west of Sarawak. It was 3,000 feet high and was often cloud-girt. Detachments of the Gurkha Signals operated these sites, thereby giving commanders much more flexibility of movement than had ever been known in the Malayan Emergency. (Colonel C. J. D. Bullock)

Right: Each base had its own helicopter pad. Here are RAF Whirlwinds at the Jambu company base. (Colonel B. M. Niven)

Right: Royal Navy Wessex helicopters were powerful and were used to change over companies as well as ferrying troops into the jungle. Operating far from their command carrier, they formed small bases far inland (not without much 'tooth sucking' by senior naval officers!). They were a battle-winning factor and had there been only a few more helicopters permanently with each battalion confrontation might have been over at least a year earlier. This is a naval helicopter base on the banks of the River Rejang. The pilots were called 'pirates' and were extremely well thought of by all. (Royal Navy)

individual characteristics on the ground, tend to look alike from the air. Flying had to remain unprovocative so there were restrictions against any escalation of tension.

One of the air's most effective contribution was to enable the ground forces to overcome the limitations and restrictions of the thick jungle. This could take the form of a logistics build-up (with arms, ammunition or other supplies being air-dropped or air-landed), reconnaissance, troop movements to a critical area and as a mobile command post.

As resources were so limited, economical tasking was only achieved by the centralized control of the air staff. The RAF became so proficient in this aspect that, even after Confrontation was over, the Malaysians insisted on RAF air-tasking officers and teams remaining behind.

Unlike in Vietnam, where the enemy could and indeed did prefer to operate under cover of darkness, night movement in the Borneo jungle was not on a scale to warrant the use of air. Patrolling the coastal areas was another matter. What is true is that it is unacceptable for an air force only to be able to operate in daylight and in fair weather.

The army also had its flight of Beaver communication aircraft. These were of immense value but their resources were stretched. The area of operations was larger than that of the Rhine Army.

The highest strip in regular use was at 3,300 feet. With the ambient of plus 29° Celsius in density, that equated to an altitude of nearly 6,000 feet. The mountains are 5–7,000 feet high. Beavers were fitted with the Decca navigator and the Search and Rescue Beacon, known as SARBE, which was carried by most infantry patrols. The Forward Air Operational Centre at Brigade was the heart of flying operations.

Armour played only a small part in the campaign as there were so few roads. (There were only two squadrons of armoured cars.) Artillery, however, came into prominence and tactics changed when, for the first time and against the grain of many gunners, pieces were used singly, based in company forts or taken to a pad on the border in a support role. There was a total of 29 guns. The Indonesians had equipment that could cause confusion at the gun positions. Using Morse for silent registration, the transmission was poached and the guns were ordered to fire. When such an order came again, the message was very carefully analysed and found to contain mistakes in procedure, so showing it was not an order to be obeyed. A corporal, leading an infantry company on a cross-border operation, suddenly found shells landing a few yards in front of him when the gunner officer was carrying out silent registration a few yards behind him.

DANGEROUS INCURSIONS

There was another deep incursion that changed the defensive stance to an aggressive one and showed up weaknesses in the way that the Border Scouts were being used. (I had arrived too late to stop them from being incorrectly slanted. Instead of being 'bare-arsed' eyes and ears who could go anywhere and be taken for ordinary longhouse dwellers on their lawful business of agriculture or hunting, they were put into uniform and co-located with a military unit, who in turn presumed they were trained soldiers. The less well-disciplined British

battalions used the Border Scouts as leading scouts on patrol, a task that they were neither militarily nor mentally prepared for.)

Thirty miles inside the Third Division and fifty miles from the nearest administrative centre and company headquarters at Belaga, is a small village called Long Jawi. Inhabited by Kayans and Kenyans, it represented the northernmost part of a migratory movement from Kalimantan with whom the inhabitants kept family and other connections. There was a detachment of Border Scouts, commanded by NCOs from the company of 1/2nd Gurkha Rifles at Belaga and a Police Field Force radio detachment. A force of Indonesian soldiers reached a point to the north of the village, prior to attacking it, at the same time as three British officers came to inspect the defences of the village. After making a new plan, they disclosed details of it to the villagers, telling them what part they had to play in the event of an Indonesian attack, unaware that some of the attackers were in the crowd, listening to what was being said.

An attack came in the early hours of the following morning, 28 September, and the small force was subjected to a barrage of 60mm mortars and heavy and concentrated fire from medium and light machine-guns. Some of the defenders were killed, some wounded and the Border Scouts, never expecting to have to face such a situation, began to slip away. They were seized by the Indonesians, disarmed and tied up. Later most of them were murdered.

The situation was only saved by Gurkha bravery and discipline. It took the corporal and his small group four foodless days to reach Belaga with the news, having hidden the wounded men in the jungle.

The Indonesians plundered the settlement before returning upstream and, on the face of it, had dealt a telling blow. Civilian morale had been severely shaken if not shattered and the Scouts decisively beaten. Faith in the security forces' ability to deal with the enemy was restored by the remarkably successful follow-up action by the rest of 1/2nd Gurkha Rifles. A platoon was flown in tactically by helicopters to a flank of the projected route of Indonesian return and the Gurkhas laid an ambush on the river, slaughtering all 26 raiders in two boats as they journeyed upriver. The Border Scouts lost the respect and backing of their community and, from a 'hearts and minds' angle, the Indonesian attack had to be counted a success.

THE TURNING-POINT

The Long Jawi incursion proved to be a turning-point in Confrontation for three reasons: it changed the concept of the security forces from being a purely defensive one into one of attack; without the helicopter, it would be impossible to control so vast an area against the Indonesians; as they were then conceived, the Border Scouts were detrimentally ineffective against such an escalation of aggression.

In Borneo there were never even one hundred helicopters (less than 60 of the troop-carrying kind for an area the size of England and Scotland), compared with the American's fleet of about 3,800 troop-carrying helicopters in South Vietnam. It was estimated that, given six helicopters to each battalion, Confrontation might well have finished a year earlier than it did. More helicopters and better maps was the cry when the minister responsible made an inspection in January 1964.

As far as reslanting the Border Scouts was concerned, a great deal of work was required, not only in more realistically defining their role and their ability to carry it out, but also in the obvious requirement of speedily completing the training of indigenous leaders to command the scouts at every level. During the course of the next few months the whole force was correctly adjusted to become as I had originally conceived it; the help the Gurkhas gave for this to happen was, without any doubt, critical and, without it, the scars of Long Jawi would never have healed.

Indonesian incursions resulted in forts being built far enough forward for the security forces to use them as bases for dominating the jungle. Defence was all-round as indeed was the patrolling. They were reminiscent of the First World War with their underground bunkers, 81mm mortars, and connecting trenches. They would be surrounded with defence stores and were not easy to take out.

105mm artillery was used in single pieces and would travel slung under a Belvedere helicopter, the gun crew and equipment being carried in a second aircraft.

Infantrymen's rifles were the FN and Armalite, both lightweight and ideal for close-range fighting. The 7.62mm was too heavy, at 11 pounds and the long barrel too cumbersome in the jungle. Bren guns were carried (although they had gone out of service by then) as the General Purpose Machine-Gun (GPMG) was only suitable for use in the forts. The emphasis was also for lightweight rations, equipment and radios.

Engineers were employed in making airstrips and helicopter landing pads in the forward areas, building roads and bridges, and furbishing company camps. They were also used where possible in a 'hearts and minds' role, in such tasks as helping local communities with water supplies and making basketball pitches.

The last few hours of 1963 were written in blood across on the eastern side of Sabah, at Kalabakan in the Tawau Residency. A platoon and a half of the Royal Malay Regiment (RMR) were surprised by 35 enemy while in their base camp near the town. They suffered heavy casualties. They had ignored all basic military requirements: their base had no defences, no alarm scheme, their sentries were negligent and their fighting spirit was not immediately obvious. There was no counter-attack. Such was the price to be paid for military slovenliness and administrative inertia. So ended the year in Borneo that started with the end of a rebellion and ended with the start of an undeclared war.

1/10th Gurkha Rifles were sent in to stabilize the situation. The area was chaotic and intelligence negligible. The operational area was immense, with large tracts of jungle that were being felled for timber and a great many tidal creeks and inlets, mud and swamp. Lieutenant-Colonel E. J. S. ('Bunny') Burnett, had these words of wisdom about the available intelligence, from the point of view of battalion commander:

> All that I could find out that first evening in Kalabakan was that the enemy had raided a provision shop at [a village called] Brantian, and that the remains of a lot of chickens, cooked and eaten a short way upriver from Kalabakan, had been found. I based all my initial plans on the single deduction that the raiders would be after more food before long. The hunch paid off.

The Gurkhas hunted the raiders remoselessly. Helicopters shifted groups of soldiers into cut-off positions to seal the enemy's escape, boats navigated the creeks and inlets, taking troops to new and from old positions, foot patrols, in the more accessible areas, knitted a web around the Indonesians to prevent them from breaking contact. By the end of January the battalion had killed twenty and captured thirteen enemy and another thirteen had surrendered. The intensity of operations was more reminiscent of Burma than of Malaya.

The ferocity of the Indonesian attack on the Malaysians added the dimension of Asian versus Asian rather than versus European. I found a sad state of nerves at the other end of the country where I met a very worried commanding officer of the Royal Malay Regiment. He, hapless fellow, was a victim of the rapid expansion of the Federation Armed Forces in that he had been over-promoted. I remembered what an Irish friend had told me about promotion, that it came in two ways – suction from above or pressure from below! Whichever way this man had got his, he was now in a mental vacuum. He had devised a tactic whereby, if the Indonesians were to attack one of his platoons on the border, he could prevent his men from being massacred. He had ordered an extra sack of rice to be put in each forward post and, on being attacked, the senior man or the sentry was to empty the rice on to the ground. The idea was that the Indonesians would be so hungry that they would go for the rice rather than for the Malay soldiers. They would need to cook the rice, by which time either they could be seen to be friendly enough for cooking facilities to be provided and thus a rapport could be established or they would not, by which time the Malay soldiers would have made good their escape. What did I think of his plan? My answer has no need of written record.

But he was not the only frightened man about. Shortly before I had had to go to where a fractious lot of head-hunting Ibans lived, straddling the border and who had been never respected any government, Dutch or British. Except for normal family feuds, quarrels about hunting rights or tempers lost over misplaced female favours, Iban had no disagreement with Iban. The larger political issues had no place in their earthly parochial lives. However, unbeknown to me, those on the Sarawak side of the border did have a quarrel with the government in Kuching. I, as commandant of the Border Scouts, was seen as a good target for them to vent their wrath by forcibly showing their displeasure. I was told, by the

Inspector-General of Police (who had earlier come in on the act and reminded me of the 'hearts and minds' aspect of my job), to go and see them.

I travelled in a longboat, skilfully navigated downstream over many rapids, by two Iban youths who looked magnificently piratical with the distinctive hair style – fringe in front and shoulder length – and 'bare-buff' with rippling muscles.

The house to which I had been invited by the headman, one Jimbuan, held twenty families. Once it was dark I was taken to the central part and told to sit down on the bamboo-slatted floor. I noticed, not for the first time, the nineteen tattoo marks on his left hand, one for each head he had personally lopped off. Gradually the men of the longhouse came and sat, in serried rows, facing Jimbuan and me. They were a strong-looking bunch and, in the dim light of the open-wicked lamps, the flickering shadows made their unsmiling faces relentlessly stern and satanic. Young and old, there were about 45 of them. They sat, silent and staring, their eyes boring into mine whenever I looked up at them.

Jimbuan launched into a litany of frustration, anger and menace: rights and wrongs, imagined or real, out they came. He spoke at me and had the sympathy of all. In twenty minutes he had worked himself into a towering rage. As he spoke in Iban, all his men understood what he was saying. In brief his message was: The enemy were not those who lived over the border. Those were Ibans who were their friends and relations. The enemy lived in Kuching and their name was Government. 'You are from Kuching,' he burst out at me, 'you are part of the government, you are my enemy. You should be killed, like I, Jimbuan, killed nineteen enemy during the war with this . . .' So saying, the old man, with surprising agility, jumped to his feet and, from behind an open door, produced a Japanese sword. He unsheathed it and brandished it over my head. He continued, his voice quavering with anger, 'I will do to you what I did to my old enemies. Look up above you!' So insistent was he and so little choice had I that I did look up, trying to avoid the stares, unblinking in their intensity, of the men in front of me. And there, previously unnoticed, was a very large bunch of sightless, grinning skulls, Jimbuan's nineteen, dumb witness to former acts of violence, hanging over my head, ready to act as witness again.

'What have you to say? Why shouldn't your head be there? Why should I treat you any differently from these?' he queried, gesticulating up at the squalid bunch of skulls.

'No reason at all, old man,' I managed to say, realizing that argument was the last thing needed – the very last, probably. 'I am your guest, but tonight I am tired and you too from working all day. Also the light is dim. Put away your sword and use it tomorrow when it is light, after you have had a good night's sleep. Your aim will be better then.'

My soft answer turned away his wrath, but I had a most unpleasant night – I was locked away. Next morning his rage had cooled and my fear had turned to anger. I was let out and made good my escape. It was a 10-hour walk to the nearest military post – a Gurkha one – and I was never more glad to see anyone as I was to see them. I also had a better night's sleep!

In January 1964 Indonesian Mustang fighters and B-25 bombers 'buzzed' towns in Sarawak. This led to the Royal Malaysian Air Force (RMAF) and the RAF setting up an Air Defence Identification Zone. There never were any air battles, and Indonesian helicopter support for its troops in the forward areas of the jungle was never a factor to cause anything but momentary concern.

CROSS-BORDER OPERATIONS

Code-named 'Claret', these were started by the British in 1964. They were very carefully controlled by the highest authority, namely the governments of Malaysia and the United Kingdom. Initially counter-bombardment was authorized, then the formation of killer squads for special 'pursuit' tasks and finally attacks in strength up to a depth initially of 5,000, later 10,000 metres, for specific operations against enemy positions were authorized – all part of the tactic of dominating the jungle.

The operations called for great courage and skill to overcome the tensions and problems of operating behind the enemy lines, hampered by severe constraints. They were to be confined to the limits of 105mm artillery range from guns located on helicopter pads just within the friendly side of the border, although it was often not possible to take any artillery pieces at all to some places opposite the area of operations. Sometimes 5.5in medium artillery also gave supporting fire. Aircraft were not allowed to overfly the border, except in a few cases of extreme urgency, and the guns could never be deployed across it.

One main concern of all commanders engaged on these operations was the portering of their casualties back to home ground. Without the use of helicopters, commanders were often faced with the tremendous task of manhandling wounded men through very rough country, continuously nagged by the danger of being engaged, on very unfavourable terms, by the enemy. The limits to which soldiers on the ground and commanders everywhere went not to leave a wounded man behind were prodigious. One particularly vivid account of two SAS men who were contacted by superior forces when on the enemy side of the border and were wounded is given in detail in the opening chapter of *SAS: The Jungle Frontier*. Briefly two troopers, Thomson and Lillico, were both badly wounded. They managed to kill two of the enemy before they started to make their separate ways back to the emergency rendezvous. Neither knew the fate of the other and both men showed stamina, determination and self-discipline of the very highest standard and of which the rest of the army was very proud. In the event both men were rescued.

'Claret' operations had very strict 'Golden Rules' and were 'top secret'. For a short time only Gurkha battalions could be used for cross-border operations and no unit was to mount more than one raid at a time. Minimum force, preventive action and avoidance of escalation were the Director of Operation's cardinal aims – raids were not to be punitive. Without these aims and constraints, the border war would have turned into something very different, costly in lives as well as being beset with international problems. If the concept of 'Claret' had been any different, that is to say had the constraints already listed not been in force, no political authority for them would have been forthcoming.

INDONESIAN AGGRESSION AGAINST PENINSULA MALAYSIA

Indonesian efforts were not confined to Borneo. There were a number of raids on the mainland, none successful and all wrongly slanted as to the reaction to be

Left: *A watch-tower, in the morning mists, at Stass, a nodal point on the route between the capital, Kuching, and Indonesian Borneo. It was first 'blooded' in 1857 (the year of the Indian Mutiny) when dissident Chinese were captured trying to flee the country after an unsuccessful insurrection in Kuching.* (Colonel B. M. Niven)

Left: *The Natives of Borneo took an active part against the Indonesian predators. Apart from the indigenous force called the Border Scouts, each longhouse had its own defence. In the village known as Piching, in the Second Division of Sarawak, a villager plants* panjis, *hardened bamboos, against intruders.* (Colonel B. M. Niven)

Left: *After enough* panjis *have been planted, they make a very strong wall that should be impenetrable under most circumstances. Kampong Piching.* (Colonel B. M. Niven)

expected from the civilian population. Two weeks after a sea-landing, the enemy dropped nearly a hundred paratroops in north Johore, from two C-130 Hercules aircraft. Although 6 Royal Malay Regiment made the initial contacts, killing six and capturing seven in the first four days, they were recalled and sent to Singapore to counter rioting and 1/10th Gurkha Rifles were sent to continue the chase. Information was sparse and extremely inaccurate: one villager reported that 25 enemy had been seen digging on a hill near a village. Trenches were even then 3-foot deep and medium mortars had also been seen. The area was cordoned off and an assault was put in at first light on 7 September. However, nothing was found at all that the Indonesians had ever been there – the only casualty was one dead owl.

Troops moved off into the thick, hilly jungle and, as aerial photography had shown the direction of the drop from the canopies still visible on the trees and debriefing of those captured was skilful, successful contacts were soon being made. One of the Gurkhas' ruses in trying to see where camouflaged enemy were was the same as the Australians' in New Guinea over twenty years before. That was throwing a stone a little way from a suspected person and, if the reaction showed it to be a man not an animal, he was shot.

New Zealand stamina was more than amply demonstrated by Captain J. Masters of Royal New Zealand Artillery who was tasked for the forward observation of a cross-border raid by 2/2nd Gurkha Rifles. After a tense battle the Gurkhas were extricating themselves when Captain Masters, a Gurkha warrant officer, CSM Hariparsad Gurung, and a signaller became detached from the main body. The signaller made a lone escape over 10,000 yards of hostile territory without map or compass. He arrived safely but covered with blood, having killed two Indonesians who had jumped on him. In fact he got back before the rest of the company!

Masters and Hariparsad were suddenly surrounded by the enemy and the Gurkha was hit twice in the leg. The enemy closed in but Masters opened fire, wounding two of them. He managed to break contact, lift the wounded Gurkha and make for where he thought the rest of the company was. He missed the way.

All that day, in the intense heat, he carried the wounded man over his shoulder as he made his tortuous way back to the border. He was constantly held back or tripped up by the undergrowth. At one place he found himself up to his thighs in an oozing, filthy swamp. It had been a nightmare journey. In the soft mud he was able to ease his aching back by dragging Hariparsad inch by inch until he felt he was strong enough to carry him over his shoulder once more. By half-past 7 that night he decided he could go no farther. He had, unbelievably, managed to bring the wounded Gurkha through 6,000 yards of thick jungle and swamp.

Next morning, soon after he had moved off again, he realized that he could no longer carry the Gurkha. He explained that he would go for help and left his second water-bottle and the remainder of his hard tack before setting off, so at least Hariparsad could assuage his thirst and hunger. By that afternoon, more dead than alive and utterly weary, Masters reached his gun position in the Gurkha camp in Sarawak whence he had set out. CSM Hariparsad Gurung was eventually rescued (after a tremendous effort) and fully recovered the use of his wounded leg.

The pinnacle of bravery was reached in November 1965 when a young Gurkha lance-corporal, Rambahadur Limbu, 2/10th Gurkha Rifles, won a Victoria Cross, the one and only such distinction won by a Gurkha since the end of the Second World War. (The full story is written up in Harold James and Denis Sheil-Small's *The Undeclared War* and the full citation in my *In Gurkha Company*.) Two points are of note: the citation was originally not, at battalion level, submitted for that supreme award, and, owing to the strictness of censorship, the location of the action was given as being inside Sarawak when in fact it was over the border. The purpose of the raid was, as were all the others, to prevent the Indonesians from making their raids into Sarawak.

In brief there was a most detailed reconnaissance of and a most cautious approach march to the ridge around which the Indonesians were constructing their camp. It was in a commanding position, on a hill that had sheer sides and three approaches only, all along steep and narrow ridges. Two of the ridges had such thick secondary jungle on their flanks that only by cutting a tunnel through it could an approach be made. There were two barriers that had been erected to prevent any assault from being successful and the Gurkhas lost surprise below the second.

There was an immediate charge uphill and, for the next twenty minutes, Rambahadur Limbu was continuously exposed to aimed fire of automatic weapons. He managed, single-handed, to rescue two of his wounded comrades who were lying out in the open as well as clear the enemy from the scene.

> That he was able to achieve what he did against such overwhelming odds without being hit is miraculous. His outstanding personal bravery, selfless conduct, complete contempt of the enemy and determination to save the lives of the men of his fire group set an incomparable example and inspired all who saw him . . . He displayed heroism, self-sacrifice and a devotion to duty and to his men of the highest order. His actions on this day reached a zenith of determination and premeditated valour which must count amongst the most notable on record and is deserving of the greatest admiration and the highest praise.

No mere military hyperbole in that citation.

THE AMBUSH

The most successful of many ambushes was one conducted by Major C. J. Pike and his men, 1/10th Gurkha Rifles, on 27 February 1966. Pike, a small, lithe man with an eye for spoor, a nose for hunting and a cold, steady nerve, moved over the border into Kalimantan with ten days' rations to ascertain whether there were any enemy using a certain river near the border to resupply his forward troops prior to their attacking units in Sarawak. By midday on 1 March three firm bases had been established and for the next three days a detailed reconnaissance of the area was undertaken, no easy task because of swamp, thick fern, long grass and jungle, to say nothing of enemy patrols and normal civilian movement in and around the area. By 4 March firm details of the enemy had been established. Pike saw that he had a very good chance of ambushing the river traffic. Plans were then drawn up for this.

From first light on 4 March, 11 Platoon watched the river for enemy movement. The rest of the company moved their base and, working their way through a swamp that was wet enough not to show traces, came on to some dry ground 300 yards from the river. The undergrowth was thick fern, often less than head height, and the men tunnelled out a firm base underneath. As all this had to be done stealthily it took time, and it was not until noon on 5 March that all three platoons were in their ambush positions.

An hour later a landing craft-type vessel carrying 35 enemy moved downstream towards 11 Platoon, who engaged it at ten to fifteen yards' range with two machine-guns, Number 94 Energa grenades and all the platoon small arms. The result was devastating. The machine-gunner fired a 200-round belt down into the midst of the troops sitting in the boat, reloaded and ran along the bank firing from the hip as he went. The 94 grenadier registered two hits at point-blank range. As the boat passed out of the ambush it was heeling to one side. No sound from it was heard.

Almost immediately enemy fire was returned from the opposite bank and 11 Platoon was ordered to withdraw. 10 and 12 Platoons stayed where they were. After waiting four nail-biting hours the units' patience and Pike's tactics paid off as, just after 5 in the evening, two boats, one with an outboard engine towing the other, with nine Indonesians, approached 12 Platoon who opened fire at twenty yards' range killing all the enemy and sinking both boats.

The result, not less than 37 killed, was the highest number of casualties inflicted on the Indonesians in one action in the whole of Confrontation – all without loss or damage to the Gurkhas. The key to success was 'impudent daring, cold courage and determination', immaculate planning and briefing based on very detailed and painstaking reconnaissance, with every soldier knowing what to do and how to do it.

THE PATROL

In June 1966 reports circulated that a man called Sumbi, a person feared by the local people, was training about a hundred volunteers in jungle warfare, over in Kalimantan, and boasting that one day he and his men would cross the border and march to Brunei Bay and thereafter sabotage the Shell oil installations in Seria. The rumours persisted. Then, on 23 July, it was reported that Sumbi with some fifty men had moved out over the border into Sarawak for 'an unknown destination'.

The battalion opposite Sumbi's probable crossing-point was 1/7th Gurkha Rifles. Men of the Gurkha Para Company were patrolling between the battalion and the border. The country was lonely, high, cold and jungle-covered. They were told to look for any movement. One morning the patrol saw something glint on the jungle floor but, in the dew of dawn, no notice was taken. On the way back it was still glinting and one of the men spotted it. He was curious, because had it been dew it would have dried out long before. He picked it up and discovered it was tinfoil. He sniffed it and it smelt of coffee. Coffee was not a feature of Gurkha rations; British troops might have it for all the patrol knew, but there were no British troops within miles. It therefore had to be Indonesians, but there were no tracks.

The patrol cast around for a while and discovered tracks of two or three men – but they had been made by British Army jungle boots, making as though from the border northwards into Sarawak. These were followed for two days, and for this time the five men of the patrol did not make any type of supine sleeping-places for themselves at night, nor did they cook anything, fearing that the noise and the smell might give them away. It is very cold at night in the Borneo uplands.

On their third day their patience was rewarded. They found not only the three pairs of jungle boots but sacking to tie round the feet, so as not to leave any distinguishable marks, for more than 45 people. How right they were not to have relaxed their precautions! Having established that their quarry had indeed continued northwards only a short time before, they opened their radio and gave a full report to their tactical commander. To make sure there was no doubt about it being enemy, the patrol was then sent back towards the border. I, as their company commander, felt saddened that their original report had not been implicitly believed.

All but four of Sumbi's men had been accounted for when *The Times* (7 December 1966) published an account of the Sumbi incursion. It was headlined 'Courage of the Gurkhas Foiled Saboteurs' and it continued: 'Details of one of the most brilliant actions in the history of the Gurkhas have just been released.' The Gurkha officer who was with his company commander when Sumbi was captured was aggrieved because he had been graded 'C' – average – on a jungle warfare course at the Jungle Warfare School yet Sumbi, who had been a student there, had been awarded a 'B' – above average – grading!

The Gurkha Independent Parachute Company was reformed into a 'Patrol Company' on its return to the mainland after it had finished training Border Scout leaders. I commanded the unit and fully supported the organization of 5-man patrols unlike the 4-man patrols operated by the Parachute Regiment, the Guards Independent Parachute Company and the squadrons of 22 SAS. Its main role was to take an airhead and for that we had to have 128 soldiers. That number could not be reduced, nor could the type of radio required on patrol be supplied in any greater numbers than would support sixteen patrols, the control element at base, sets required on detachment and a couple of spares. We also had to operate in a conventional rifle company role. Tactically we preferred one commander and four men (medical orderly, two combat pioneers and radio operator): all were linguists and patrol commanders could manage all three skills. In emergencies – carrying a man on a stretcher, for example – the fifth man was very useful. Finally, had we only had four men in each patrol, we would have had to find something else for the remaining sixteen men to do!

THE END OF CONFRONTATION

In October 1965 a Communist *coup* to seize control of the Government in Indonesia had been foiled within five hours. Sukarno's powers were then curtailed. On 23 May 1966 an Indonesian goodwill mission went to Kuala Lumpur with a message of peace and, after considerable discussions and not a little face saving, Confrontation officially ended at noon on 11 August 1966, 'not with a bang but a whimper'.

After it was over, everyone in Malaysia had to stay in camp, waiting for orders for the peacetime pull-out. We, in the Gurkha Para Company were not in Malaysia, but in Brunei where these cease-fire orders did not apply. We were, therefore, still operational. The Brunei Government wanted to know if the last of Sumbi's gang, the four men, had infiltrated into Brunei or had died in the Sarawak jungle. In an area of wild country that could have been anything from 500 to 2,500

Right: A view of an Iban longhouse by the Sungei Menuang. More than one hundred families live in it. Each family has its own fighting cockerel which is looked after with great care. Of an early morning the air is made cacophonous as each tries to out-crow the others. Entrance into these houses is made either up steps, as here, or up a pole with notches cut in it. Part of the troops' task was to ensure that the inhabitants of longhouses were sufficiently pro-government to give early warning of any incursion or suspicious happenings. (PR FARELF)

Right: An airstrip was fashioned at Belaga, many miles up the River Rejang. It was because there was an airstrip here that reinforcements were able to be flown into Kampong Jawi, miles to the south and the nearest habitation to the Indonesian border, after a successful Indonesian attack that heavily outnumbered and killed Gurkhas and Native Border Scouts. (Museum of Army Flying)

Right: 248 Gurkha Signal Squadron manned a re-broadcast site at the top of a 2,988-foot mountain, called Gunong Serapi, in Sarawak. It was a most uncomfortable existence as there was nowhere easy to go for any exercise, the site would be cloud-girt and clammy for most of the time and a strict watch had to be maintained. Patience, diligence and skill were all required for success. (Royal Signals Museum)

square miles, the odds against finding four men were infinitely remote. None the less, a patrol was sent to the border of Brunei and Sarawak, a ridge of hilly jungle, to see what it could pick up. One of the soldiers needed evacuating and, pressure of other duties off, I flew in to take his place.

The corporal in charge of the patrol put me as number 4 and off we went along the border ridge. The jungle was dark and damp. It had been raining. We travelled slowly, keeping our eyes skinned. And then I saw it! A single leaf, one of a myriad in all that vast expanse of jungle, caught my eye. It had an unnatural crease making its outline straight. Nature abhors anything straight so the crease in this leaf was not the produce of nature. Man must have made it, yet we were the only people supposed to be anywhere in the area. There was a very slim chance that it was Sumbi's last four men; one of them might even be a 'leaf doodler' – one who picks at leaves and sticks, plays around with them without realizing it, then discards them. I called the corporal's attention to it and we cast around even more thoroughly. Our search revealed more suspicious signs, moving away from us into the area of the Royal Brunei Malay Regiment (RBMR) on our flank. A message was sent to them, alerting them as to the possibility of trespassers.

I got a message the next night from their commanding officer, an old friend of mine, who had spent all his life till then in the Gurkhas. 'Why', I was asked, 'are you frightening my soldiers by pretending to be a ghost?' Working, as we were, on Morse Code prevented me from sending a fitting retort. All I could do was to send a 'Wilco . . . Out'.

We met soon after I left the jungle. The RBMR soldiers knew that I was on their flank. The day we found the leaf they had sent a few men to get water from a stream to cook their evening meal. Approaching a thick bush, a voice, speaking in English, ordered them to stop, turn round and go away. This they had done and, on reflection, reported that a ghost had spoken to them; how could a voice, disembodied and unexpected, have been made by anything else? The commanding officer knew better but, still unconvinced that what we had found was correct, presumed that I had tracked the prints of some local Ibans into his company's area and, out of sheer impishness, pretended I was ethereal.

In fact four Indonesians did emerge from where we had been patrolling and, almost dead from starvation, went to an Iban longhouse in the valley below to ask for food. As they were eating, the soldiers were fetched and captured them. They were indeed the last of Sumbi's gang and, at their interrogation, one of them admitted that he did have a habit of plucking leaves, folding them and then discarding them.

I have yet to find out the exact wording of the citation for RBMR's only battle honour.

The ratio of Gurkhas to British troops was about 2:1. Peak strengths of the security forces in Borneo were 14,000 Commonwealth troops in country, with a further 10,000 immediately available. Service casualties were 114 killed, 118 wounded, while civilian casualties were 36 killed, 53 wounded and 4 captured. Minimum enemy casualties were 590 killed, 222 wounded and 771 captured. There could have been as many as 24,000 Chinese sympathizers giving support to 22,000 Indonesian regular troops.

In the House of Commons, the Secretary of State for Defence had this to say about Confrontation: 'In the history books it will be recorded as one of the the the most efficient uses of military force in the history of the world.' He also paid tribute to the men of the British and Commonwealth nations who fought in Malaysia:

> . . . the campaign has been a model of inter-Service co-operation; all three Services have worked as one. We should pay tribute to all those, from the highest to the lowest rank, who have served alongside the forces of our Commonwealth partners and who have made so signal a contribution to the settlement that has been achieved. I should like to add a special tribute to the Gurkhas.'

In November 1975, as the defence attaché in Laos, I watched the Pathet Lao Communists consolidate their political victory – after the North Vietnamese Army had won their military fight for them. I was talking to the Indonesian chargé d'affaires, who had been on the army staff during confrontation, about CRW. He told me that, in retrospect, the Indonesians regarded 'Confrontation' as excellent practice for any future war against the Communists and were grateful to the British for teaching them to be better soldiers.

THE EMERGENCY AND CONFRONTATION: A PERSPECTIVE

This is the title of a foreword to the 7th Gurkha Rifles regimental history (*East of Kathmandu*, by Brigadier E. D. Smith) written, in 1976, by the Colonel of the Regiment, General Sir Walter Walker, who was the Director of Borneo Operations from December 1962 until March 1965. Although it was written for a Gurkha history, its message extends to all infantrymen. It is a trenchant piece of writing by a man who has a better understanding both of Communist aims and of jungle warfare than most and, for brevity, clarity and depth of knowledge I know of none better. It was he who chose me to be Commandant of the Border Scouts. As not many readers of this book will have read it in its full and original form, and as I never had any experience at any level above colonel, I can do no better than to quote from relevant passages:

> No one in his right senses would expect me to indulge in whitewashing or to conceal the truth. My aim . . . is to highlight the lessons to be learnt in the hope that those who follow, and who undoubtedly will find themselves involved in future similar contests, will be able to profit from the successes and failures of their predecessors.
>
> . . . the fundamental trouble was that within two years of defeating the Japanese in Burma [where the General commanded 4/8th Gurkha Rifles], all our military training and thinking had become focused on nuclear and conventional tactics for a European theatre against a first-class enemy. So, when the Malayan Emergency broke out, we had forgotten most of jungle warfare techniques and expertise, learned the hard way at such cost in the Burma campaign. The authorities fell into the same trap in the short interval between the end of the Malayan Emergency and the outbreak of the Brunei revolt followed by Indonesian Confrontation.
>
> The Whitehall Warriors imagined that 'Jungle Exercises Without Trees' on Salisbury Plain were a suitable rehearsal for jungle operations, forgetting that the jungle is such that if a soldier loses sight of the sweat-stained back of the man in front, he loses his way. The military tactics of guerrillas was something quite new within the accepted pattern of warfare – surprise attack by the enemy against soft targets, then withdrawal in the face of opposition to the sanctuary of the jungle. In the West, the army's training in nuclear and conventional tactics depend for its

Left: River crossing in Borneo was an essential part of operations and it involved many methods, most of which got one wet. In this instance, the man pulling the improvised stretcher has tied it round him to prevent it drifting apart; the casualty with a bandaged arm is thereby kept dry. (Colonel B. M. Niven)

Left: In Borneo troops had to dig in; this was more reminiscent of Burma and never needed in the Malayan Emergency. Here troops of 'B' Company, 1/10th Gurkha Rifles, dig in at the Jambu base, in the Second Division of Sarawak. In Jambu live some of the most intractable of all Ibans – the headhunters of Borneo. It was in this area that the author was nearly decapitated. (Colonel B. M. Niven)

mobility on roads, railways, water and air. By contrast, in guerrilla warfare roads, railways and rivers are the ambusher's paradise, even when convoys obey all the safety rules. But troops who are able to move secretly, mostly in small groups, making rendezvous only at the precise moment of battle, cannot be ambushed.

That was the way our Gurkhas [and, indeed, every well-trained infantryman] learned to move and they learnt to do it better than the guerrillas. They were able to out-guerrilla the enemy in every department of the game, through sheer good training and tremendous self-discipline, based on operational experience. Although this was mainly the platoon and section commanders' war, nevertheless it was the company commander who had to be able to set the example and do everything that his men could do, do it better and do it for longer.

Unlike the American policy of 'Search and Destroy' and then return to base, the Gurkha technique in Borneo was 'Clear, Hold and Dominate'. Results could not be achieved merely by attacking and shooting the enemy and then returning to base. He had to be played at his own game, by living out in the jungle for weeks on end, by winning the hearts and minds of the people and planting our own agents in villages known to be unfriendly. In these conditions, the Gurkha carried his base on his back, and it consisted of a featherweight plastic sheet, a sockful of rice and a pocketful of ammunition. The jungle belonged to him: he owned it, controlled it and dominated it by day and night for nights on end.

Domination of the jungle was achieved via the ambush which was at one and the same time the guerrillas' and our most potent weapon. Whether on a small or large scale, it was the key element. An ambush is merely another word for 'fighting

Right: The west of Sarawak was much thinner than the centre and the east. There space could not be sold for time and early warning against Indonesian depredations was at a premium. Near Tebakang, in the Second Division, 'B' Company, 1/10th Gurkha Rifles, manned an operations/communications tower in their base camp. (Colonel B. M. Niven)

from ground of one's own choosing', but with the difference that it depends on complete surprise. The enemy must be unaware that he is walking into a trap. An ambush required all the tricks of the Gurkhas' trade: an eye for country, tracking skills, marksmanship, guile, cunning and, above all, self-discipline. It required constant training and rehearsal. There was no chance of ambushing the enemy if the Gurkha smoked, chewed gum, washed his hands with soap, 'Brylcreemed' his hair, whispered or coughed. In ambush, a man is lying in wait for a dangerous, hunted animal whose sense of smell and keen eyesight were phenomenal.

The Regiment[s] gradually devised tactical techniques and battle skills which would have done credit to a cat-burglar, gangster, gunman and poacher. The Gurkhas were able to do so, and became so well-trained that they were able to fight the guerrillas both in the jungle and out of it, and to kill and harry them until they were utterly exhausted. The type of fighting, the type of country and the climate called for individual stamina and fortitude, stout legs, stout hearts, fertile brains, and the acceptance of battlefield conditions almost unimaginable in their demands on human endurance.

. . . the Gurkha made great use of deception and guile, never doing the same thing twice. His objective was to dominate and own the jungle and the frontier, week in, week out, day and night. Unlike the Americans in Vietnam, there were no 'Prince Rupert' tactics of galloping over the jungle canopy in helicopters. Company and platoon commanders used all their skill and guile (for example by contour flying to get within striking distance of the enemy by helicopter), but without being seen or heard. Then the Gurkhas tracked him down, stalking and closing in on their feet for the kill. The sure way to beat a guerrilla is to operate more quietly, smoke less, and talk less to possible enemy agents before an operation. Victory in guerrilla warfare goes to the tougher, more resourceful soldier and the more gadget-filled our life becomes the harder it is to produce him . . .

The lesson to be learnt from counter-insurgency operations is that terrorists fighting a guerrilla-type war can tie up lavishly equipped, modern, regular forces ten times their number in strength. Moscow and Peking have never under-estimated guerrilla power [this was written before the Russian invasion of Afghanistan]. Russian and Chinese hands . . . are pulling strings of terrorism. Revolutionaries everywhere are all in the Communist net. This is what the Russians and the Chinese call 'revolutionary war by proxy' – getting the local Communist Party to do their dirty work for them. The lesson of Cambodia, of the French in Indo-China, of the Portuguese in Africa and the Americans in Vietnam, is crystal clear. It is that well-equipped armies, sophisticated military operations and air power, are no protection against guerrilla tactics. By contrast our counter-insurgency operations in Malaya and Borneo were a complete success.

In Vietnam an over-sophisticated American Army and Air Force, which dropped four times more bombs than they did in the whole of the Second World War, failed to win a limited guerrilla war against puny men of a puny nation . . . They were outfought and outwitted not only in battle but also at the Paris peace negotiations and in their evacuation plan with their mighty rescue armada. In Washington they were divided and paralyzed as well. The United States poured into Vietnam eight years of effort, the lives of 50,000 young men, the good health of another 300,000, $150 billion of their hard-earned tax money and the honour and prestige of their nation.

It is easy to see why the Soviets wanted to keep the war going. While America spent $150 billion on weapons that are now down the drain in Vietnam, the Soviets spent an equivalent amount on nuclear weapons to control the world. History will be left to explain America's decision to fight a costly no-win war (or could it have been won?) that left South-East Asia in far worse condition than it was before American intervention began.

In both Malaya and Borneo the enemy was at least as formidable as the Vietcong in the early 1960s, and Indonesia just as strong militarily as North Vietnam. If either campaign had been mismanaged, we too could have had a Vietnam on our hands. The Borneo campaign stands out as being a notable example of how highly trained professional infantrymen can achieve a decisive victory against a well-armed, aggressive and unscrupulous enemy with little bloodshed to ourselves, little destruction of the countryside and with so little disruption of normal life of the civilian population that reversion to peacetime conditions at the end of hostilities was virtually automatic.

There was no bombing interdiction, no napalm or defoliation of the jungle. No wonder the Commonwealth Forces were welcomed for the social and economic benefits they brought to the jungle villages. By mastering the physical conditions, by securing the willing help of the inhabitants, the campaigns . . . were won without the people at home or the world at large realizing the extent of the fighting soldiers' achievements.

So whether an unconventional or conventional war is fought, it is the man on the ground who is the final arbiter of success or victory, if he is allowed to politically by the civilians or militarily by his generals. Yet, without training, the soldier is as nothing. The few units that can still train in the jungles of Brunei and Belize must remember the General's words – there is *no other way* to win wars at CRW level in the jungle. Sweat still saves blood.

IV
JUNGLE CRAFT AND
THE FUTURE

Previous page: The jungles of Belize are 'dirtier' than much of Asia's, with more than their share of poisonous insects. Water can be a problem, both for drinking and crossing. (British Army PR)

Left: Brunei is an ideal place for training, there being both jungle, swamp and open spaces. The General-Purpose Machine-Gun (GPMG) is here being fired in the Sustained Fire role by men of Support Company, 2/2nd Gurkha Rifles. During Confrontation these weapons were used to defend company bases, known as forts. In the jungle they were too heavy to carry under normal circumstances and the Bren gun, then no longer in service, was reissued for foot operations. (Colonel C. J. D. Bullock)

Left: Belted ammunition is loaded into the GPMG by two soldiers of Support Company, 2/2nd Gurkha Rifles, undergoing training. (Colonel C. J. D. Bullock)

Left: One Support Company weapon was the 84mm Carl Gustav, a recoilless anti-armour weapon which fired High-Explosive Anti-Tank, High-Explosive or Illuminating rounds. In Brunei it was looked on as a 'bunker buster'. Men of Support Company, 2/2nd Gurkha Rifles, practise firing it in 1968; it was due to be replaced by the Light Anti-Armour (LAW) 80 during 1987–8. (Colonel C. J. D. Bullock)

10
Jungle Craft

Threats to governments can come both externally and internally. Since 1945 many governments have been threatened by guerrillas based in the jungle. In simple terms, the ingredients seem to have been like this: the victim country had at least one border across which was a sanctuary, probably a long sea coast, jungle or mountains and guerrilla-dominated areas. The government of the victim country invited another friendly government to help it. The ensuing pattern was a forward operational base being established by seizing and holding small areas of terrain suited for such a task. It was then expanded. This was often known as 'clear and secure'. Once this area had been dominated, offensive operations and deep penetration were carried out, searching for the enemy and destroying him while the police tried to eliminate his infrastructure. Once advances became critical, another forward operational base was established, the area previously having been seized and held. Thus the cycle developed. (Sir Robert Thompson's book *Defeating Communist Insurgency* is an exemplary dissertation on the whole problem.)

As have already been described, the main ingredients in jungle warfare, especially CRW, are the enemy, terrain and climate. I see the fighting in three categories: first, the security forces maintain a presence in the threatened area, dominating the jungle by constantly patrolling and ambushing against an enemy who does not want to stand and fight so must therefore be found and surrounded before being eliminated by being killed or captured. Then there is the enemy with an aggressive nature who still has to be hunted, but who will fight it out when met up with, so must be overwhelmed by conventional fire and movement, even though the advance is yard by yard, from tree trunk to tree trunk. The third category is when the security forces are the hunted and anyone who has been hunted will know that it is a most adrenalin-pumping experience.

For success in all three, surprise, secrecy and security, often in complete silence, are essential. This results in new or modified drills being used for observation, formations, hand-signals, fields of fire, halt procedures, weapons at the ready, sentries, harbouring, immediate action drills when ambushed on foot, in motor transport and in river craft or when faced with a sudden head-on contact. Fire discipline is vital. The enemy must never be helped by security forces making more noise than is necessary, by not leaving smells behind when cooking, shaving or smoking, by disguising true strengths, by not leaving any litter and by not doodling with leaves and twigs. Over and above all military requirements, intelligence, integrity and self-discipline are at a permanent premium.

All this is inculcated by hard, rigorous and realistic **training** for full combat-worthiness – to allow immediate and instinctively correct reaction to any situation, despite being tired, wet, hungry, afraid and outnumbered. The principles remain constant, but the unusual factors demand a deep and detailed knowledge of navigation, patrolling, ambushing, ability to infiltrate, stay-behind techniques, tracking (with or without dogs), crossing obstacles, watermanship, combat engineering and continuous battle security; the correct use of information either by radio or patrolling for a pattern of enemy movement to be established; correct use of air and armour; and, ever important, soldiers must know not only how to treat the civil population but they must understand the government's 'hearts and minds' programme. This is a difficult, protracted experience and a frustrating job which should be sponsored and controlled by government. The soldiers' job is to treat the civilians normally and help where possible: all this must be enhanced by being a crack shot, good health, jungle fitness and high morale, with self-discipline an indispensable prerequisite. A soldier must not only know his enemy, he must know his friends and he must know himself. None of this can happen overnight.

The British Army's Jungle Warfare School, which was located north of Singapore island in peninsula Malaysia, had a reputation for simple, sensible and basic infantry training at platoon and company levels in tropical rain forest terrain. It was constituted in 1948 but had its roots as a battle school and reinforcement unit in Burma. In Malaya its first commandant was Lieutenant-Colonel (later General Sir Walter) W. C. Walker – the first Director of Operations in Borneo against Indonesian Confrontation – and I its last. I recently came across a quotation I used there when lecturing soldiers: 'The greatest risk in living dangerously, rock-climbing, motor-racing, big-game hunting or operating against an enemy, is, through over-confidence or exhaustion, to relax vigilance, and not to take every little precaution on which life depends.' That is ever true.

The way the school operated was to train both individuals and instructors to train their men of their own units. During the Malayan Emergency battalions from Africa, Australia, New Zealand and Fiji as well as from the United Kingdom were employed on operations. Each battalion sent a training advance party of 20 to 30 men and these would spend six weeks at the school. They would then train their own men when the unit arrived in a camp near the school, which provided training areas and umpires on exercises. As regards individuals, students from eighteen countries came to the school.

Techniques were constantly evolved and improved on as information of enemy tactics and methods became available. Lessons from Vietnam were incorporated in the syllabus as Australians and New Zealand instructors with Vietnam experience joined the staff.

In addition to 'straight' infantry courses, visual tracking and tracker-dog handlers' courses were run. The Americans sent their soldiers for combined tracking courses and, once back in Vietnam, these men had a bigger price on their heads than other Americans. I gather that none was lost. The school also established South Korea's dog tracking school.

The nearest equivalent that the Australian Army has is the Jungle Training Centre in Canungra, Queensland. This is a bigger set-up and copes with much more than mere jungle training, despite its name. The Americans had a similar

Above: In swamp it is never easy to get into a 'copybook' fire position. In the words of the company commander, who took the photograph, '. . . so I gave the signal for each man to take up the best fire position he could in the mud and water'. One rifleman of Support Company, 2/2nd Gurkha Rifles, takes aim . . . while **(below)** another keeps his powder dry although he has wet feet. (Colonel C. J. D. Bullock)

Below: Three men of the Gurkha Independent Parachute Company training to crossing a river in Brunei prior to going on a long-range patrol over the border into Indonesia. There were always many more volunteers from the recruits than could be absorbed within the company. The company had three roles: capturing a lightly-held airstrip by parachute descent; deep reconnaissance in 5-man patrols; and conventional infantry. It was the author's turn to cross after this. (Gurkha Museum)

jungle training place in Panama until it became too political an issue to keep it there. Florida now has similar training facilities. In the early 1980s state National Guard units were sent to Honduras, during their annual 2-week tours of duty. As they were engaged in jungle warfare training as well as making airstrips and roads many thought that they were preparing for military action against Nicaragua. Similar combat training in Honduras was refused to 450 Californian guardsmen in 1985.

I have visited Royal Thai Army Special Force junge warfare training centres – a joint effort with the US Green Berets – and was quizzed on it afterwards by the Deputy Supreme Commander of the Royal Thai Army. Similarly, I have visited ARVN Ranger and US Special Force jungle warfare training establishments in South Vietnam, the latter using live ammunition. I have had dealings with training or operations in Communist-held jungle by the Royal Lao Army. I have debriefed a surrendered Pathet Lao and a North Vietnamese adviser in Vientiane ('ralliers') about their tactics and have come the conclusion that the tactics we taught at the Jungle Warfare School for CRW at the active phase and low-intensity operations as occurred in Borneo (as opposed to a major war at Burma campaign standards) and the services provided for the British Army were better than any other. After

Below: Royal Air Force air crews had to be taught how to survive if they were forced down in jungle – hostile or friendly. Many of them were trained at the Far East Air Force (FEAF) Survival and Parachute School in Changi on Singapore Island. In the early 1970s the Jungle Warfare School took over this commitment. 10-day courses were run in south Malay(si)a. An overnight sleeping platform and shelter have to be constructed. A jack-knife and webbing are kept in the roof, while the fine nylon cord used to tie things up has the dual purpose of being used for fishing nets. (Major H. V. Gilpin)

Below centre: Flight Lieutenant 'Kip' Gilpin, the Chief Instructor, slept on a bed made from a stretcher. The cloth was impervious to leeches, and Signal markers, blue and orange, were used as a canopy. (Major H. V. Gilpin, alias Flight Lieutenant 'Kip' Gilpin)

Far right: *The fireplace, shielded from the wind by wood, which is also drying. Tins were burnt to prevent animals from rootling after they had been buried. (Major H. V. Gilpin)*

the Jungle Warfare School left Malaysia it was re-established on more modest lines in Brunei.

I have already mentioned how cavalier is the French approach to jungle operations. (When, in Laos, American advisers asked the Lao generals why there were always so many details left unplanned the answer was always, 'Oh, we learnt it that way from the French.') One of the major differences between American and British attitudes to training is the ratio of instructors to students. For the former it is one instructor for 100, or at times 200, soldiers, except for special forces, when it is one to ten. This is the British ratio for all training.

Another difference is the emphasis that the British put on human endeavour rather than on machines. British training is hard – as the good little girl said to the bad little girl, 'Is it hard to be good?', the bad little girl said to the good little girl, 'It's got to be hard to be good!' – and results show the wisdom of making mistakes on training rather than in action. This is one reason why standards, especially in oriental armies where junior officers are reluctant to expose their inexperience in front of their soliders, are not as high as might be expected because 'face' – 'that display of public potency which makes for personal credit' – can be lost when mistakes are made.

An infantry soldier's job is one of the very few that does not provide for dress rehearsals before the real thing. As in almost no other activity, the youngest and most inexperienced command in the army, the platoon commander, is the one that contacts the enemy first. The more experienced a commander becomes, the farther away from the enemy he serves.

Realism in training has its risks to be sure. Balancing safety precautions without frustrating an exercise is not easy. At the end of our last exercise for South Vietnamese army officers, the Gurkhas were dressed as Vietminh, that is to say, in black pyjamas. One of the attacking Vietnamese saw one such man lying 'dead' at the edge of the camp and, such was the realism, went up the 'body' and kicked it in the teeth. There was a struggle: it took three of us to keep the Gurkha under control. He then said that he either had to kick the Vietnamese equally

Left: There was a jungle village in the Jungle Warfare School grounds which was modelled on the lines of what the Vietminh did: there were false walls, false fireplaces and false ceilings to the houses and there was a well with a connecting passage below the water level that emerged some distance away in the scrub. Next to it was a 'booby-trap lane' in which all types of traps found in Vietnam were exhibited and could be activated. In 1970 the author discovered that local 'baddies', reinforcements for guerrilla activity to the north of the country, were using the facility for themselves. Here demonstration troops (from the Gurkha Independent Parachute Company) search suspects, having first rendered them 'safe'. (Gurkha Museum)

Left: Vietminh-type tunnels were a feature of training in the Jungle Warfare School. A visiting General talks to the author (the Commandant) about various aspects of training troops under these conditions. (PR FARELF)

Left: An all-party Parliamentary delegation learns the difference between the various types of south-east Asian combatants at the Jungle Warfare School. The author points out the finer points of Gurkhas dressed as: an Indonesian Border Terrorist (IBT), a Vietminh guerrilla and a 'main force' Vietnamese soldier. To other audiences a film was also normally shown, with noisy sound effects: no bangs were allowed this time as they might have caused unwarranted by-elections! (PR FARELF)

hard in the teeth or cut his head off with a kukri. His eyes were red: the Vietnamese looked green. The Gurkha then tried to draw his kukri from his scabbard but was restrained by a man specially detailed to prevent him. It was an ugly and tense situation that I (only) just managed to contain by getting the two to shake hands. It was like trying to get the knotted handkerchief in the middle of a tug-of-war rope over the centre mark!

Apart from details of platoon organization and equipment – some of the items carried were specially for the jungle* – each army had its own inventory of **weapons**.** Silent weapons were not carried: a few were kept for very special tasks but they were not of general value. A silently shot bullet lacks distance and velocity and, in the case of an automatic, the working parts clattered so loudly it was not worthwhile using them. It is to be noted that nowhere is any mention of British Army booby-traps; these were specifically forbidden although teaching was given. Jungle clothing and equipment were as light as could be, with a view to durability. The major training aspect in weaponry was not so much the inventory – although a proper understanding of their characteristics in tropical jungle had to be realized – but their firing. The construction of jungle ranges was always of prime importance, not only from an ordinary shooting point of view, but with the aim of speeding up reflexes.

Fire discipline is ever important. A British battalion fresh from England completed its training and, as a final exercise, was given the task of laying a night ambush on a road running through jungle. It was possible that guerrillas might cross over it. At 10 o'clock that night one of the sentries thought he saw enemy movement and opened fire. The enemy returned the fire, using tracer and a battle royal developed. In the morning the brigadier told me about it, confident that the battalion had been well bloodied and that many of the enemy should have been killed. No bodies had been recovered. I suggested that, before going to have a look himself, he send a message to the commander of the troops to collect the empty cases of the ammunition that the enemy had expended. A message to this effect was sent. The brigadier (brave, pompous and always right) told me to get into his Land Rover and we drove out to the scene of the action.

Nothing. No empties. No casualties. No guerrillas. The man who first fired had mistaken shadows for men, The sound of his shots for enemy fire and his own tracer bullets ricochetting as that of the enemy's. Disgruntled we drove away, the brigadier driving, I sitting next to him. We passed a group of rubber trappers laughing.

'Do you know why they are laughing?' I asked.

No, he didn't. 'Because, when they saw the flag fluttering, they thought that you were the driver and I the brigadier.'

---

*These included hexamine cookers, water sterilizing outfits, mite repellent, canvas 'Millbank' bags (to filter water), bags for food, water and packs, mosquito-nets, a folding saw, 100 feet of nylon rope and a large cutting knife.

**British Army platoon weapons that were 'special to theatre' included: 7.62mm self-loading rifle, AR 15 (Armalite) rifle, 7.62mm Bren LMG, 7.62mm GPMG, 9mm SMG, Shot-gun (various types), 3.5in rocket-launcher, 84mm anti-tank gun (Carl Gustav), 2in mortar, M26 grenade, 36 grenade, 80 (WP) grenade, 83 (coloured smoke) grenade, 94 grenade (Energa), Claymore mine and Very pistol.

Fire control is not the only sort of control required, as I later learnt to my cost when I read what the brigadier had written about me in my annual confidential report!

Booby-traps, cunning contrivances usually of an explosive and lethal nature designed to catch the enemy unawares, are savage practical jokes. Their use reduces morale and mobility by creating fear, uncertainty and suspicion in the minds of those against whom they are used. They work by pressure, pulling, release or delay. In Burma simple booby-traps with grenades were used, some types of which are shown on the opposite page.

In the 'tinned' or 'canned' method, one end and part of a side of the tin were cut away. A hole was made in the remaining end of the tin through which the trip-wire was attached. The operation of such traps was simple. The safety-pin was removed after the grenade had been primed, with the striker lever held down so that the grenade did not explode. It was then inserted into the cut-out can so that the striker lever was held inside the remaining circular portion of the can. The grenade and the can were held together and placed so that a pull on the trip-wire withdrew the grenade from its holder, when it would explode.

Refinements could be introduced by balancing the container so that the grenade fell out when the can fell over.

Apart from animal traps, which were adapted for use as booby-traps, seven improvised types are shown on the facing page as examples of what could be done. The information is taken from posters prepared by the United States 7th Air Force for distribution to its squadrons in Vietnam.

Barbed spike plates were common. They were easily made and were placed anywhere and it was most unlikely that the trap was seen before damage was done. The points could be tipped with poison, such as human excrement. Bamboo arch traps were usually found along jungle trails and were suspended in the overhead foliage. Once the trip-wire was pulled, a man had from 3–5 seconds to get out of range of the blast. Fragments from the grenade were thrown great distances due to the height above ground. These traps were particularly effective at night.

In grenade daisy-chains, the trip-wire was camouflaged across the track and, when pulled, the first grenade detonated. This broke the wire to the second grenade whose safety-pin had already been extracted. This second grenade broke the string to the third and so on. Apart from being a trap, it was an excellent warning device. Bridge spike traps were positioned so that, when weight was exerted on the bridge, the weakened portion collapsed and the victim was impaled on the *panji* stakes below. *Panji* 'bear' traps were concealed under brushwood or leaves on the track. When the victim walked over the trap, his leg plunged down into the pit, pivoting on the boards, which closed on his leg, which, in turn, was wounded by the spikes above the level of the ankle. These traps were found mainly along tracks, dykes and around heavily foliaged areas and were particularly effective against a lone traveller. Cartridge traps were easily set up and were very effective. The head of the round was the only part exposed; pressure exerted on the tip set the round off. These traps were capable of killing, wounding or removing a foot and were also particularly effective against a lone

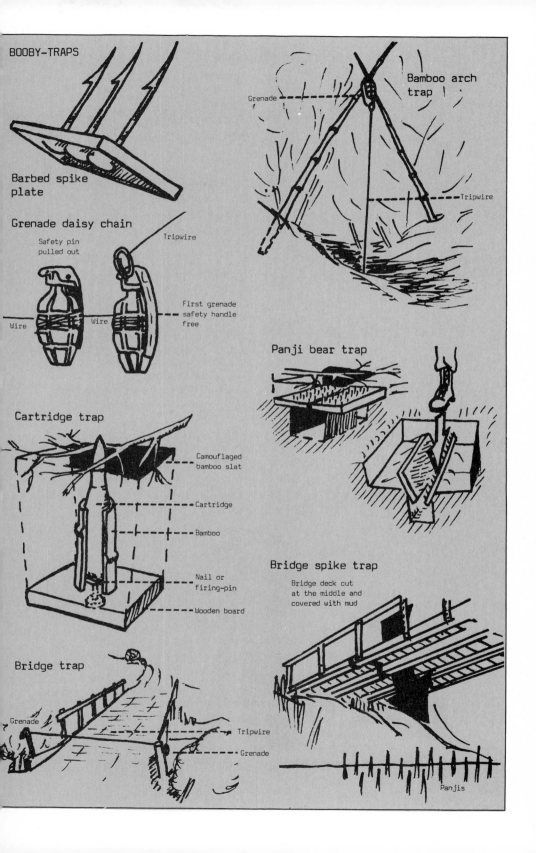

BOOBY-TRAPS

Barbed spike plate

Bamboo arch trap

Grenade

Tripwire

Grenade daisy chain

Safety pin pulled out

Tripwire

Wire

Wire

First grenade safety handle free

Panji bear trap

Cartridge trap

Camouflaged bamboo slat

Cartridge

Bamboo

Nail or firing-pin

Wooden board

Bridge spike trap

Bridge deck cut at the middle and covered with mud

Bridge trap

Grenade

Tripwire

Grenade

Panjis

traveller. They were found on tracks, dykes, paths or anywhere where natural foliage is available. In Bridge traps, when the trip-wire was pulled, the grenades on each side of the bridge entrance exploded within 3–5 seconds and fragments hit the victim from both sides. Traps were also found along a trail. They were used extensively in the Mekong delta area, rather than in thick jungle. The use of booby-traps was forbidden to British and Commonwealth troops in Malaya and Borneo, but the Indonesians did use them.

Navigation is something that needed constant practise and, initially in thick jungle, it seemed as though no method of finding the way really worked. A commander needs a map and compass as a blind man a white stick and a guide-dog. The elements of navigation are keeping direction and knowing the distance travelled. Study of up-to-date air photographs always pays dividends. Everybody has a bias, to right or left, when walking. To find out which, bind the eyes and walk across a flat piece of ground. Checking features from the map is a good way of knowing where you are, but accuracy should never be taken for granted without collateral evidence. During one operation in Malaya I once found myself trying to meet up with another company on a specific hill feature but neither of us met the other. It was only much later that we discovered that an 'extra' hill existed on the ground! The flow of a stream is a much surer guide than any track, which should always be treated with suspicion.

Speed of movement is another aid in navigation: very roughly, tactical movement through primary jungle is about 1,000 yards (a map square) an hour, but slows down to as little as 100 when moving through swamps. Obstacles, such as a swamp, need to be bypassed. This is easy enough only if compass work and counting paces are accurate.

Radio communications need to be known about. Atmospheric conditions are bad in the high-frequency band. A lot of interference, especially at night, is experienced and this often makes the set unworkable. Similarly, dense vegetation often makes it difficult to erect efficient antennae. Very-high-frequency sets suffer from being screened. Re-broadcast stations, allowing for direct 'line of sight'

Left: A rifleman of 2/2nd Gurkha Rifles demonstrates a man trap. It would crash down from its hidden position in a tree and impale the person below. (Gurkha Museum)

Right: Senior officers from the Royal Thai Army are briefed about British Army methods. Men from all five continents came to the Jungle Warfare School. In his 3½ years there, the author had an average of eight visitors, of all sorts, every five working days. (PR FARELF)

communications as used in Borneo, are one answer. With the spread of modern technology better sets are being produced.

Living off the land is a subject in itself and survival techniques can only be touched on here. On occasions individuals and groups of men will find themselves in a situation where normal food is either in short supply or is totally lacking. This can happen when lost on a patrol, when enemy action has disrupted normal methods of supply or when 'on the run' from being captured or being chased. In my own experience, you either survive successfully and forfeit tactical advantages or you remain tactically sound but cannot survive properly.

Food can be got from animals, fish, insects and vegetables and, unless eaten raw, has to be cooked, so fire making and food preparation are needed. Finding potable water, the prime life giver, must not be taken for granted. The type of food available obviously depend on the habitat searched. The way I used to test if the plant I did not know was poisonous was to rub it gently on the inner side of my lip and if it burnt I would not touch it further. On a more complex level numerous traps can be constructed which will enable animals of widely varying sizes to be caught – this however is an art which takes time to acquire.

Overnight shelters are of different types, depending on how many people they must house. It is as valid as ever to state that the better the night's sleep, the more favourable are the chances of a decent performance the next day. It is vital when making temporary shelters to ensure you remain dry; the poncho or Australian light-weight sheet offers the soldier the opportunity to create some six basic designs which, if properly built, will ensure sleep uninterrupted by weather.

Harbouring, that is to say the establishment of an overnight halt, is essential in jungle where frequently there is no obvious enemy line of approach and an attack could come from any direction. No unit can consider itself secure when it stops for the night unless it ensures it has all-round protection and that there are no enemy in the immediate vicinity. The technique was used in New Guinea with battalions, in Burma with brigades, notably in Chindit columns, and adapted for use in Malaya and Borneo by small units. It is a long process and I found that a

Above left: Men of the Gurkha Independent Parachute Company, who acted as demonstration troops/exercise enemy at the Jungle Warfare School at the very end of their existence (they were disbanded in 1971) had a distinctive uniform: the red beret and badge of the airborne forces and a rifle-green flash with the colours of the Brigade of Gurkhas behind it. Sergeant Bhuibahadur Rai, 7th Gurkha Rifles, had served with the author ever since he joined the army, some fifteen years earlier. (PR FARELF)

Above right: 'Happiness is an open parachute'. Th airstrip at Kankar Kahang, in south Malaysia, allowed drops of simultaneous twenties, making 4C men in the air at once. Dropping in trees was not part of the official training requirement, nor was HALO (high opening, low-altitude 'free falling'). Earlier on in the Emergency all this area was dominated by Chinese guerrillas. (PR FARELF)

unit new to the theatre thought it cumbersome. However, when I was in Vietnam, I was told that American units had disregarded it, at their peril. Ideally, there are ten stages: breaking track, reconnaissance, occupation, perimeter check, clearing patrols, putting out a screen, work period, withdrawal of the screen and posting of sentries, routine and stand-to. All that takes 175 minutes, nearly three hours. It is seldom possible to allow so much time to be spent; the degree of security required, that is to say the amont of work needed, will depend on whether the harbour is protective for a halt, or clandestine.

Visual tracking as stated previously, is another aspect of jungle warfare that needs constant training. It is an art that, like survival, needs a book to itself. It is axiomatic that knowledge of enemy movement is required in as much detail as possible. I have known a Gurkha track one man through a rubber plantation that was cleared of undergrowth half an hour after he had walked through it and where rubber tappers were working.

It is almost impossible to walk through the jungle and leave no signs at all. Signs to be looked for are known as ground signs and top signs, the dividing line being ankle level. Examples of ground signs are: foot or boot marks, broken twigs or leaves on the ground. bruised or 'bleeding' roots, disturbances of insect life, of grass or ground vegetation, mud left from boots, leaves, stones and twigs distrubed, debris dropped beside a track and disturbed water.

Right: The United Kingdom was coy about the aid given to the South Vietnamese. Six courses every year were run for the Army of the Republic of Vietnam (ARVN) in the Jungle Warfare School. These photographs were taken during the last-ever course to be run for ARVN. It was surprising that many of the students had never been in the jungle before! All found the course hard, not only physically but also because procedures were so different from those they had already been trained on, which were US Army in concept. The hardest point for any Vietnamese student to grasp was the need for tactical flexibility at every level and so how to exploit any particular situation. Junior commanders had never been taught to think for themselves. Being ambushed in road convoy was part of the final week-long exercise. (Lieutenant-Colonel J. P. Cross)

Right: RAF Whirlwind helicopters took part – good training for their crews also – with tactical moves of troops during the exploitation phase of the exercise. (Lieutenant-Colonel J. P. Cross)

Right: Students took it in turn to have command appointments. Orders are being given to a platoon. The attachments on the rifles allow for 'bulleted blank' to be used, adding much realism. Members of the Directing Staff discreetly monitored events. Most of the students had some knowledge of English, but interpreters were used extensively. Discipline was harsh: one ARVN Lieutenant-Colonel Guiding Officer, who was slack when at the Jungle Warfare School, was reported by his own officers (Majors!) on return to Vietnam and gaoled as a punishment. (Lieutenant-Colonel J. P. Cross)

Left: Silent hand-signals were essential for movement in the jungle to be as quiet as possible. There were many signs that had to be learnt so that correct information could be sent back from the leading scout to the commander who could then give out basic orders quickly and silently. Observation – of a flank and where to tread, as well as keeping an eye on the man in front – was all-important. Here the 'Halt!' sign is being given. (Lieutenant-Colonel J. P. Cross)

Left: Two men lie in fire positions, one a Bren gunner, the other a rifleman. Camouflage nets for hats or helmets were not issued here, but the Vietminh were insistent in camouflaging their headgear with the type of foliage of the terrain they were travelling through at any particular juncture. (Lieutenant-Colonel J. P. Cross)

Examples of top signs are: broken twigs or leaves, scratches on trees, bruised moss on trees, hand-holds on trees, changes in colour and natural position of vegetation and cutting.

Information that can be gleaned from accurate tracking is diverse: direction of movement, number of persons making the track, time when made, loads carried, the sex of the person, speed and type of food eaten.

Movement by road transport is a constant and lucrative source of weapons for guerrillas. Training in counter-road ambushes is needed by everyone and even then there is always a risk of being overwhelmed by an enemy superior in cunning and guts. I have talked to one middle-aged, innocent-looking, schoolmasterly Pathet Lao who went into raptures, eyes sparkling at the memories of his younger days at the way the Pathet Lao and the North Vietnamese took advantage of French slackness in thick country to the west of Hanoi, using such weapons as poisonous arrows, traps and mines as well as small arms, and the prizes gained.

Time and again the same mistakes were made, owing to the innate laziness of the troops who felt safe in their vehicles.

Even harder to extricate oneself from is an ambush on a large river, as was evidenced many times by Indonesians when chastised by the SAS the other side of the Borneo border and the Gurkhas on both sides. Even crossing a large water obstacle is a hazard – hence the carrying of the 100 feet of nylon cord by all soldiers on patrol.

Flotation is needed to cross many of the wide waterways found in tropical jungle and there are a number of ways crossings can be made. Even when there is no enemy and normal training is being undertaken, the power of these rivers should never be under-estimated. The techniques are quite basic and easily improvised: the individual can use trousers tied at the ends, soaked and thrust downwards overhead to create an airbag; groups can create larger floats with ponchos and coconuts or jerry-cans; and of course there are the obvious lifelines and logs to be employed.

Left: It was not often possible to take up prone firing positions in the jungle due to undergrowth which obstructed vision. If fire lanes were cut (as they would be for a position that had to be defended) the firer would be able to take the attacking troops by surprise. More often than not, however, the heads of the observers had to be off the ground to see anything.
(Lieutenant-Colonel J. P. Cross)

Left: The 'dead' had to be searched very carefully as it is an old trick to lie doggo. The 'exercise enemy' were Gurkhas and it was hard always to have to lose! They were dressed in 'Vietminh' black to add realism. Capture of the guerrilla camp and warding off a counter-attack was the finale of the exercise.
(Lieutenant-Colonel J. P. Cross)

Ambushes are one of the oldest forms of successfully killing an enemy and are basically of two kinds, deliberate and spontaneous. They can be linear or area in design, depending on the terrain. Killer groups must be detailed and where possible, a reserve must be held. For success control and surprise are paramount. This means that the siting of a deliberate ambush position should take the following points into consideration: the site selected should be easy to conceal, so that from the enemy point of view it is unoccupied; it must not offer an early escape to those enemy not killed when the ambush is first sprung; it must allow sentries to give due warning before the first enemy enter the ambush; be capable of being covered by all weapons; and have a good covered approach avoiding contact with known enemy positions or local inhabitants. Discipline is essential for success; almost every British batallion that served in Malaya suffered casualties when soldiers left their ambush positions without orders and were shot by their own men.

In the Jungle Warfare School, we experimented with geometrical patterns, such as a △, an X or a Y. Live goats were used to see the effect such devices as Claymore mines would have in any one pattern.

A diagramatic example of a very successful ambush over the border during Confrontation is given in Appendix 3.

Patrolling has been stressed countless times during jungle operations. As regards jungle patrolling, there are basically four methods to be used. One is to leave a central point on different compass bearings (the 'fan' method), one is to

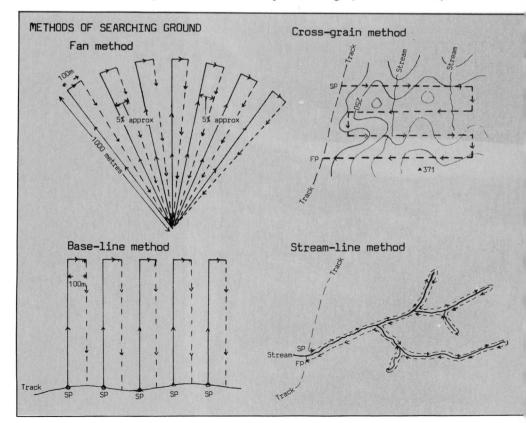

Right: *There were occasions when the GPMG was carried in the jungle, despite its weight. Although heavy and cumbersome, this weapon proved devastating in ambushes with its very high cyclic rate of fire and shock effect. The gun number 2 carried a rifle and most of the ammunition belts, acting as loader and assistant when firing.* (Colonel C. J. D. Bullock)

leave from different points on similar bearings (the 'base-line' method). Yet another is known as the cross-grain method, while the fourth (the one I disliked most) is following streams ('stream-line').

Close reconnaissance of an enemy camp follows on from a successful patrol and is one of the hardest manoeuvres to execute properly. It must be done by the person who is going to do the assault. Words of wisdom, taken from the Jungle Warfare School teaching of that time, in turn gleaned from the experiences of many, successful and otherwise, are:

1 Stop and listen for ten minutes every ten minutes or every hundred metres.

2 Once you have located the general area try to circle the camp 100–200 metres out. This should enable you to locate the sentry posts and the water point. Stop and listen frequently.

3 Avoid ridges and valleys. Where the going permits travel halfway down a slope. You are less likely to bump a sentry or water party by doing this.

4 Be patient. Do not hurry. Listen and listen again.

5 If an enemy appears to look straight at you, 'freeze' and he will probably not see you.

6 Check all sides of the camp objective. Go in, withdraw, go round, go in, withdraw, go round and so on, up to three or four times. Do not move round too close in.

7 When going in, go alone but covered by a cover man 5 to 15 metres in rear. Go slowly, stop, look, listen frequently. Leave the rest of the party in dead ground to your rear.

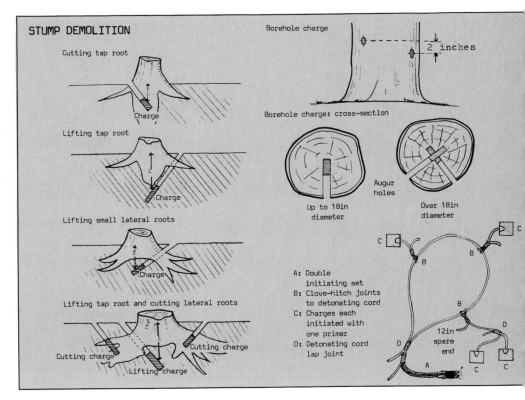

STUMP DEMOLITION

Cutting tap root

Lifting tap root

Lifting small lateral roots

Lifting tap root and cutting lateral roots

Charge

Charge

Charge

Cutting charge

Cutting charge

Lifting charge

Borehole charge

2 inches

Borehole charge: cross-section

Augur holes

Up to 18in diameter

Over 18in diameter

A: Double initiating set
B: Clove-hitch joints to detonating cord
C: Charges each initiated with one primer
D: Detonating cord lap joint

12in spare end

8 Do not use tracks of any sort. Conceal any marks you make on wet soil, especially when withdrawing.

9 Don't forget to check your compass frequently as you go round.

10 Patience, patience, patience and yet more patience is the secret of success.

Night lighting is a most useful adjunct in attack, defence and ambush. It can be as small as illuminating flares fired by 2in mortars and Very pistol or flares dropped from aircraft or set off electrically on the ground.

Tree demolitions, including the removal of stumps, are needed when blowing sites in the jungle for a helicopter to land or hover and useful when taking an airdrop or evacuating casualties. The teaching in Borneo was as shown in the diagrams.

Jungle ranges are essential to enhance marksmanship. Made into 'jungle lanes' they can contain moving targets, those that expose themselves vertically and those that are moved laterally. In Burma there were jungle lanes to teach jungle lore. These included demonstrations of patrols, sentries, tree signs, booby-traps, footprints, leaves, false movement by snipers, cooking, shelters and weapon emplacements; examples of noise made by men in occupation of a position and various bird and animal calls, including that of a frog, which was a very good one to imitate to attract a person's attention. Such lanes, modified for the terrain and enemy involved, are a valuable adjunct to training. In the 1980s such electronic devices as 'Small Arms Battlefield Engagement Simulators' have been introduced. These, along with 'umpire pistols' which monitor 'hits' on 'enemy' soldiers – although not yet efficient in leafy terrain – point the way to

Above: *At times a Landing Site for rescue helicopters had to be blown. In this instance the Officer Commanding the School, Squadron Leader Jim Davis, demonstrates how (not) to take out stumps and reduce a hillock – too much explosive was used. For the technically minded, detonators and fuzes were carried in Packs Echo and the explosive was Notal 808, in sticks. The man in the peaked hat is a member of the Royal Thai Police; these men also came on jungle warfare courses and could be very good. (Major H. V. Gilpin)*

Centre right: *In 1984 men of the 2nd Battalion, Grenadier Guards, went to Belize, to deter Guatemalan aggression. Routine patrolling to ensure that no Guatemalan incursion occurred was a constant. Even when the terrain was not jungle covered there was much obstructive undergrowth. (British Army PR)*

Right: *Packs have to be kept dry, so are encased in waterproof bags. An inflatable mattress can be seen on the bank; these are of great help to weak or non-swimmers. (British Army PR)*

future training aids. The old maxim that 'sweat saves blood' is ever true and can only be learnt by hard, realistic and vigorous training and whatever aids there be are only a substitute for the real thing.

Searching a built-up area or a village needs much practise, especially when faced by the type of situation found in Vietnam. There are two types of operation: one when a normally friendly or neutral village is searched. Then it is wise to bring in as many civil police as possible and keep males and females separate for searching. The other is when enemy are known to be in the village and an assault has to be mounted. In Vietnam especially, villages contained elaborate hide-outs which were nigh impossible to find and very difficult to penetrate.

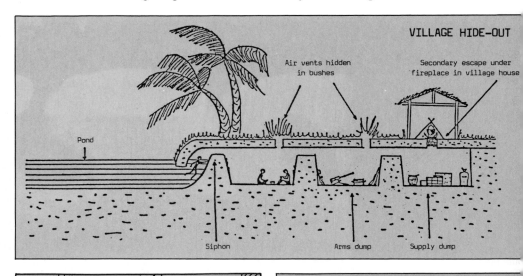

VILLAGE HIDE-OUT

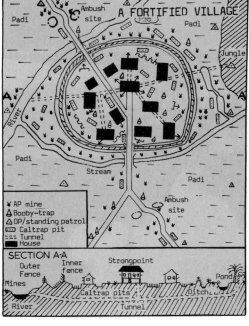

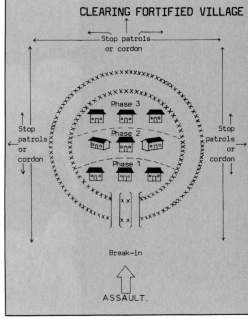

ght: US Special Forces, the een Berets', helped train diers of the Royal Thai Army, h for operations against rrillas in Thailand and for ting in Vietnam. A camp is ng built for this purpose in the gle near Lop Buri, in central ailand. (Captain Crummy, US ny)

ft: Wherever possible, villages uld be searched by civil police her than by soldiers. However, re are times when the army s to clear fortified village by lf. The Vietminh were rticularly successful at hiding ring such searches. This stration is taken from Street thout Joy.

ght: Erection of simple huts m bamboo only had to be ught to Thais from the towns; lage men knew how already. e US instructors, who later nt out in an advisory role, uld have to remember that the fference in size of 'furniture' uld give an intelligent snooper clue as to the nationality of the er. (Captain Crummy, US my)

ght: Booby-traps were a nstant fear. Physical ones pped on, swung at or impaled victim. The author is studying iations of this deadly theme h the assistance of a Green et instructor. (Captain mmy, US Army)

War dogs, like everything else in the army, come with varying roles. There are guard dogs, security dogs and infantry patrol dogs. A dog can be best trained for one task only and I believe that what I call the 'multi-purpose police dog' is expected to do too much. One of the key elements in all dog work is the correct relationship between dog and handler. Dogs have limited uses in the jungle, due to the climate, thickness of country, inability to tell the difference between friendly forces and enemy, and making 'points' at monkeys. That having been said, there are undoubted uses for dogs. The British soldier makes an excellent handler.

There are other aspects of basic training for operations at this level, some of which are **attacking an enemy camp, air supply, helicopter marshalling, making helicopter landing pads** and **first aid.**

I have not included learning languages of the people in whose country operations are taking place. Certainly, as regards the British Army, learning languages at soldier level is not taught. The French seem to think likewise (but, I expect, for cultural reasons) and the Americans had an extensive language training programme that was slanted towards 'advisers' and 'specialists'. I regard languages as a tactical weapon, which properly used, pays as big a dividend as any other I know.

Training for specialist roles is in a different category and embraces a higher degree of competence as well as some new skills. The Gurkha Independent Parachute Company, for instance, had three roles: seizing an airhead; patrol company, based on SAS tactics and methods; and conventional infantry. Patrol company skills that were required for each soldier, in addition to whatever he had to have for the other two roles, included sending and receiving Morse, infantry pioneering – particularly the use of explosives – first aid and languages.

Left: In 1970 to prove that troops from Britain were capable of operating after a 6-week acclimatization period with the three other nations committed to Malaysia's defence (Singapore, Australia and New Zealand), a large-scale exercise code-named 'Bersatu Padu' (Unity) was planned. Before the troops took to the jungle much training had to be undergone. Here, at the Jungle Warfare School, in Johore, Malaysia, troops run to emplane in Wessex helicopters. (Gurkha Museum)

Left: One lot of troops was carried away to another destination in six helicopters while a platoon sat in 'sticks' (sometimes called 'chalks') waiting for their turn. (Gurkha Museum)

No tree jumps have been undertaken since they were made in the mid-1950s by the SAS.

Where the Borneo Border Scouts were concerned, it was information that they were expected to produce and they were looked on as the 'eyes and ears' of the security forces. Apart from teaching them how to memorize details and to describe what they saw, they were taught how to shadow a body of troops. One group under training successfully shadowed an operational Royal Marine patrol that was using dogs for a considerable distance. At the end of this exercise I asked the Marines what they would do if they found themselves being followed. It could not happen, they said, but if it did, 'we'd have shot them'. They never did believe what I told them!

Large-scale jungle warfare exercises were sometimes held: I remember one during 'Confrontation' that took place on the east coast of peninsula Malaysia. In essence it conformed to the scenario I painted at the start of the chapter, with a parachute assault on the beach-head and even the Royal Navy taking part. A United Nations observer was also introduced into the 'conflict'. Although nothing official was announced, we on the ground took it as a warning to the Indonesians not to escalate their operations against Malaysia and, if they did, here was a demonstration of what was on our side.

In 1970 there was much argument about Britain's role 'east of Suez' and the army's ability to come to the aid of any country threatened. A 5-nation exercise was held in Malaysia, involving Australia, New Zealand, Singapore, Malaysia and Britain. My task was to run the training for the battalion instructors (to train their own men) before it all started. Eventually the exercise drew to a close. The culminating point was an attack on the 'baddies' (represented by the Gurkhas) by the 'goodies'. It may have been more bad luck than bad judgement that the assaulting troops were about 10,000 yards away from where they should have been. It was certainly bad everything that they refused to come down from the hill they had wrongly attacked before they had been sent more trousers, which had all had been tightly fitted around the crotch, and the strain of actually going into the jungle had split them in all the wrong seams. Bad soldiering was not the only wrong attribute they showed. They had not been nicknamed 'the coffee-shop cowboys' for nothing.

After 'Confrontation' was over the only possible role envisaged for Gurkha battalions was against a 'Vietminh'-type enemy. Accordingly each Gurkha battalion was made to hold one jungle exercise a year. Vietminh-type tunnels were dug, command posts were rendered invisible and paths into the 'enemy's' stronghold were cleverly camouflaged with elephant droppings. On one such exercise all the 'enemy' had to be in their positions by 10 o'clock when the commanding general was to make his inspection. Nothing, but nothing, was to give the position away. At two minutes past 10, to the general's great annoyance, he saw a pair of socks hanging from a bush, thereby making it obvious that 'enemy' troops were in the immediate vicinity.

The general was very angry and made pointed remarks about the owner being a bad soldier. It so happened that the owner of the socks was the VC-winner, Rambahadur Limbu.

There is **no** subsitute for the real thing!

Left: *A 120mm battalion anti-tank gun is camouflaged, sited looking down a road. Very often the threat of being fired on by such a weapon can dampen the ardour of troops whose discipline is not their strongest feature. (British Army PR)*

Below: *This vehicle is a Combat Vehicle Reconnaissance (Tracked), CVR(T), operated by soldiers of Queen's Own Highlanders on patrol in Belize. It is the Scimitar version of the vehicle and had superb cross-country mobility, aluminium alloy armour and protection from nuclear, bacterial and chemical weapons. (British Army PR)*

Right: The Scorpion version of the CRV(T) is able to travel along shallow rivers. Men of Queen's Own Highlanders are on patrol: without escorting infantry on the flanks, such a vehicle could be a target for ambush in such close country. (British Army PR)

Below: Troops return from a routine patrol to Salamanca Camp, Belize; here seen deplaning from an RAF Puma helicopter. (British Army PR)

11
The Future

It takes a braver man than I to stand up and say where and when the next campaign in the jungle will take place. I find it hard to think that there will ever be one, but I find it still harder to think that there won't be one. The jungle will run out altogether before man really settles down and stops fighting – despite reforestation programmes in some countries!

Except possibly for some special force training, rather than intervention, in aid of a friendly power, I cannot see the British Government (or the Australians and New Zealanders) wanting to become involved in a jungle war ever again. Other nations that have had their fair share of jungle fighting, France and USA, may be tempted to send troops to the jungle, either their own or those whom they think can act as their surrogates. As for the Russians and the Cubans, who knows what they won't be up to? Whatever it is, I cannot imagine them in the Amazon fastnesses or the Borneo uplands.

Malaysia will be faced with a guerrilla problem for a long time to come, despite all protestations to the contrary. There was more banditry in 1937, so statistics would have us believe, than there was twelve years later in the Emergency. In the rest of Asia where there is jungle, some of it is almost bound to be used for some nefarious purpose or other – opium growing, clandestine routes for contraband, big-game poaching – so that an energetic government will need to take action against it, if it is not to become the type of running sore that is to be found in Irian Jaya as the result of Indonesia's transmigration policy or the dissatisfaction in the Philippines. As regards CRW, surface it will from time to time but probably not in jungle. It would be risible if an anti-Communist campaign were to be carried out in the jungles of, say, Vietnam by patriots who had backing from . . .? Anyone's guess! Nevertheless, periodical 'tunnel hunting' could pay dividends.

All that having been said, I still advocate that jungle warfare training be continued for as many soldiers as can be made available to take advantage of what facilities there are – and facilities there must be. The reasons are all not strictly military, germane though such training be to a professional soldier's skill. The jungle is an antidote to the rush of modern life and the rash of trivia that seems so indispensable to our discomfort; it is an ideal place for a man to come to terms with himself and it is also superb in teaching young commanders what command really entails.

Because the jungle teaches people how to be dependent on others to a degree it does, and because of the self-reliance it engenders, it is also an ideal training ground for survival were the unthinkable to happen and a nuclear strike rendered all normal life – now so blithely taken for granted – a thing of the past. I started off by saying that the earliest records of self-reliance in overgrown, if not actual jungle, conditions were recorded in Genesis: maybe that is how those few who remain will one day find themselves at the very end. But at least I won't be there to prove or disprove my hypothesis – nor will there be any survivors at all if people disregard all the teaching and training points I have made in this book!

Below: Troops here wade over the Rio Grande, keeping their rifles dry. Crossing rivers is not as dangerous from ambush as travelling along them, but there is not a lot that the men in the water can do if ambushed. (British Army PR)

Appendices

1. IMMEDIATE ACTION DRILLS

Encountering the enemy unexpectedly at short range is always a possibility in jungle terrain. This is when, Grant Taylor says, there are either 'the quick or the dead'. With no time to make a plan, **immediate action drills** have been evolved to get out of a tricky situation, inflicting casualties on the enemy while doing so. These three options were used by British, Australian and New Zealand forces in Malaya and Borneo.

Immediate ambush drill is designed for when the enemy is heard before he hears the security forces. It is decided that an ambush is possible so the silent signal is given for this. The scout group must immediately take cover from view and remain still, even though their positions are not the best from which to fire. The rifle and LMG groups have more time to get to good fire positions, with the LMG position being of critical importance. The ambush is sprung when the commander reckons the maximum number of enemy is caught in the ambush area. If, however, the enemy sees the troops before the ambush is sprung, fire will be opened by any member of the ambush position. As it is probable that the strength of the enemy is not known, all troops must be ready to act on the commander's orders.

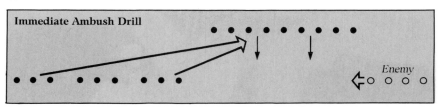

Encounter drill is used when recognition of one another is simultaneous. Then everything happens at once. The leading scout shouts 'Contact front!' and the scout group takes cover from where the enemy can be observed and fired on.

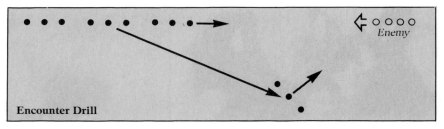

The LMG group, in the absence of other orders, moves to the high ground or *to the right* and engages the enemy. The rifle group covers the flanks and rear and waits further orders. They must not be pinned down by enemy fire. The commander moves forward to observe.

Counter-ambush drill is used when some of one's own troops are caught in an ambush by the enemy. Those men caught in the ambush return fire and call out 'Ambush left/right' and those not caught move off the track, form up and attack the flank of the enemy ambush position.

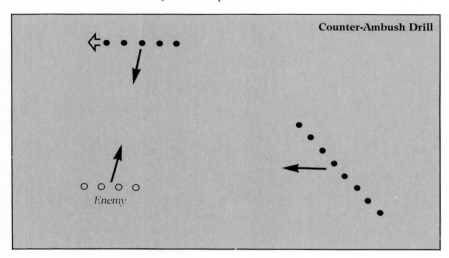

Counter-Ambush Drill

Enemy

2. JAPANESE TRAINING

Japanese archives hold only limited information regarding training for tropical warfare in the Imperial Japanese Army in the Second World War. In none of the headings does the word 'jungle' appear. Translated extracts include only three aspects of warfare:

'*Study of 'Education and Training to adapt Army troops for operations in Southern Theater (or Area)';'*

'*Part of Lessons from the experience of operations in South (Imperial Head-quarters, Army Section, 1942, August);'*

'*Detailed record of operations by the 5th Division.'*

'*Education and Training' includes **'Tropical operations in general, Application of troops, Weapon, supply, sanitation, etc., Miscellaneous'.**

Subjects that applied to troops are:

1 *Activities of troops on vehicles;*

2 *Reference for anti-airborne combat;*

3 *Reference for landing combat;*

4 *Reference for landing combat by field artillery;*

5 *Reference for commanding motor bicycles;*

6 *Reference for transportation commander mission while in the ship transportation.*

Subjects covered by 'Weapon, supply, sanitation, etc.' include;

7 Reference for maintenance of aviation (equipment) in tropical area;

8 Reference for handling of signal equipment in tropical area;

9 Reference for handling of ammunition in tropical area;

10 Reference for sanitation (management) while in ship transportation;

11 Reference for handling of tank, trailer and automobile in tropical area;

12 Reference for medical facilities when staying in tropical area;

13 Warning (or advice) for temporary piling and storage of weapons and ammunition in tropical area;

14 Warning (or advice) for usage of weapon in tropical area;

15 Reference for aliment duties in tropical operations;

16 Reference for supply duties in tropical operations;

17 Reference for accounting duties in tropical area.

'Miscellaneous' covers

18 Reference for ideological warfare aiming Southern area (Thailand edition) October 1941;

19 Reference for ideological warfare aiming Southern area (Burma edition) December 1941;

20 You can win the war just reading this;

21 Reference for the identification of aircraft of UK, USA and USSR, September 1941.

'You can win the war just reading this' was prepared to spread the results of research and study by the Taiwan Army Research Department to all the officers and men participating in the (tropical) operations. It was distributed to each individual on board the troopship. Someone says that the pamphlet was printed 400 thousand copies, and in this case almost all participating soldiers received it. The pamphlet was written in easy colloquial Japanese with 70 pages in 18 clauses. On top the aim of publishing the pamphlet and the items to be well considered are stated and then the following contents are stated.

1 What place is the Southern operation area;

2 Why you have to fight and how to be fought;

3 How will proceed the war;

4 What you should do on board the ship;

5 Landing combat;

6 March in tropical area;

7 Stationing and bivouac in tropical area;

8 Scouting (reconnaissance) and security;

9 Combat;

10 Protection of gas;

11 For signal soldiers;

12 For automobile soldiers;

13 Love your weapon;

14 Aliment;

15 Sanitation;

16 Sanitation of horse;

17 Manoeuvre at specific terrain;

18 Conclusion.

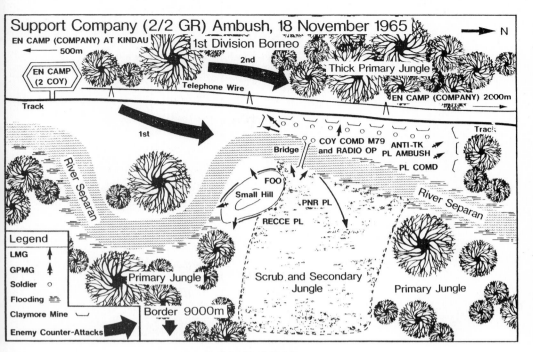

Support Company (2/2 GR) Ambush, 18 November 1965
1st Division Borneo

EN CAMP (COMPANY) AT KINDAU

← 500m →

EN CAMP (2 COY)

2nd

Thick Primary Jungle

EN CAMP (COMPANY) 2000m

Telephone Wire

Track

1st

Bridge

COY COMD M79 and RADIO OP

ANTI-TK PL AMBUSH

Track

PL COMD

River Separan

FOO

Small Hill

PNR PL

RECCE PL

River Separan

Legend

LMG

GPMG

Soldier   o

Flooding

Claymore Mine

Enemy Counter-Attacks

Primary Jungle

Scrub and Secondary Jungle

Primary Jungle

Border 9000m

N

3. AMBUSHES

Ambushes can be of any shape but basically they are **linear** and **area** in concept. Refinements in design can always be made when the killing-ground has been selected and the availability of 'area weapons' (such as Claymore mines) determined. Some commanders like a △-**shaped ambush,** some an **X**, others a **Y**, but whatever the layout, the basic tenets must never be forgotten: for success, surprise, silence, security, a rehearsal whenever possible and a reserve, are paramount. One very successful company ambush was carried out during Confrontation by Major C. J. D. Bullock of 2/2nd Gurkha Rifles, as shown in the diagram. This site was 9,000 metres over the Borneo border in Kalimantan, just within range of supporting 105mm artillery. At least 24 Indonesians were killed (out of one rifle company) for two Gurkhas wounded. The ambush was area in concept although the actual killing-area was linear. For the record, the Pioneer Platoon constructed the bridge over the River Separan, a remarkable achievement under the tense conditions.

4. LIFE ON THE LINES OF COMMUNICATION IN BURMA

Major Mike Roberts remembers some of the problems suffered by the staff on the L of C up to Imphal.

> Rail to Tistamukh, steamer up the Brahmaputra, rail to Dimapur, then a one-way-traffic-only road over the jungle-covered mountains to Imphal.
>
> One interesting fact emerged on this last bit. At first vehicles travelled in one-way convoys, but the delivery and accident rates were awful. The Powers-That-Be set an up time and a down time on the Dimapur–Kohima section and the Kohima–Imphal section, with plenty of passing places. Drivers set off individually at their own best pace and the delivery and accident rates improved dramatically. After the Japanese attack, all delivery was by air to one strip in Imphal.

As an example of conditions, Major Roberts remembers how he made a journey from Manmaw in the Kabaw Valley to Ceylon on leave in either late 1943 or early 1944. It took 12 days and involved a journey by foot and road transport before reaching the river steamer at a place called Pandu. While there he found:

> 600 IORs [Indian Other Ranks] waiting 3 days for transport. Some urgent duty, some courses, some leave. Food insufficient in rest camp.
>
> 9th 1800 hours all lined up outside barrier awaiting orders to embark. No one in charge.
>
> 9th 2100 hours 16 BORs [British Other Ranks] pick up kit on MC [Movement Control] Sergeant's orders and proceed to boat taking coolies. Take up all 1st class accommodation irrespective of whether there were officers or any other BORs travelling on more urgent duty. This was signal for remaining 500 IORs to pick up baggage and rush the gangplank, blocking it completely, and stopping the unloading of the ship altogether. 2 Sergeants MC staff trying to keep control.
>
> 10th 0930 hours I took control and cleared the beach with a party of 40 Gurkhas I had collected, returning all IORs back behind barrier, telling them not to move till ordered by MC staff.
>
> 1000 to 11th 0300 unloading proceeded and coolies embark. Another boat comes in and is unloaded. The MCO says there is accommodation for 700 and I endeavour to pass this on to IORs waiting.
>
> 0300 hours. 2 officers take their kit on board. This is a signal for IORs again to rush gangplank. Again cleared until report from MC Sergeant received. Ship clear and ready to receive passengers. The MC Captain only appeared once during the whole proceedings, at about 0930 or 1000.
>
> 0400 hours order BORs on then GORs [Gurkha Other Ranks] then remainder. They rush gangplank again so with 2 GORs with rifles let them through one by one.
>
> 0500 hours. All aboard. Was handed and signed as OC ship, statement of numbers on board. A remarkable piece of guesswork by the MC staff. Received one day's rations to be issued.
>
> 1000 hours. Sailed. Began issuing rations. The usual rush, slightly allayed by forming one-way traffic. Some men had not had a decent meal for two days. Issuing rations to 600 men representing most of the races and creeds of India is not easy, especially as the rations cannot be split into one-man units.
>
> 1900 hours. Get stuck on sandbank for 35 minutes.
>
> 11th 0200 hours. Pull up for night on orders . . . owing danger of sandbanks.
>
> 0700 hours. Proceed.
>
> 0800 hours. Heave to. Ship ahead on sandbank. Takes 2 hours to refloat. 6 boats waiting to pass.
>
> 1000 hours. Move on.
>
> 1830 hours. Arrive Tistamukh. Move to train. Very few have had any food today. Report this to MCO. Rest camp has 7,000 waiting transport upstream. Capacity 1,500.
>
> 2200 hours. Train comes in. Entrain. Move to another siding. Get rations for one day. Issue during the night up to 0300 hours . . . also sign, with assistance of 6 other officers on train, IORs' leave certificates. I did not even ask the MCO to sign them. He had had no sleep for 36 hours.

An Advanced Guard Action in New Guinea.

A typical engagement where minor hostile resistance was encountered in the advance over KOKODA track is described below.

The main column was restricted in its movements to one track through the jungle. One AUSTRALIAN battalion, consisting of four Rifle Coys., formed the Advanced Guard. At 1400 hours, contact was gained with troops disposed as shown in Sketch 1.

The leading elements of the Advanced Guard immediately fixed the enemy and attempted to dislodge him. After the deployment of the Van Guard, which was unable to dislodge the hostile resistance, an attempt was made to determine the strength, extent and depth of the position. The Advanced Guard Commander, who was well forward where he could obtain all the available information, after making a rapid appreciation of the situation, ordered a double envelopment according to a pre-arranged plan as shown in Sketch 2.

Two companies were employed on the right flank and one company on the left flank. The two companies were sent round the right flank so that the advance of the Main Column would be uninterrupted if only minor resistance was encountered.

The units making the encirclement laid telephone lines as they advanced through the jungle. In this manner, the Advanced Guard Commander was in constant communication by telephone with all units, and knew all developments in the situation. The encircling forces advanced and encountered only hostile patrols which were driven in. Based on these reports, which indicated that the enemy position was fixed, the Advanced Guard Commander reported to the Column Commander the extent of the hostile position. By nightfall the position was completely encircled as shown in Sketch 2.

The final attack was ordered at first light the following day. During the night the Battalion Commander received reports from the Company Commanders. As a result of constant pressure throughout the night the enemy made no attempt to break through the position. The attack went according to schedule at first light the following day, and was over within five minutes, except for "mopping up".

The casualties in the battalion acting as an advanced guard, resulted in 24 men being killed in developing the attack. In the co-ordinated main attack the following morning, only 6 men were killed. After the battle was over, between 150 and 200 dead Japs. were found a useful credit balance.

In the meantime, based on the prompt, decisive action of the Advanced Guard Commander, the march of the Main Column was uninterrupted. As a result, the Brigade Commander after detailing the new Advanced Guard, was able to continue the uninterrupted advance with security and by-pass this hostile resistance, since he had been informed that the two companies encircling the right flank had fixed the enemy and would protect his left flank in his advance. In addition he knew exactly the location of the enemy as well as our own troops.

(Reproduced from The Jungle Book, *Military Training Pamphlet No. 9 (India), 4th edition, September 1943.)*

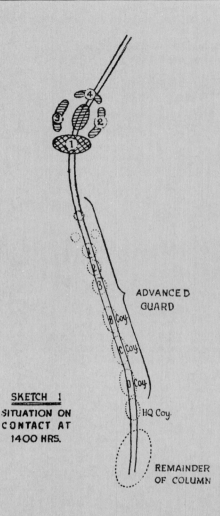

DEVELOPMENT OF
ACTION.

1. Leading platoon of leading company, locates enemy astride the track in hostile area No. 1. Deploys to hold track against enemy action

2. Second platoon of leading company deploys to right flank to locate the enemy's flank when it is stopped by fire from hostile areas Nos. 1 and 2.

3. Third platoon of leading company deploys to left flank to locate the enemy's flank when it is stopped by fire from hostile areas Nos. 1 and 3.

ADVANCED
GUARD

B Coy

C Coy

D Coy

SKETCH 1

SITUATION ON
CONTACT AT
1400 HRS.

HQ Coy.

REMAINDER
OF COLUMN

ENEMY LOCALITY FIRST ENCOUNTERED ———

ENEMY LOCALITIES SUBSEQUENTLY
LOCATED DURING OUTFLANKING MOVEMENT ———

OUR FORCES ————————————————

ROUTES TAKEN ——————————————

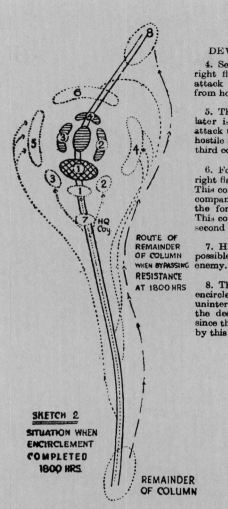

**ROUTE OF
REMAINDER
OF COLUMN
WHEN BYPASSING
RESISTANCE
AT 1800 HRS**

SKETCH 2

**SITUATION WHEN
ENCIRCLEMENT
COMPLETED
1800 HRS.**

**REMAINDER
OF COLUMN**

ENEMY LOCALITY FIRST ENCOUNTERED —

**ENEMY LOCALITIES SUBSEQUENTLY
LOCATED DURING OUTFLANKING MOVEMENT**

OUR FORCES

ROUTES TAKEN

DEVELOPMENT OF ACTION—*contd.*

4. Second company, on arrival, is sent to the right flank by B. N. Commander to locate and attack the enemy's flank. Stopped by fire from hostile areas Nos. 2 and 4.

5. Third company, on arrival three minutes later is sent to the left flank to locate and attack the enemy's flank. Stopped by fire from hostile areas Nos. 3 and 4. Both second and third company lay field cable as they advance.

6. Fourth company, on arrival, is sent around right flank to block track in rear of enemy. This company, in conjunction with the second company provides flank and rear security for the force during its uninterrupted advance. This company extends the field cable from the second company as it passes.

7. H.Qs. company is placed in reserve for possible use in the destruction of trapped enemy.

8. The remainder of the column by-passes encircled enemy position and continues the uninterrupted march. Bde. commander leaves the destructions of the enemy to the one Bn., since the hostile strength and depth was known by this time.

Bibliography

National archives hold vast quantities of books, papers and pamphlets relating to aspects of wars that were fought in the jungle or similar conditions. Military histories are also found at:

United Kingdom
Ministry of Defence Whitehall Library
Old War Office Building
Whitehall
London SW1A 2EU

United States of America
The Chief of Military History
Headquarters
Department of the Army
The Pentagon
Washington,
DC 20310

US Army Center for Military History
Carlisle Barracks
Pennsylvania 17013

Australia
Australian War Mamorial
Canberra
ACT 2601

France
Monsieur le Général
Chef du Service Historique de l'Armée
de Terre
Château de Vincennes
94 304 – Vincennes Cedex

Japan
General Staff Defence Force
Protocol and Liaison
The National Institute for Defence
Studies
2-2-1 Nakameguro
Meguro-ku
Tokyo 153

Material (MOD sources) consulted for this book includes:
Book List Series 56: Jungle and Bush Warfare
Fitzgerald, Lieutenant-Colonel T. O. *Bush Warfare; Notes from Lectures*, 1918
Heneker, Lieutenant-Colonel W. C. G. *Bush Warfare, 1907*, vol. vi
Momtanaro, Lieutenant-Colonel A. F. *Hints for a Bush Campaign*, 1901
Morgan, Major C. B. *Hints of Bush Fighting*, 1899
Rowan-Robinson, Major-General H. *Jungle Warfare*, 1944
Royal West African Frontier Force. *Notes on Training in Bush Warfare*, 1938
Book List Series 537: Malayan Emergency, 1948–60
Archer, Major T. C. R. 'Medical Problems of the Operational Infantry Soldier in
  Malaya', in *Journal of the RAMC*, 1958
Miller, D. 'Jungle Warfare', in *War Monthly*, 1977

Norris, Air Vice Marshal C. N. F. 'Air Aspects of Operations against 'Confrontation", in *Brassey's Annual*, 1967

R. (B.N.). 'The campaigns in Malaya: Tactics of Jungle Fighting', in *World Today*, 1949

Slater, Group Captain R. R. C. 'Air Operations in Malaya', in *Journal of the RUSI*, 1958

Book List Series 1445: Malaysian Confrontation, 1962–66

Riggal, Major J. S. 'RCT Light Aircraft Operations in Borneo', in *RCT Review*, 1966

Book List Series 1883: Vietnam War: Armoured Operations

Battreall, Lieutenant-Colonel R. B. 'Armor in Vietnam', in *Armor*, 1965

Book List Series 1856: Vietnam War: Australian Forces

Jackson, Brigadier O. D. 'The Australian Training Team Vietnam in 1965 and early 1966', in *Australian Army Journal*, 1973

Book List Series 2258: Vietnam War: Airmobile Operations

Bashmore, B. T. 'Vertical Attack by Counter-insurgents', in *Armor*, 1962

Gillette, Captain S. G. 'Airmobile Operations in Vietnam', in *Armor*, 1966

Other works recommended include:
MALAYA, 1941–45

Barber, Noel. *Sinister Twilight*, Eyre & Spottiswoode, 1969

Chapman, Spencer. *The Jungle is Neutral*, Chatto & Windus, 1949

Percival, Lieutenant-General A. E. *War in Malaya*, Eyre & Spottiswoode, 1949

BURMA

Allen, Louis. *Burma, the Longest War: 1941–45*, Dent, 1984

Bickersteth, Major A. C. *One Damned Thing After Another*, pubd. privately

Brett-James, Antony. *The Ball of Fire*, Gale & Polden, 1951

Calvert, Michael. *Prisoner of Hope*, Collins, 1952

Carew, Tim. *The Longest Retreat*, Hamish Hamilton, 1969

Fergusson, Bernard. *Beyond the Chindwin*, Collins, 1945

— *Wild Green Earth*, Collins, 1946

Masters, John, *The Road Past Mandalay*, Michael Joseph, 1961

Mead, Peter. *Orde Wingate and the Historians*, Merlin Books Ltd., 1987

Slim, Sir William. *Defeat into Victory*, Cassell, 1956

Tuchman, Barbara. *Sand against the Wind*, Macmillan, 1970

History of the Second World War: The War against Japan, vol. III, HMSO Army in India Training Memorandum: *The Jungle Book*, 1943

—*Jungle Omnibus*, 1945

NEW GUINEA

Carlton, Henry (Jo) Gullet. *Not as a Duty Only: An Infantryman's War*, Melbourne University Press, 1976

Dexter, David. *The New Guinea Offensive*, Official War History series

White, Osmar. *Green Armour*, Wren, Melbourne, 1972

MALAYAN EMERGENCY: 1948–60

Barber, Noel. *The War of the Running Dogs*, Collins, 1971

Cross, Lieutenant-Colonel J. P. *In Gurkha Company*, Arms & Armour Press, 1986
Henniker, Brigadier M. C. A. *Red Shadow Over Malaya*, Blackwood, 1953
Smith, E. D. *Counter-Insurgency Operations: 1 Malaya and Borneo*, Ian Allan Ltd., 1985

INDO-CHINA/VIETNAM
Fall, Bernard. *Street Without Joy*, Schocken Books, 1972
Herr, Michael. *Dispatches*, Pan (Picador), 1978
Karnow, Stanley. *Vietnam: A History*, Century
Patti, L. A. *Why Vietnam? Prelude to the American Albatross*, University of California, 1980
Westmoreland, William C. *A Soldier Reports*, Dell, 1976

FRENCH SOURCES
Allemand, T. *Evolution des sections de combat d'infanterie de 1871 à 1982*, Thèse 3ème cycle, EMESS, 1985
Bergot, E. *Bataillon Bigeard. Cas concrets de combat – Guerre d'Indo-Chine*, Fayard, 1966
Ferrandi, J. *Les Officers français face au Vietminh*, Fayard, 1966
Schoendoerffer, P. *La 317ème Section*, Folio, 1978

BORNEO
Dickens, Peter. *SAS: The Jungle Frontier*, Arms & Armour Press, 1983
Geraghty, Tony. *Who Dares Wins: The Story of the SAS*, Arms & Armour Press, 1980
James, Harold, and Sheil-Small, Denis. *The Undeclared War*, Leo Cooper, 1971
Smith, E. D. *Counter-Insurgency Operations: 1. Malaya and Borneo*, Ian Allan Ltd., 1985

COMMUNIST REVOLUTIONARY WARFARE
Bateman, Michael-Elliot. *Defeat in the East*, OUP, 1967
Corbett, Robin. *Guerrilla Warfare from 1939 to the Present Day*, Orbis
Langer, Paul F., and Zasloff, Joseph J. *North Vietnam and the Pathet Lao – Partners in the Struggle for Laos*, Harvard, 1970
Thomson, Sir Robert. *Defeating Communist Insurgency*, Chatto & Windus, 1967
Mao Zedong (Tse-tung). *The Selected Works*
— *Selected Writings*
Giap, Vo Nguyen. *People's War, People's Army*. These last three works are fully described in Bateman's *Defeat in the East*.

GENERAL
Bloodworth, Dennis. *An Eye for the Dragon: South-East Asia Observed*, Secker & Warburg, 1970
— *Chinese Looking-Glass*, Chaps. 26, 27, Secker & Warburg, 1967
Pocock, Tom. *Fighting General*, Collins, 1967
Swinson, Arthur. *Illustrated History of the Second World War*, Purnell

Index